THE
TAX & LEGAL
PLAYBOOK

SECOND EDITION

Game-Changing Solutions to Your Small-Business Questions

MARK J. KOHLER
CPA, Attorney

Entrepreneur Press®

Entrepreneur Press, Publisher
Cover Design: Andrew Welyczko
Production and Composition: Eliot House Productions

© 2019 by Entrepreneur Media, Inc.
All rights reserved.
Reproduction or translation of any part of this work beyond that permitted
by Section 107 or 108 of the 1976 United States Copyright Act without
permission of the copyright owner is unlawful. Requests for permission or
further information should be addressed Entrepreneur Media Inc. Attn: Legal
Department, 18061 Fitch, Irvine, CA 92614.

This publication is designed to provide accurate and authoritative information in
regard to the subject matter covered. It is sold with the understanding that the
publisher is not engaged in rendering legal, accounting, or other professional
services. If legal advice or other expert assistance is required, the services of a
competent professional person should be sought.

Entrepreneur Press® is a registered trademark of Entrepreneur Media, Inc.

Library of Congress Cataloging-in-Publication Data
Names: Kohler, Mark J., author.
Title: The tax and legal playbook: game-changing solutions to your small
    business questions / by Mark J. Kohler.
Description: Second edition. | Irvine, California: Entrepreneur Press, [2019]
    | Includes index.
Identifiers: LCCN 2019013449| ISBN 978-1-59918-643-6 (alk. paper) |
    ISBN 1-59918-643-8 (alk. paper)
Subjects: LCSH: Small business—Taxation—Law and legislation—United
    States. | Tax planning—United States.
Classification: LCC KF6491 .K64 2019 | DDC 343.7306/8—dc23
LC record available at https://lccn.loc.gov/2019013449

Printed in the United States of America

23 22 21 20 19   10 9 8 7 6 5 4 3 2 1

*This book is dedicated to all of those trying to make their
American Dream a reality in the face of stress, frustration,
and opposition, yet stay committed and determined to not give up.*

CONTENTS

PART II
GETTING THE MOST FROM YOUR BUSINESS ENTITY

PART III

GAME-WINNING TAX STRATEGIES

PART IV

PROTECTING YOUR ASSETS

PART V

THE PROPER APPROACH TO PARTNERS AND INVESTORS

PART VI

PLANNING FOR THE NEXT SEASON

ACKNOWLEDGMENTS

I can't thank my family enough for their support during the many hours I spend at work and on projects such as this book. My amazing wife, Jennifer, and wonderful children, Dillon, Allison, Sydney, and Molly, truly believe in my mission to share this important information with our fellow Americans and taxpayers. I couldn't do it without them. Please thank them if you see them.

Thanks to my law partner, Mat Sorensen, who contributed a tremendous amount of content, support, and resources on various topics. His book, *The Self-Directed IRA Handbook*, has set a high bar for me in my writing efforts. He is truly brilliant. Thank you to my accounting firm partners LaDell Eyre, Brian Brown, and Rick Taylor, who supported me in my dream to write the update to this book. Their work verifying strategies and tax law was a huge help.

BUSINESS PLANNING WITH GAME PLANS

Even if you aren't a sports fan, the concept of having a "game plan" before heading into an athletic event shouldn't be a foreign concept. In fact, I think we can all agree that if a team or an individual taking part in a serious competition doesn't have a game plan before starting, the likelihood of success will be minimal. Even in a friendly backyard game of one-on-one basketball, you would quickly devise your plan of attack whether it's focusing on outside shots or taking your buddy to the hoop with aggressive layups.

Well, the game has changed, hence the reason for this update to the first edition of this book. With the passage of the Tax Cut and Jobs Act (TCJA) at the end of 2017, we are still understanding its impact on the economy and the strategies small-business owners can exploit and take advantage of in the fine print. Bottom line, it's arguably the biggest tax reform package since Ronald Reagan's presidency and the Tax Act of 1986. Thus, the rules have changed significantly, and business owners would be smart to take notice and learn the basics.

Understanding the rules of tax planning couldn't be more similar to understanding the rules to a winning game plan. Thus, it is absolutely critical to have a variety of plans in place for the different "games" you may play in the tax and legal arena. Just as in sports, if you don't research and devise well-thought-out strategies as you build your business, you could lose not just your shirt (or thousands of dollars), but also years of your life with wasted time and stress.

But where does a small-business owner turn? There has to be a playbook with strategies that can help you in your struggles and decisions. But how do you know if those answers fit your situation? How can you trust what you're reading? Regrettably, millions of entrepreneurs across the U.S. face these problems each year, never quite finding the comprehensive analysis of their tax and legal structure they desperately need.

The unlucky ones are instead bombarded by self-proclaimed gurus who use coaching systems run by unlicensed and unqualified staff to sell their overpriced game plans without tailoring them to the client's situation. Others are trapped in relationships with CPAs and lawyers inherited from their families—advisors they can't fire out of loyalty, even though they are stuck in a rut of outdated strategies. If these situations weren't troubling enough, add to the mix the do-it-yourself websites and software that enable entrepreneurs to screw up their tax or legal planning with the click of a button.

Do any of these situations sound familiar? Like millions of entrepreneurs across the country, you may very well be searching for the best tax and legal approach to running your business. You deserve regular consultations and game plans that are comprehensive, understandable, affordable, and tailored to you and your business. Sadly, too many entrepreneurs never get such advice.

Athletes facing the same struggle of how to win turn to coaches with credentials and experience for guidance in training and building their game plans. You can do the same. You can learn the basics to become the captain of your own team, directing your players with a broad understanding of the rewards and pitfalls of quality tax and legal planning.

As a certified public accountant and lawyer, I can say with great confidence that finding a professional skilled in both legal and tax matters is a rarity in the small-business world. Most professionals with my training end up in big business, working for Fortune 500 goliaths. However, I chose to dedicate my career to helping small-business owners. Not only have I spent 19 years helping both new and seasoned entrepreneurs, I myself have started, failed, and succeeded in several enterprises. I know the challenges small businesses face, and understand the legal and tax strategies that can help you save on taxes, protect your assets, plan for retirement, and succeed in your version of the American Dream. Watch out for any coach or advisor with lesser credentials.

The Concept Behind the Complexity of the Tax Cut and Jobs Act

2018 brought sweeping changes to the tax code, changing our "playbook." These changes will rock our world for the next few years until 2024, when Congress will most likely be foreced to revisit the code once again. Most of those changes affect and benefit larger corporations, but small businesses are reaping strong benefits as well. The key is that you have to know how to make the system work for you.

Anything that is out there that might help us save on taxes is great, but with this tax legislation there are winners and losers. And some small-business owners are going to be winners, while some will be losers, and that will be the case no matter what tax bracket you're in.

Frankly, the concept of this tax law was to implement some *permanent* corporate tax law, and in order to sell it to the American public, Congress gave individuals and small business some *temporary* tax benefits. Yes, that sounds a little jaded. Not that the corporate provisions are all bad, but it's regrettable that the legislation couldn't have focused more on individuals, included all small-business owners (more to come on that), AND made the entire law permanent. Oh well. I plan to exploit and take advantage of everything I can and, in turn, share all I have learned about this complex law with you.

So, for our purposes in this book, we're not going to concern ourselves with the C corp (big corporation) tax issues, or the individual 1040 tax return issues. Clocking in at over 517 pages long, the joint committee House and Senate Reconciliation Report (the basis for the tax law) is a lot to digest, and approximately 75 percent of it affects big corporations. But the remaining 25 percent and individuals personal taxes.for small-business owners is absolutely critical for your "playbook." My focus is on the small-business owner, you and me!

Building and Implementing a Game Plan

I'm a firm believer in setting regular goals or plans to take your business to the next level. These plans have been and can be called by many different names. For the purposes of this book, a "game plan" refers to any written agenda with a list of tasks that comprise a strategy to address a particular goal or dilemma in your business. As you consider the topics in this book, you may create one broad tax and legal game plan or a variety of game plans to tackle specific issues you are facing in your business. These game plans could be created in meetings with a partner or simply by the sole business owner on a regular basis. They should be implemented over a specific time period, such as a day, week, month, quarter, or year, with lists of projects and tasks to complete.

As you read this book, I encourage you to work on building game plans for your business and personal financial goals that can evolve and that you can update regularly. It is so difficult to manage all the loose ends and chaos that can occur when running a small business. Even experienced business owners can benefit from using game plans as an integral part of their business.

Here are a few issues to consider when building, updating, and implementing game plans based on the ownership of your business and its legal structure:

- *Individual owners.* Anybody who has owned a business knows that success can often turn on one simple principle: self-discipline. When you own a business, there is usually no one leaning over your shoulder making sure you are working the hours you need to and focusing your energy on the right tasks. Take the time on a regular basis to sit down and work on your various game plans to ensure you are staying on target.
- *Partnerships.* Game plans in a partnership don't have as much to do with self-discipline as they do with accountability. It is so important for partners to meet on a regular basis to discuss, strategize, decide, assign, and then document every decision they are making as a partnership. It is so easy to forget who is doing what and why you decided on a certain course of action. In difficult as well as successful times, game plans will often be the glue that holds a partnership together.
- *Board of advisors.* Whether you are an individual owner or have partners, a board of advisors can be a huge resource in implementing your game plans, reviewing them on a regular basis, and holding you accountable. Your board can simply be the professional advisors you rely on and meet with regularly, or it can be a formal board that you have invited to meet with you on pre-set dates and times to collaborate and provide feedback and support. This can be a group of peers with experience in your industry, or a group of family and friends you treat to dinner once a month to get their ideas and support and to report your accomplishments. Everyone loves to give free advice over a nice dinner. Don't underestimate the power of this resource.

Think about these scenarios and players when you craft your various game plans.

What You'll Learn in This Book

The purpose of this book is to address your tax and legal issues and to propose game plans that can offer a **starting point** for an individualized consultation with your CPA or lawyer. Each chapter presents a real-world case study that will set the stage for the consultation and the game plan that follows for that particular situation.

What this book is NOT is a comprehensive guide to the TCJA. This book provides a look at how the tax code has changed and how it may apply to you as a small-business owner. Always consult your CPA or lawyer before making any decisions.

You'll learn the ins and outs of fundamental decisions you need to make for your business—from choosing the proper legal entity to saving the most you can on taxes. I will also highlight some of the scams and deceptions on the market that all too many entrepreneurs fall victim to when it comes to tax and legal planning.

In the pages that follow, you will find concise and straightforward answers to some of the most important tax and legal questions out there. These are questions entrepreneurs from around the country have asked me countless times in my career. Armed with this book, you will never again walk out of your CPA or lawyer's office with your head spinning with unanswered questions.

How to Read This Book

This book is more than a how-to guide. I've taken all the pain points of business owners I've worked with as well as case studies from similar entrepreneurs to tackle the issues most relevant to your tax and legal needs. You can read this book one of two ways. You can read it straight through front-to-back for a comprehensive look at the tax and legal issues your business will face from founding to exit. Or you can use the book as a reference guide, reading chapters as needed to answer your questions as they arise.

Consider each chapter your personal consultation and opportunity to start building a game plan. Use the critical alerts and action-item checklists to meet your own needs. You'll come away wiser and better equipped to make the best decisions for your business, your family, and yourself.

PRE-SEASON PLANNING

In the pre-season, all coaches consider their teams'
overall strengths and weaknesses to create a general
game plan for the upcoming season. We, too, need
to understand our situation has a general game plan
for success and then work towards building smaller,
detailed game plans for specific areas. I'll present the
number-one way to build wealth and save taxes that
should be both part of your general game plan and the
foundation for your more specific game plans.

YOUR GAME PLAN
FOR SUCCESS

—— CASE STUDY ——

A young couple walked into my office. As I joined them to introduce myself and learn what their objectives were, the significance of this meeting quickly became apparent.

They had never met with an attorney before, and although they had worked with an accountant to complete their taxes in years past, they had never requested from their CPA what they planned to ask of me.

They wanted a game plan.

They knew they were paying too much in taxes, and they sincerely wanted to start building more wealth—not so much for their retirement per se, but to feel more financially secure and have the financial independence to someday achieve their own personal American Dream.

I felt a huge responsibility to conduct a positive meeting. It was crucial to not only give them practical ideas and suggestions, but also to provide encouragement, direction, and hope as well. I wanted them to believe in themselves and know their goals weren't out of reach.

As I had anticipated, after some cordial introductions and a welcome, they anxiously asked (like many clients do): "Is there a plan we can actually implement to save taxes and build wealth, or do we just need to keep our heads down and hope for some sort of retirement with our employer and Social Security?"

This is certainly not an uncommon question, and it isn't limited to the young and the restless either (please excuse the pun). I meet with clients on a regular basis who are in their retirement years and still looking for answers.

We are living longer. Costs are going up. The real "security" of Social Security is questionable, and we expect more from our hard-earned income and savings than ever before.

I feel there are answers. I know there are answers. And to find them, you need to start by looking at yourself.

Six Characteristics for Success

Over the years, I have discussed with clients countless times the successful characteristics of those who are financially independent or are living their American Dream.

I have concluded that my successful clients have six primary characteristics. I will briefly discuss each characteristic below, but the remainder of this book contains chapters discussing in much more depth how you can develop, implement, and incorporate these habits into your own life.

1. Entrepreneurship and Owning a Business

I realize this may sound cliché or even crazy, but during my career as an attorney and CPA, I have learned that the first step toward building wealth and saving taxes is to start a small business, which could certainly involve some rental real estate as well. My successful clients have always had a small business at some point on their path to financial independence.

Please hear me out. For those of you who work a regular job and don't want to be an entrepreneur, I'm not asking you to quit your day job. I'm just asking you to at least have a small business on the side.

There are so many good reasons to have a small project brewing on the back burner and very few reasons not to. Some say it is too risky in today's economy to start a business. I say it is too risky *not* to start a small business!

I could go on and on about the benefits of starting your own business: having another source of income to fall back on, embarking on a project you love, turning your hobby into a business, gaining the independence to run a business the way you want, and even hiring your family members to save taxes. But let me just mention the two most important reasons for starting a small business: It gives you 1) an opportunity to build wealth and 2) a way to save on taxes.

When you think long and hard about it, you would probably agree that it is very difficult to build significant, self-sustaining wealth when working exclusively for someone else building *their* wealth.

With a small business, your potential is unlimited. Again, I'm not asking you to quit your career, job, or the trade or skill you have been cultivating for years, but please *at least* start building a project on the side that can give you additional income to invest in the market, buy real estate, or simply build equity in the business itself.

This is the number-one method to build wealth and save taxes! Throughout the rest of this book, I will build on this foundation. As you will quickly discover, a business will allow you to legitimately convert otherwise personal expenses into valid business expenses. There are expenses such as travel, a home office, dining, auto, mobile phones, and computers that you can write off legitimately with a business purpose.

2. Living Below Your Means

My wealthy clients have learned to live well within or even below their means. They know the secret to building wealth isn't living paycheck to paycheck.

Conversely, most of my high-income-earning—but not necessarily wealthy—clients are good salespeople, but they tend to lean on creating additional revenue when an IRS bill or a creditor is looming, rather than having the foresight to save for it beforehand or tightening their belts to adjust. I suggest you consider proactive austerity first, rather than reactive salesmanship to help you out of a bad situation.

The problem with thinking we can always make more money to solve our economic problems is that we can never predict when we'll have ups and downs in our income. Ill health, an economic downturn, embezzlement—a variety of factors could blindside us when we are living paycheck to paycheck. Rather, we should be cutting expenses and living within a reasonable expectation of our means.

The wealthy set aside money to invest and thereby create more passive income in the long run and hence more financial freedom. Yes, you already know this! I'm just reminding you.

3. Investing in Real Estate

The wealthy own real estate. No way to get around it. Yes, we should all be diversified in our investments, and the wealthy certainly invest in a variety of assets. I'm not dismissing marketable securities, brokerage accounts, and market liquidity. But real estate also boasts a variety of incredible wealth-building characteristics.

A February 2014 *Bloomberg* article reported that according to Morgan Stanley, 77 percent of investors with at least $1 million in assets own some type of investment real estate.

4. Managing Retirement Accounts

The wealthy understand and know what is in their retirement accounts. They know that retirement accounts like a 401(k) or IRA are simply vehicles; they aren't "investments."

Some people say, "Oh, I don't want a retirement account. I don't trust the stock market." This is a complete misunderstanding of what a 401(k) and IRA are and how they operate. An owner of a retirement account can invest in a variety of assets including real estate, notes, and small businesses. How you invest in your 401(k) or IRA is up to you—unless your company-sponsored plan limits your choices. However, this isn't because of legal restrictions. Rather, certain plan underwriters don't want to give you an option to "self-direct" because of their policies.

The wealthy understand that they can shift opportunities to their retirement account and self-direct their investments by changing the sponsor or custodian of their plan. I talk about this in detail in Chapter 25 and encourage you to contribute to the retirement account that fits your needs and then invest in what *you* know best. You'll see your wealth grow faster when you control it, not when you blindly leave it up to someone else.

5. Continuing Your Education

The wealthy not only continue to learn about wealth-building and moneymaking strategies, but also continue to learn about money-saving tax and legal strategies. They appreciate what Benjamin Franklin said: "A penny saved is a penny earned." It's just as important to learn about ways to save money as it is to make money.

You may think I'm being self-serving discussing why it's important to continue to learn about tax strategies. Yes, this is a book about tax savings, but I've sadly learned that many people would rather pick up a book at the airport or attend a seminar on money-making strategies than learn about saving money or taxes. I get it. I understand.

However, let me remind you that the greatest expense in your life, not on an annual basis but over your lifetime, will be taxes. So maybe you should learn something about it.

The wealthy subscribe to print and email newsletters on tax and legal strategies. They attend workshops, listen to podcasts, watch webinars, and, most importantly, schedule a consultation with their tax planner at least annually to strategize. Moreover, if they hear about a unique, exotic, or expensive strategy, they get a second opinion from their trusted advisors.

Remember, you are the captain of your team. You don't have to know all the techniques and have the same skills of your team members, but you need to at least understand the big picture. You can't build a game plan if you don't continue to educate yourself on both the basics and cutting-edge strategies.

6. Seeking Professional Advice

The wealthy know their limitations and what they're good at. They delegate technical matters to those with the skills to complete the project. However, they still understand the big picture and their game plan. Those who try to do everything themselves typically make mistakes and miss out on better strategies because they're not experts.

I realize some may find it offensive that our U.S. tax law and business legal system is so complex that an average individual can't prepare their own taxes or legal documents with a little work or research (and it's become even more complex since the new tax law changes went into effect in 2018). I agree with you—it's sad. But, like anything else that is a trade or skill, that doesn't mean we should throw caution to the wind out of spite to prove that we can and should be able to do it ourselves. For example, my home electrical system is so complex that I'd rather hire an electrician than spend my weekends and evenings at Home Depot trying to become expert enough to repair it myself.

I also realize that many of the wealthy got to that point in life because they pinched pennies. However, they don't step over the dollar to pick up the nickel. What this means is that you can certainly save money by shopping for the best service at the most competitive rate, but you don't do it yourself and risk all your hard-earned assets on the chance that you'll miss something.

The internet certainly hasn't helped, either. Online incorporation websites have done a masterful job of dumbing down the process and importance of business planning to the point where everyone thinks it just takes a mouse click and a piece of paper to have a quality asset-protection plan. This couldn't be further from the truth, and extreme caution needs to be taken when using web-based services to seemingly cut corners.

Finally, the wealthy realize that you get what you pay for, further underscoring the fact that building a team to best serve your needs requires work to seek out and interview the right professionals. This entails finding the right CPA who will suggest strategies and match your risk tolerance when addressing gray areas. This also means using the proper attorney for each type of legal issue you may be facing. Gone are the days when a general practitioner attorney could handle all your needs. Asset protection and estate planning attorneys have very different skills and expertise from litigators, divorce lawyers, or bankruptcy attorneys.

Game Plan Takeaway and Action Items

A tax and legal game plan is much more than just learning what the best tax strategy is for the year, like the flavor of the month. Building a game plan is only the precursor to playing the actual game. Building wealth, saving taxes, and protecting your assets requires the right mindset, strong habits, and ongoing procedures.

The wealthy respect the process of tax and legal planning. As I met with the clients in the case study above, their attitude quickly changed to understand the long-term nature of our planning and future relationship. Throughout the rest of this book, I will specifically target aspects of a quality game plan that embrace and exemplify the six characteristics above. They include:

- Embrace entrepreneurship
- Buy real estate
- Live within your means
- Engage with your retirement plan
- Continue to learn tax and legal strategies
- Hire competent professionals

GETTING THE MOST FROM YOUR BUSINESS ENTITY

Your business entity can be the most valuable player on your team. It's critical to choose wisely which entity is best for your business, make changes when necessary, and take advantage of the benefits of your business structure.

SOLE PROPRIETORSHIPS

—— CASE STUDY ——

I was excited to have a follow-up call with Tom, a client who had recently taken my advice to heart and started his own internet-based business. Tom had a corporate job he was very skilled at and was on track to eventually make a very comfortable living. But the tax bill he faced each year was killing him, and he was determined to save on taxes and hopefully make some additional cash flow at the same time.

This strategy was a perfect fit for Tom. His new business was similar to that of millions of other American business owners. It was something he loved doing, he could do it from home, the startup capital was minimal, and it was flexible enough for him to fit into his busy schedule.

The purpose of our call was to determine whether he could simply start as a sole proprietor or if he needed to form a formal entity, like a limited liability company (LLC) or corporation. He had seen and heard various advertisements enticing him to set up his entity easily and inexpensively online, but he wondered whether this would create a domino effect of additional tax and legal reporting requirements in the future.

Within minutes of getting on the phone, he asked in an exasperated tone, "Mark, can I just use a sole proprietorship for now?"

On the face of it, this might seem to be a pretty straightforward question with an easy answer. You might suggest I say, "Sure, just get rolling as a sole proprietor and, in the words of Bob Marley, 'Don't worry about a thing.'"

However, in a quality tax and legal consultation, it's important to consider a variety of issues.

Examine Your Business Needs

For many people, starting out as a sole prop could be a perfect fit, but for equally as many, it could be a disaster.

There isn't a one-size-fits-all approach or answer to a business such as Tom's. You could most certainly have a set of circumstances that are different from Tom's, mine, or anybody else's. For example, consider the following issues that could have a major impact on your entity decision:

- The amount of your earnings and deductions
- Tax planning to avoid paying too much self-employment tax
- Liability exposure from your product, services, or location
- Whether you have a partner or investor in the business
- Where you live and are conducting business

- Business goals and marketing plans
- The administrative costs and demands of setting up certain entities

A custom-tailored consultation and game plan takes all these issues into consideration and applies them to your situation. Let's break down these topics one by one and see what information may trigger additional planning strategies.

GOOD TO KNOW:
WHAT IS A SOLE PROPRIETORSHIP?

A sole proprietorship (sole prop) is the simplest form of doing business. All you need to do is just start selling your product or service. An Employer identification Number (EIN) is required. No "doing business as" (dba) registration is required, although one is recommended for marketing purposes. No business bank account is required, although one is recommended for bookkeeping and audit protection. No extra tax return is required. All your income and expenses are reported on your 1040 Form, Schedule C.

The Self-Employment Tax

One of the primary disadvantages of a sole prop is the self-employment (SE) tax of 15.3 percent on the ordinary net income generated by your business. In 2019, the entire 15.3 percent is applied on the first $132,900 of net income. The SE tax is comprised of a 12.4-percent Social Security tax along with a 2.9-percent Medicare tax. After $132,900, the Medicare tax of 2.9 percent continues to apply, and then at $250,000 (married filing jointly) or $200,000 (single filers) of net income, it climbs up to a total of 3.8 percent in perpetuity. Bottom line, this tax adds up quickly!

Keep in mind, "ordinary income subject to SE tax" includes items such as sales of products or services, commissions, or short-term income in real estate if you are a real estate professional. SE tax doesn't apply to passive income, such as rent, dividends, interest, or capital gain.

Ordinary income can blindside many new business owners with a big SE tax bill in the spring of the following year. Again, the tax benefits of owning a small business are fantastic! But after you write off all your business expenses (see Chapter 9), and the business still has a profit, the SE tax will kick in. However, if your net income is small, don't worry about the SE tax and move on to consider the next issue that may impact whether or not you form an entity.

RUN THE NUMBERS

Assume you hit a home run and earn $45,000 in sales the first year. You write off $15,000 in expenses in a cautiously aggressive manner, which leaves you with $30,000 in profit. Depending on your situation, an S corp (or an LLC taxed as an S corp) could create significant savings by avoiding a portion of the SE tax. (See Chapter 4.)

Sales:	$45,000
Expenses:	$15,000
Profit:	$30,000
SE tax:	$4,590

When evaluating the possible tax ramifications and planning options of your sole prop, it's critical to distinguish between ordinary income and passive income, as I described above. Figure 2.1 on page 17 is a visual representation of how I distinguish between ordinary and passive income for asset protection and tax planning. I'll elaborate upon this diagram and build upon it in future chapters.

Liability Exposure

Another primary disadvantage of the sole prop is the owner's personal responsibility for the liabilities of the business. Thus, carefully analyze what risks exist and if you indeed have exposure. If you do, you may

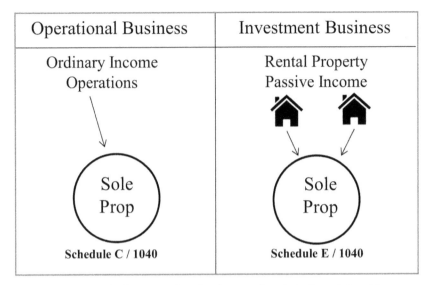

Figure 2.1 – **Ordinary vs. Passive Income in a Sole Proprietorship**

want to consider setting up an entity even if it is unnecessary for tax purposes or any other reason.

One strategic option is setting up an LLC but taxing it as a sole prop. This way, you get the asset protection of an LLC, but you don't have the cumbersome tax reporting of an S or C corporation. However, if you are running a low-to-zero liability exposure business, setting up an entity for liability protection purposes probably isn't necessary. Continue to address any other issues or reasons that would make setting up an entity necessary.

Business Partners or Investors

If you have a partner or investor in your business, it's almost a given that you will form an entity rather than operate as a sole prop. Simply by definition, having a partner means you need to file a partnership tax return, will be taxed as a partnership, *and* have personal vicarious liability exposure for your partner's actions. Additionally, you will want to legally document your relationship with the individuals you are doing business with and be careful not to open yourself up to a lawsuit with a "handshake deal" (see Chapter 22).

CRITICAL ALERT!
THE DO-IT-YOURSELF SCREW-UP

I recently had a consultation with a client who was the mirror image of a client I met with the previous week, and the week before that, and the week before that. They had one thing in common—they attempted to try a do-it-yourself (DIY) entity formation online. In fact, I meet with clients on a regular basis who have tried to form their entity online and now have a myriad of problems that include any and all of the following:

- There is only one sheet of paper showing the formation of the entity and no supporting documents.
- The entity is set up in the wrong state.
- The entity has expired because it wasn't renewed on time and with the proper method.
- The wrong entity was registered altogether.

Using the sole prop may be exactly what you need to do and rushing into setting up an entity on your own without consulting the proper professional could waste your time, money, and energy.

With the introduction and onslaught of online incorporation services, thousands of people think they now have a way to save big money and play lawyer. But consider this: My law firm employs a full-time paralegal to clean up entities for clients who attempted to do it themselves online.

Don't get me wrong. If you have set up multiple entities in the past and/or consulted a professional who comprehensively analyzed all of your issues, *and* you actually implement all of the proper documents to form an entity (not just filing basic articles online for an LLC), then go ahead and form your own entity online.

However, for the rest of you entrepreneurs and new business owners, please have a real law firm (one that's affordable and gives a proper consult) set up your entity for you.

Location

Please know that if and when you set up an entity for an operational business, it's absolutely *critical* that you establish the entity in the state where you are doing business. (It's a different scenario when establishing an entity for a rental property.) If you don't, you won't receive any asset-protection benefit from the structure in the state where you are doing business. So when you do your cost-benefit analysis, look specifically at your state and determine whether operating as a sole prop is more advantageous. For example, the filing fees for an entity can be extremely high in states like Texas or Illinois, and the ongoing minimum tax for an entity can be expensive in states like California. Do your homework.

Business Goals and Marketing Plans

If you are investing in a robust marketing plan and working hard to brand your company name or product, setting up a formal entity early may be a wise move to protect your name (at least in the state where you are doing business). In the short run, a dba (doing business as) registration could certainly protect your name until you set up your entity. However, in some states, it costs just as much—and is just as big of a hassle—to file for a dba as it is to set up an entity. Moreover, you won't be able to use the initials "LLC" or "Inc." at the end of your company name or in your marketing materials until the entity is established.

There is also an image issue. You may desire the legitimacy and image of having a more established entity like an LLC or a corporation. If it's important in your field or industry, having the initials of an entity after your company name could be more strategic than looking like a garage startup doing business under your personal name or a dba.

Business Credit

As I discuss more fully in Chapter 7, setting up an entity is essential to establishing and building business credit. When you create a formal entity, you will obtain a Tax ID number and eventually be able to establish credit and borrow funds solely in the name of your company.

Building business credit takes time, but when done properly, it can be a huge asset to a small-business owner. This alone could be your reason for forgoing a sole prop and setting up an entity right out of the gate.

Administrative Costs and Requirements

It's important to do a cost-benefit analysis during this entity research process to ensure it makes financial sense to set up an entity. Keep in mind that each state's filing fees and annual reporting procedures and costs will vary dramatically. Moreover, some states impose taxes specific to certain types of entities that you wouldn't typically realize exist. Your attorney should be able to easily cite the costs to you. You can also visit the various state websites, starting with the tax commission and secretary of state sites, to gather this information.

Typically, there are four costs to consider: 1) filing fees and setup costs, 2) annual maintenance fees and services, 3) any state entity taxes on gross or net income, and 4) tax return preparation and services throughout the year. Again, these costs will vary dramatically based on the state and type of entity. Make sure to get several quotes, and don't think doing it online is always the best move. You get what you pay for.

If you discover after this cost-benefit analysis that the costs of setting up and maintaining an entity far outweigh any benefits it offers you, then a sole prop could be the perfect fit as long as you don't also have tax, liability, or partner issues.

Game Plan Takeaway and Action Items

In Tom's situation, we ultimately decided to go with a sole prop for now and review his situation at the beginning of the next year. We didn't anticipate a tax problem, there was no real liability threat, and he had no partners. The sole prop was a great fit for Tom, and he was off and running.

I often tell clients that unless there is a major liability, partnership, or tax issue, starting out as a sole prop is a great fit. Don't get too complex too quickly. Make sure your business concept is viable and become familiar with entrepreneurship before investing in a more advanced structure. But if you begin making more money (or believe you will) or have liability exposure, you should consider other options.

If you still want to do some DIY planning, I get it. It sounds great, and I realize all of us are on a budget. But at least have your structure reviewed by an attorney and a tax professional who know this area of the law.

- If you anticipate making more than $30,000 in ordinary net income before year-end, consider the S corp (see Chapter 4).
- If you have liability exposure, consider forming a single-member LLC to establish protection, but report your taxes as a sole proprietor to simplify things (see Chapter 3).
- If you have partners or investors, consider an LLC so you can avoid the vicarious liability for your partners' actions, and have the operating agreement for the LLC to document the agreement between each of you (see Chapter 22).
- If you plan to establish business credit quickly, setting up an entity will be critical (see Chapter 7).
- If you plan to invest in your brand and image, and you need the credibility and image of a formal corporation or LLC, setting up a formal entity from the outset could save you a lot of headaches down the road trying to rebrand your company name and image.
- Carefully consider a cost-benefit analysis of setting up an entity vs. operating as a sole prop before deciding.

3

LIMITED LIABILITY COMPANIES

—— CASE STUDY ——

I recently had lunch with two incredible women in my local area who had just started a cleaning business. I was impressed with their idea and dedication to hard work. My wife and I owned a janitorial business for seven years as we worked our way through college and graduate school, and I know that running this type of business is no small venture.

As best friends, they were anxious to make sure they were doing everything correctly and as "officially" as possible. Their intentions were admirable, but in their zealousness to get started, they fell prey to one of the current doctrines in small-business culture: "If we are going to be in business, we had better set up an LLC."

So they set up a limited liability company (LLC). They didn't know why, what the tax ramifications were, or how to set it up correctly. They simply went online, and after a few mouse clicks, they assumed they were now in business because they had an LLC.

Regrettably, this is not an uncommon experience. Some of you reading this book may be thinking, "So . . . what's the problem, Mark?" Frankly, the LLC isn't the be-all and end-all for small businesses. One of these dedicated ladies must have already had this gut feeling because as soon as we sat down for lunch, she asked, "Should we have an LLC?"

Far too many people rush out to set up an LLC because it seems like the "common" or "right" thing to do once you start a business.

I don't know where this fad originated or who started the spread of misdirection and misinformation, but the LLC, for all its pros and cons, is here to stay for the foreseeable future. Thus, I would be remiss not to tackle this important topic and set the record straight.

An LLC is a fantastic entity for certain reasons, but it can also have some major drawbacks. Some of the benefits of an LLC are:

- Personal protection from the operations of the business (i.e., lawsuits)
- The ability to reserve a business name and create a formal brand
- Documentation of the relationship in a partnership via the LLC operating agreement

However, an LLC may surprise new business owners in the following ways:

- An LLC does not save taxes in any way, shape, or form. However, a taxpayer *still gets* the 199A pass-through deduction as a sole prop. The LLC doesn't change that. (You'll read more about the "pass-through deduction" in Chapter 6.)

- Business owners still pay the SE tax with an LLC. I can assure you that you will be shocked by SE taxes if you generate ordinary net income (and don't think your accountant can save you with a "guaranteed payment" to try and right this wrong). The IRS has been very clear that you can't fabricate a salary for an active business owner of an LLC to get around the dreaded SE tax; this only works for an S corp. (Read about the S corp in Chapter 4.)
- Many states have additional operational costs and/or high filing fees or taxes for an LLC. (Think of California, where the LLC minimum tax is a "gross receipts tax," while the franchise tax rates for an S corp are based on the net-income.)

The bottom line is: Make sure you have a full picture and understanding of the LLC before you commit to one.

Three Major Reasons to Use an LLC

I believe it boils down to three reasons why an LLC might make sense in certain situations for a new business owner. Let's take a look at those.

1. Liability Protection With Rental Property

The number-one reason thousands of LLCs are created and used around the country every year is to hold rental property. The LLC protects the owner and manager of the property from the operations of the business/rental. In order to have this protection, the manager and owner (referred to as the "members") of the LLC need to act responsibly—without negligence and within the scope of their duties and responsibilities. (See Chapter 8 for more information on how to protect the corporate veil.)

The well-established laws and statutes of LLCs across the states will protect the members of the LLC from liabilities that could arise with contractors, tenants, and guests of tenants on the

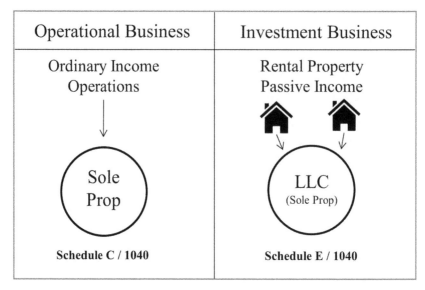

Figure 3.1 – **Investment LLC**

property. Thus, if you even own *one* rental property, an LLC should be a serious and important consideration. Figure 3.1 shows where an LLC would be used on the investment side of your business structure.

Moreover, LLCs can be used for higher-level asset protection when trying to protect the "asset" as well as the owner from the liabilities of the rental property. This is generally referred to as a COPE (Charging Order Protection Entity) and applies to LLCs in approximately 20 States. (See Chapter 21 for more details on this type of entity and strategy.)

2. Liability Protection in an Operational Business and Ability to Convert to an S Corporation Later

Sometimes an LLC can be a great stepping stone for a new business owner when they have an operational business. As I discuss in Chapter 2 regarding sole props, SE tax applies to *ordinary net income* in an operational business. Just because you form an LLC doesn't mean you can limit the SE tax on that ordinary income. Here is a list of typical kinds of income, divided into ordinary or passive:

Ordinary Income	Passive Income
Sales of product	Rental income
Sales of services	Interest
Commissions	Dividends
Wholesaling real estate	Capital gain
Fixing/flipping real estate	Royalties

SE tax applies to ordinary net income but not passive income. The best way to limit SE tax is to implement an S corp. However, one of the major benefits of an LLC is that you can obtain asset protection early in the life of your business while your ordinary net income may still be low or inconsequential and later retroactively convert to an S corp when the time is right. This is because under the tax code, an LLC can be converted to an S corp retroactively by filing an IRS Form 2553. (This type of situation typically involves a single-member LLC.)

Let's look at an example. Figure 3.2 illustrates how an LLC could work as an operational LLC and as a sister company to another LLC holding rentals. The LLC on the left gives the owner/member asset protection for their operational business and can evolve to an S corp as needed.

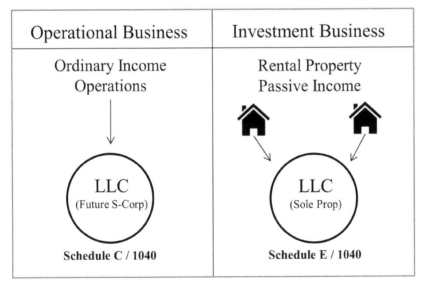

Figure 3.2 – **Operational LLC**

> ### GOOD TO KNOW:
> ### WHAT IS A SINGLE-MEMBER LLC?
>
> A single-member LLC (SMLLC) is an LLC owned by one individual (or entity) and offers a unique cost-saving benefit. The owner gets asset protection yet no extra tax return. The owner can report the LLC's operations on their tax return (typically a Schedule C if an individual or on a consolidated tax return if another entity owns 100 percent of the LLC). Also, if the owner is an individual, they can choose to convert to an S corp retroactively to the beginning of any tax year without a timing problem.

It's important to note that forming an LLC doesn't simply mean filing a single piece of paper with the state. It's crucial that the owner treat the formation and maintenance of an LLC similar to that of a corporation to receive the same type of protection. Many new business owners fall prey to the false belief that an LLC is simpler to set up and maintain. In Chapter 8, I discuss corporate maintenance, applicable to all entities, as one of the basic and important asset protection practices when setting up and maintaining an entity.

3. Advantageous for Partnerships

An LLC is excellent for partnerships. It protects each partner from the actions of the other partner and allows for more efficient tax planning. Most important, the LLC creates a mechanism to document all the agreements and terms of the partnership. Far too many business owners partner with others based on agreements made by a handshake, email, or some scribbles on a napkin at Denny's or Waffle House.

An LLC can be designed so that each partner holds their share in the form of an S corp. As I mentioned above, an LLC can be used on the operational side by an individual owner for at least protection and the *potential* to convert the entity to an S corp later, but the LLC can also be used in a significantly creative manner with partners. This allows each partner to take additional tax write-offs utilizing their

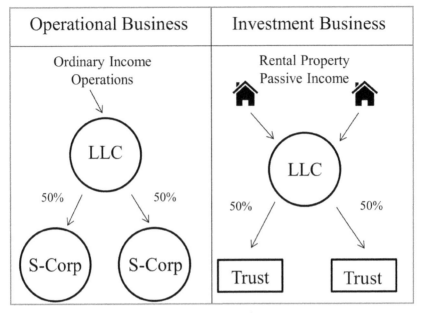

Figure 3.3 – **Partnership LLCs**

own S corp as an *owner* of the LLC, receive other sources of revenue, establish his or her own payroll levels to save on self-employment tax, and even create a 401(k) or health plan tailored to their situation. The possibilities seem almost endless. Figure 3.3 shows how an LLC can help protect both the ordinary income and the passive income of a partnership.

An LLC is just as important when investing in rentals with partners on the passive side of the equation. With the LLC, the partners (or members of the LLC) are not only personally protected from the actions of the other partners, but the entity also provides documentation for the terms of the partnership. Moreover, partners can *also* integrate the estate planning for each partner into the LLC with their trust/estate plan. Typically, the ownership of the LLC would be held in the name of each partner's revocable living trust.

I discuss this ancillary benefit of estate planning and the LLC further in Chapter 26. Just because a partner has stepped up to the plate in terms of an LLC and asset protection, it does not necessarily mean the partner has considered who will inherit their share of the LLC upon their passing, whether it be family, loved ones, or charity. The title of any property or assets would be held by the LLC for asset protection purposes, but the ownership of the LLC would be in the respective trusts, which eases the inheritance process should one partner die.

Series LLCs

Most business owners understand the concept and importance of isolating assets or ventures that may expose them to personal liability. As a result, business owners have historically had to pay to create and then manage separate LLCs for each property, group of properties, or business venture.

Various states have tried to resolve this problem by enacting "Series LLC" laws. When structured properly and respected, a Series LLC gives members limited personal liability from claims arising from multiple properties or operations without having the extra costs of multiple LLCs.

What makes a Series LLC different is its ability to establish designated "series" or "mini-LLCs" within the original LLC ("parent LLC"). Each series within the parent LLC can have its own specified property, assets, investment objective, or business purpose. The debts, obligations, and liabilities of each series are only enforceable against the assets of that series, not against the assets of the parent LLC or any other series.

CRITICAL ALERT!
THE DELAWARE/NEVADA/WYOMING CORPORATION

This is probably one of the biggest scams in the asset protection industry. For convenience, I'll refer to this as the "Nevada entity" because it has been sold for years as the supreme state for small-business owners to incorporate in. However, Delaware, Wyoming, and even New Mexico are also sold as great states to incorporate in due to their favorable business laws.

CRITICAL ALERT!, CONTINUED

Essentially, Nevada entities—whether an LLC, S corp, or C corp—are oversold to thousands of people each year using scare tactics, misinformation, and half-truths. Promoters will try to prod, push, and scare new business owners into making a rash decision and setting up their entity too quickly, while promising unrealistic tax and asset benefits.

Yes, if you are living or doing business *in* one of these states, you might save state taxes or even receive better asset protection. But if you live or do business elsewhere, and in a state that imposes state tax, you will most certainly not save on taxes by incorporating in Nevada, Wyoming, or any non-income state tax jurisdiction, for that matter. You will still pay tax in the state where you live or do business. (Don't get sucked into the C corp sales pitch either. I discuss this scam in a separate alert in Chapter 5.)

Is the asset protection better in some of these states? *Yes, if you are doing business in that state!* If not, you won't get any extra asset protection at all. In fact, if you don't take the time to register your entity in the state where you are operating the business (an extra cost, mind you), you will be personally exposed and have no protection whatsoever.

For example, if you are doing business in Colorado, you will need to register your company there anyway and pay the necessary state taxes. By incorporating in Nevada, all you do is increase your administrative costs and headaches with additional state filings. Set up your company in the state where you are doing business and follow your state laws for maintaining the corporate veil. The *corporate veil* (which you'll read more about later) is the legal principle that a barrier or veil of protection exists between the business and its owners and officers or managers, thus offering them personal asset protection from the operations of the business. You receive this protection with an LLC or corporation, and if you maintain it properly, you won't need to waste your hard-earned dollars registering in a state where you aren't operating.

In addition, if the Series LLC is properly created, the owner can avoid filing separate tax returns for each series. For an entrepreneur with multiple investment properties or business ventures, the Series LLC may be an extremely useful tool. (See Appendix C for a list of states that have enacted Series LLC laws.)

Do I Need an LLC for Every Rental Property I Own?

In my opinion, the answer to this question comes down to the amount of equity you have in each of your properties, where they are located, and which properties carry the highest risk of a potential lawsuit. Some people say the safest bet is to create a new LLC for every property. However, in many states, this can be expensive, and the bookkeeping and records for the LLCs can lead to cumbersome headaches.

It should really be an issue of quality rather than quantity. For example, you may want to keep your high-equity properties separate from your high-risk properties. Consider grouping low-equity properties together in one LLC with high-equity properties in another LLC. Or when the equity in your first LLC gets too high, transfer some of the properties out to a new LLC, separating your eggs into different baskets to reduce your risk. If you have properties in different states, you could also group them into state-specific LLCs. Or if you have properties in a state that allows it, consider setting up or converting to a Series LLC. For more on this see Chapter 8.

Doesn't a Corporation Give Me Better Asset Protection than an LLC?

No. You might even hear the opposite: that LLCs provide better protection than corporations. Myths prevail on both sides of the aisle as to which entity provides the best protection. The truth is that the protection the corporate veil provides owners, officers, and managers is a legal concept applied uniformly across LLCs and corporations across the U.S. under statutes and years of case law. Real asset protection from your entity's operations comes down to following corporate procedures, not commingling funds, using the company name on all documentation, and managing your company responsibly. (See Chapter 8 for more information on protecting the corporate veil.) This is the same legal principle and concept no matter which entity you choose.

Game Plan Takeaway and Action Items

The LLC is primarily for asset protection, holding real estate, and/or to document and operate a partnership. An LLC does not save taxes in and of itself; however, you can have an LLC taxed as an S or C corp if appropriate.

With my amazing cleaning business partners, we were able to use the LLC for now but with some tweaking to the formation documents to better memorialize the terms of their agreement. Moreover, we had to get creative on the tax planning side until their profits dictated the need for each of them to have their own S corp. Luckily, we were able to use what they created and not "throw the baby out with the bath water;" however, that isn't the case for everyone setting up their entity on their own.

For new entrepreneurs, simply clicking a button on an incorporation website can do more harm than good without some comprehensive planning behind the decision. Moreover, without proper formation documents, the LLC articles of organization may not even be worth the paper they're printed on. Every LLC needs to have all the correct pieces and parts, or the asset protection and corporate veil will be missing. By cutting corners, you won't get the proper protection, and you'll have to spend more money later to have an attorney clean it up and provide the necessary documentation.

With all that said, an LLC can be extremely powerful and helpful in a well-designed tax and asset protection plan. Consider the following factors if you're thinking about an LLC:

- If you own rental property, you should consider an LLC.
- If you need asset protection and have ordinary income operations, but want to convert to an S corp, you should consider an LLC.

- If you are in a partnership, you should consider an LLC.
- Don't feel pressured to set up an LLC for every rental property.
- Watch out for companies and self-professed gurus suggesting that you should create entities in states other than where the property is, where you are doing business, or where you reside.
- Stay away from online incorporation unless you have done it before. If you do choose to incorporate online, make sure to get all the documents and corporate book that come with a complete package.

4

S CORPORATIONS

——— CASE STUDY ———

Cynthia was a marriage and family therapist with an all-too-familiar story. She was a successful professional paying far too much in taxes while working with an archaic tax advisor.

As a sole proprietor, Cynthia had built a nice practice over the course of six years. She was now close to breaking $100,000 in net income, and her situation was similar to that of many other consultants, sales reps, realtors, dentists, doctors, real estate flippers, and internet marketers I advise.

She was writing off every expense she could think of, but her net income was still getting a major haircut with the 15.3-percent self-employment tax. She anticipated that this year she would make more than $75,000 after expenses and her SE tax bill would be more than $10,000 . . . and *then* she would pay federal and state tax.

The exasperating part of the story for me was to hear that her current CPA had never even suggested an S corp. This was a travesty and was costing her thousands of dollars every year.

She summarized the situation simply and quickly. Then, with hope in her voice that I would give her a positive response, she asked, "When is the right time to consider an S corp?"

Most small-business owners with operational businesses should at some point consider organizing their ventures as an S corp. The asset protection could be critical and the tax savings significant, depending on their situation.

Reasons to Choose an S Corporation

Thanks to the new Tax Cut and Jobs Act (TCJA) legislation that passed in 2017 and took effect in 2018, there are now four major reasons why you may choose to form an S corp. First, shareholders and officers of an S corp are not personally liable for corporate debts and liabilities. Second, the S corp's net income will not be subject to self-employment tax (SE tax is a combination of Social Security and Medicare taxes, also referred to as FICA). Third, there is now an interplay between maximizing the 199A pass-through deduction and the FICA savings unique only to an S corp. Finally, many new business owners misunderstand or underestimate the power of building corporate credit with an S corp. The significance of these four benefits cannot be over emphasized, and it's my opinion that the *vast* majority of operational small businesses should be operating as an S corp.

In fact, many small-business owners already take advantage of the savings that an S corp offers in regard to the SE tax. However, some tax planners advise business owners to stay away from the S corp because the strategy to save on SE tax is subject to abuse by some unscrupulous business owners and sometimes comes under fire by legislators. Please don't listen to this advice without getting a second opinion.

Bottom line, the S-corp strategy works when it is used properly and not abused. The majority of our legislators know this. The S-corp SE tax-saving strategy has been around for years, it's only been more validated and its benefits expanded under the TCJA, and I feel strongly it will continue to be so for many more years to come. Now, let's dig deeper into the reasons why an S corp may be right for you.

Asset Protection Benefits

As with the LLC and corporation, asset protection is one of the major benefits of the S corp. In fact, the same protection of the corporate veil is afforded to C corps, S corps, and LLCs, provided they are established and maintained properly. I discuss asset protection procedures for maintaining an entity more fully in Chapter 8.

Saving on Self-Employment Tax

S corps can save immensely on the dreaded SE tax. If you're operating as a sole prop or an LLC and creating ordinary income from operations (i.e., sales of services or products), all of your net income is subject to FICA/SE tax. As I explained in the Sole Proprietorship section (Chapter 2), in 2019, the entire 15.3 percent is applied on the first $132,900 of net-income. The SE tax is comprised of a 12.4-percent Social Security tax along with a 2.9-percent Medicare tax. After $132,900, the Medicare tax of 2.9 percent continues to apply, and then at $250,000 (married filing jointly) or $200,000 (single filers) of net income, it climbs up to a total of 3.8 percent in perpetuity. Bottom line, this tax adds up quickly!

However, in an S corp, the SE tax does not apply to the net profit like it does in an LLC or sole prop. As long as the S corp owners take a reasonable payroll (i.e., salary) through a W-2, the tax law allows the owner to take a good portion of their profit as net income under the K-1, thus saving on SE tax. The beauty of this strategy is that the

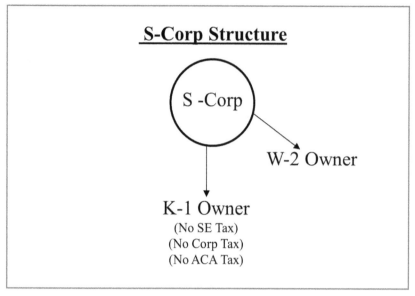

Figure 4.1 – **S Corporation Structure**

business owner only pays SE tax on their payroll and not on the flow-through income or net profit. Figure 4.1 is a visual representation of how the S corp generally functions and the benefits of splitting income into payroll and pass-through or K-1 income.

GOOD TO KNOW:
S CORPS VS. C CORPS

S corps are designed for small businesses; this election restricts companies to no more than 100 shareholders. The big benefit is that the S corp isn't subject to corporate tax. As a result, shareholders avoid corporate tax (often referred to as double tax) on their net income. Net income, after all business expenses are deducted, flows through to the shareholders of the S corp and their personal 1040 tax return on a Form K-1. In contrast, C corps are subject to corporate tax and are built for large corporations that need to raise capital via thousands, if not millions, of shareholders.

199A Pass-Through Deduction

Thanks to the 2018 tax law changes, small-business owners are now able to take advantage of the 199A deduction, which allows pass-through entities (like an S corp) to take a 20-percent deduction off the net profit or bottom line.

Although this deduction also applies to LLCs and sole props, it is even better with an S corp. The reason why is that the S corp allows you to save *both* on SE tax while maximizing the 199A pass-through deduction at the same time. In fact, a wise and strategic tax planner will carefully plan the optimal salary for the S corp owner, while at the same time calculate the 199A deduction. (Please see Chapter 6 for an in-depth discussion and analysis of how to take advantage of this strategy.)

Business Credit

As I mentioned earlier, many small-business owners establish an S corp to start the process of building business credit (sometimes referred to as "corporate credit"). When you create an S corp, you will obtain a Tax ID number and immediately will be able to start implementing steps to establish credit and borrow funds solely in your company's name. It takes time, but when done properly, it can be a huge asset to a small-business owner and is a notable ancillary benefit to operating an S corp. (See Chapter 7 in regard to building personal and corporate credit.)

S Corporation Tax Abuse

The problem with this strategy is that some small-business owners abuse it by taking too little or no salary, thus ruining it for the rest of us. Because of the abuse, Congress occasionally takes up this issue and debates this strategy.

Many people consider these bills terrible for business and the economy, and typically the Senate will shoot them down. In fact, there are several major advocacy groups lobbying behind the scenes to make this happen, such as the American Institute of CPAs, the Chamber of

Commerce, and the National Association of Realtors. S corp FICA/SE tax strategy has been around for years, and it will continue to be so for many more years to come.

RUN THE NUMBERS

If you gross $100,000 and net $75,000 after expenses, the tax savings with an S corp could be significant. Keep in mind that half of the self-employment tax is an above-the-line deduction—i.e., a deduction taken when calculating your adjusted gross income—so each taxpayer's case will vary. Here is a basic example to show the potential savings:

Sole Proprietorship		S Corporation	
Sales:	$100,000	Sales:	$100,000
Expenses:	$25,000	Expenses:	$25,000
Profit:	$75,000	Profit:	$75,000
SE Tax:	$11,475	Payroll:	$36,000
		FICA Tax:	$5,508
		K-1 Income:	$36,246
+ State and Federal Taxes		+ State and Federal Taxes	
		Savings:	$5,967

Choosing the Proper Payroll Level

In regard to payroll and net-income planning, we consistently encourage our clients to allocate at least one-third of their net income to "wage earnings," and the remaining amount can flow out as "net income" not subject to SE tax. However, please know this is a starting point; every taxpayer is different. Moreover, it's important to maintain this procedure through proper payroll planning, especially in light of the TCJA pass-through savings of 20 percent you're going to get. The reason being is that the IRS knows

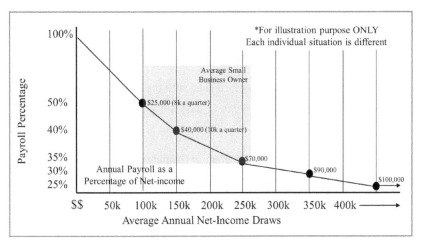

Figure 4.2 – **Kohler Payroll Matrix**

that S corp owners are now even more motivated to take a lower salary in some instances in order to maximize the 199A deduction. Thus, taking a proper and *reasonable* salary is more important than ever.

Figure 4.2 is a useful visual guide in determining the proper payroll level in your S corp from year to year. Keep in mind as you look it over that each individual's situation is different. That said, I've been using this type of matrix in my accounting firm and law firm for almost 20 years, and we've never had a client audited for taking too little of payroll. I'm confident it's a great starting point for considering the proper payroll level.

The Future of S Corporations

S corps have a far-reaching effect on our economy. The IRS estimates that there were 4.6 million S corp owners in the United States in 2014—over twice the number of C corps. Moreover, according to the S Corporation Association of America, pass-through companies contribute more to the bottom line of the economy than do C corps, and the percentage of entrepreneurs choosing this type of business entity is growing.

CRITICAL ALERT!
THE TOO-CONSERVATIVE PLANNER

The abuse of the S corp strategy, coupled with the fact that many CPAs are overly conservative, causes clients to miss out on this strategy time and again.

If your CPA is discouraging this strategy or claiming that your salary needs to be so high the savings won't be worth it, the problem isn't the strategy; the problem is your CPA's definition of "too high."

There have been hundreds of published cases giving examples of abuse and IRS enforcement for low salary levels. Ninety percent of these cases are instances where the taxpayer took no salary at all! In the other cases, where owners took a salary yet were still audited, their payroll fell outside the guidelines I set in the Kohler Payroll Matrix on the previous page.

Some practitioners will also argue that the S corp is going away, so why bother? This makes no sense to me. Use the strategy as long as it's available, and if Congress limits the S corp, we can all modify our approaches at that point.

If you have a profitable business as a sole prop, your CPA or tax advisor could be costing you thousands. Do they have the same risk tolerance as you? You are the captain of your ship. Take control of your business and get a second opinion.

Avoiding the Affordable Care Act Tax

Many taxpayers have forgotten or don't realize that there is an additional .09-percent tax based on the Affordable Care Act (ACA) on any net income above $200,000 for single taxpayers, or $250,000 combined net income for married couples. This applies to any ordinary net income you generate in your sole prop or LLC.

Another unique benefit of the S corp is that this additional ACA tax does not apply to the net flow-through K-1 income of an S corp—

WORD OF WARNING

It is absolutely critical that once you start to operate as an S corp, you implement a payroll procedure *and* make sure it functions at a reasonable level. Quarterly payroll reports are required, but the system can be simple and affordable. There are many national, regional, and local payroll companies that provide this service as well as CPAs who provide one-stop shopping for their clients.

If you are operating as an LLC and decide to make a retroactive S-election at the beginning of the year, you need to make sure your payroll is processed before the appropriate deadline for the year (typically January 15 for the prior year at the latest). If you try to pull off the election in a subsequent year without making the payroll cutoff or by not having payroll at all, your risk of an audit, penalties, taxes, and interest increases dramatically.

---

only to the W-2 portion over the $200,000/$250,000 limits. Thus, if you plan your payroll level properly, you can structure your business to save even more on taxes.

How Do I Create an S Corporation and Make the S-Election

First, you set up a "standard corporation" or LLC with your Secretary of State. This is where I recommend the new business owner get a little support or advice in the process. It's not as easy as clicking a mouse with an online incorporation service.

I literally have two full-time employees doing "clean-ups" for clients who set up their own entity. This means we are either explaining why and what they did, re-doing the documents, or completely starting over because they checked the wrong boxes during the online set-up process. Oftentimes, they end up spending more later rather than if they had just called our law firm in the first place (where we charge a fair and reasonable price).

Now once the entity is set up, it's all about the "election" or paperwork that needs to be filed with the IRS. The next step is to file Form 2553 within 75 days of incorporation. This form declares that you want your entity taxed as an S corp and the date you want that change to be effective. Nonetheless, don't be discouraged if you miss this 75-day window. For example, as I mentioned in Chapter 3

WHO QUALIFIES AS AN S CORPORATION SHAREHOLDER?

If you aren't already a U.S. citizen, you must at least be a resident alien to be an S corp shareholder. There are two tests to determine if you can qualify as a resident alien:

1. *The Green Card Test.* If you are a lawful permanent resident with a green card (Immigration Form I-551), it doesn't matter how long you've been present in the country; you can qualify as an S corp shareholder.

2. *The Substantial Presence Test.* This test is essentially mathematical. It is satisfied if the individual is physically present in the U.S. for the requisite amount of time. For the purposes of the test, presence during any portion of a day is considered presence for a full day. The Substantial Presence Test is met in either of the following circumstances:

    a. the individual is physically present in the U.S. for 183 days or more during the target calendar year, or

    b. the individual is present in the U.S. for at least 31 days for the year in question and has been present for 183 days which are the sum of a) days during the target year counted as full days, plus b) days in the first preceding year counted as one-third days, plus c) days in the second preceding year counted as one-sixth days.

In summary, if you have a green card or if you have been living in the U.S. for 183 days or more during the calendar year, then you are eligible to be a shareholder of an S corp. Remember, you need to pass this test every year until you get your green card.

regarding LLCs, it's oftentimes an excellent strategy to backdate an LLC to S-corp status back to the beginning of the year even though the 75 days have long passed.

In 2013, the IRS provided regulations under Revenue Procedure 2013-30, which allows a small-business owner to convert their current business entity to an S corp retroactively to the beginning of the year, even if you miss the 75-day deadline. However, keep in mind that once you make this election it's extremely important you report payroll and follow all the steps required under S-corp status. It's more complicated than filing Form 2553 and thinking all is well. If you make a mistake, you may not get your election made effective.

Game Plan Takeaway and Action Items

I'm convinced that the S corp has to be the single most influential tax and legal strategy for a growing small business.

Over the years that followed, Cynthia, the therapist I mentioned in the case study earlier in this chapter, never once regretted her decision to implement an S corp. If you are considering creating ordinary net income, it's only a matter of time until you take advantage of the S-corp structure.

- Asset protection is the primary benefit of incorporating; the tax savings are an added benefit.
- If you plan to build business credit, an S corp can be a good choice.
- If you need asset protection and are not sure about your income level yet, use an LLC and then make an S-election when the time is right.
- If you are making more than $30,000 in annual net income in your business or plan to make that much before year-end, an S corp could be a perfect fit for you.
- Make sure to look at the overall cost of the setup and mainte-nance of the S corp in your state (it varies) and compare this cost to your potential savings.

- Find a payroll service as soon as you start operating as an S corp, and make sure you're on top of the procedure.
- Have your CPA walk you through the proper payroll level, and don't be afraid to be cautiously aggressive.

5

C CORPORATIONS

—— CASE STUDY ——

I met with a couple in a hotel lobby in downtown Seattle. They were new clients, and we were meeting to discuss their recently purchased tax and legal plan that had cost them several thousand dollars—more than $5,000. This elaborate tax and legal entity plan came complete with a limited liability corporation (LLC), C corp, limited partnership, and trust. On its own, each structure or entity was properly set up and legitimate. However, the plan as a whole was far more than the clients needed, and the cost to maintain it would certainly outweigh the purported benefits.

My clients only had two rental properties, and while one spouse was maintaining a W-2 day job, the other was pursuing short-term real estate deals with fix-and-flip and wholesale properties. I agreed they needed some asset protection planning and tax advice, but they had been oversold the C corp as the entity that would solve all their problems. C corps primarily exist to serve large companies selling stock to thousands of shareholders. My new clients were lied to about the benefits of a C corp in their situation and what they really required. To add insult to injury, the entities weren't formed or registered in the state where they lived or owned rental properties and added operational costs to their budget.

While it was initially a very sad and frustrating meeting for my new clients, they were ultimately relieved and grateful to receive advice they knew they could rely on—and not have to worry that they were being scammed again.

Regrettably, the above experience is all too common. The lawyers and CPAs in my firms meet with new clients in this predicament on a regular basis. I understand we are all searching for tax and legal strategies that provide significant benefits, but some promises are far too good to be true. While some products and services are outright scams that offer no asset protection or tax benefits, another dilemma is that although some of these complex strategies may work, the costs far outweigh the benefits for the small-business owner.

When the C Corporation Makes Sense

It is true that almost every Fortune 500 company is set up as a C corp, and they have specific reasons for doing so, such as raising capital and abiding by securities laws in order to go public. But for the average small-business owner or startup, this is completely unnecessary. Large corporations have different goals from small-business owners, the least of which is saving money on taxes. A small-business owner's needs are *very* different, and most of the time they can skip the complications of corporate double taxation (which I explain in more detail later in this chapter) and just use an LLC or S corp.

Myths about C Corporations for Small-Business Owners

In my opinion, the C corp is one of the greatest pitfalls in tax planning for the small-business owner, and it astonishes me how many lawyers promote it. If they want to sell setting up a new corporation, that's fine. However, I wish they would sell the S corp, which might actually help people achieve their business goals.

Essentially, there are three myths used to sell entrepreneurs C-corp packages they do not need:

1. The myth of extra tax deductions
2. The myth of lower corporate tax rate vs. personal tax rates
3. The myth that they can avoid the double-taxation problem with a higher salary

Let me briefly address each of these myths and suggest you use them as a starting point for a mindful consultation with your CPA or tax attorney.

Myth 1: Extra C Corporation Tax Deductions

Advocates for the C corp will contend that because of all the entity's extra tax deductions (discussed below), you'll be able to dramatically reduce your net income far more than you could with any other type of entity. I have grave concerns with this argument.

There is a list that tax book authors, self-professed gurus onstage, and call centers with scripts will present that contains all of these "cool" tax deductions that can only be used by a C corp as opposed to an S corp.

Now, their point is valid in that owners of S corps cannot take certain write-offs. The rule is that if you own more than 2 percent of an S corp, neither you nor your spouse can take the following write-offs:

- Disability insurance
- Health reimbursement arrangement
- Day-care assistance plan
- Educational assistance program
- Cafeteria plan

While these sound like good write-offs you'll miss out on, consider that 1) not everyone can use these write-offs anyway; 2) they don't add up to enough to make a long-term difference; and 3) if you have other employees, you have to give them the same benefits you receive in order to take the deductions.

Can you afford to and are you planning to purchase disability insurance? Do you have kids in day care, or are you going back to school and need a write-off for tuition besides the other available education write-offs (such as the lifetime learning credit)? Are you aware that you can write off health-care expenses in other creative ways using a Health Savings Account (HSA) or Section 105 Health Reimbursement Arrangement? (See Chapter 11.) And finally, have you thought about how much it will cost you to provide these fringe benefits to your other employees you may have?

The list goes on and on as you get closer to the bottom line. I am convinced that promoters and other authors who address this topic fluff up the benefits of C corps for small-business owners either because they can't think of anything else to discuss or they want to sell you a corporate entity setup.

But to be fair, I'll consider both sides. I'll take a leap of faith and assume you can get $15,000 more in write-offs in your C corp that you couldn't get anywhere else—an assumption, I think, that is extremely aggressive.

First, let's compare apples to apples when it comes to your income and the expenses you may incur before we add any expenses to the C corp strategy. Figure 5.1 on page 51 compares an S corp and a C corp with the same income and expenses. Assume you have $100,000 in gross income, $25,000 in general expenses, and thus $75,000 of net income. Then you take out your salary of $25,000, which you would have to do in both an S corp and a C corp.

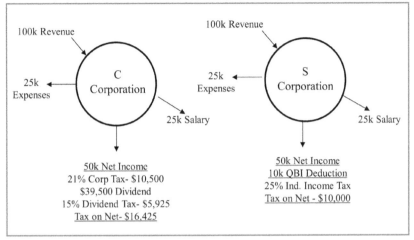

Figure 5.1 – **S Corp vs. C Corp with Same Expenses**

This leaves you with a $50,000 dividend taxed at a 21-percent corporate tax rate—*before* you take your dividend and are then taxed again on your individual return.

But what if the C corp digs up $15,000 more in expenses? What would it look like? This is what self-professed gurus will suggest, although they will be long gone when it's time to actually prepare and file your tax return. I strongly disagree that the average business owner is going to be able to find $15,000 more in expenses. These types of expenses are extremely unique, especially when you take the health care expense out of the equation. (See Chapter 11 on how health care expenses can be deducted more strategically.) But nonetheless, I'll give these gurus the benefit of the doubt to still make my point. Figure 5.2 below shows that the S corp still wins and has more net tax savings even after the C corp hypothetically comes up with $15,000 more in expenses (see Figure 5.2 on page 52).

To make a fair comparison, I assume you have an individual federal income tax rate of 25 percent in both figures. This is even an easier comparison now after the passage of the Tax Cuts and Jobs Act that created a flat 21-percent corporate rate. Previously, C corp advocates would tout the lowest corporate rate of 15 percent—no longer! As such, we can compare apples to apples when we make the assumption

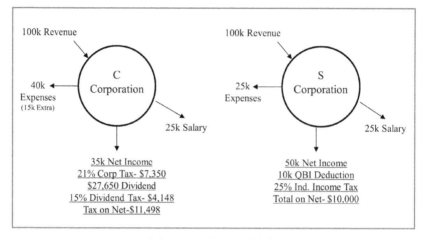

Figure 5.2 – **S Corp vs. C Corp with $15,000 more C Corp Expenses**

that the individual has the same individual tax rate under each scenario. I feel that 25 percent is a good compromise.

As you will note in both diagrams above, the individual pays a flat 15 percent tax on the qualified dividends from the C corp. However, coupled with the 21 percent tax rate on the C corp profit "before" dividends, the double-tax is a killer. Thus, ultimately S corp wins the tax savings battle . . . and furthermore, the more money you make the more you save with the S corp.

CRITICAL ALERT!
RED FLAGS FOR LEGAL SCAMS

Most small-business owners don't need an elaborate structure, and many Americans are being sold products or services that don't provide any asset protection whatsoever. To help you avoid scams and the issues my case study clients faced, here is a list of red flags that can alert you to a potential legal scam or poor advice:

• *A nonlawyer giving advice.* This is a classic situation wherein after a new investor or entrepreneur attends an event, an "incorporation service" reaches out to them from a call center and gives legal advice,

---

CRITICAL ALERT!, CONTINUED

trying to justify their position because they may have one lawyer on staff. This is not a professional consultation you can rely on.

- *Talk of a "silver bullet" structure or plan that is "a must for you!"* Some promoter or professional is out there today promising, "If you do the following . . . no one can touch your assets, and you will be protected." They do not mention the administrative costs or tax consequences of what they're prescribing, or how the structure or strategy is actually executed. They only present the half-truths of a few successful-but-unique situations and then oversell complicated structures to the unwary.

- *Multiple entities when you don't have the assets or businesses to justify them.* For example, if you have a day job and two to three rental properties, you certainly don't need a corporation as a management company, an LLC, a limited partnership, and an elaborate irrevocable or land trust.

- *A recommendation to set up an entity in a state other than the one where you live or where your rental properties are located.* This often brings up the Delaware, Nevada, or Wyoming sales pitch. As I discuss in Chapter 3, this is typically a scam and completely unnecessary for the average small-business owner. If someone is selling this strategy to you, suggesting these states offer additional perks or benefits, please get a second opinion.

- *The one-size-fits-all "standard" package.* If someone tries to sell you a standard setup package, this is another red flag. There is no one-size-fits-all asset protection plan. Asset protection requires a comprehensive approach to procedures and structures tailored to your situation, and the plan should evolve at the same pace at which you acquire your assets. Often, the C corp is a part of these "standard" plans, and the entrepreneur owner is left with a tax filing and bookkeeping mess.

Moreover, you will notice I calculated a corporate tax rate of 21 percent on the dividend, which is now a flat rate the C corp advocates have to live with.

So here is the bottom line: When giving the C corp advocate a generous $15,000 in additional deductions and keeping tax rates fair and reasonable, it's still a break-even proposition.

What this tells me is that if you have any more income in the C corp than expected or a lack of write-offs, you're hosed. The S corp wins again.

Now, could you wipe out all the corporate income with additional deductions? I doubt it—and if you don't, there won't be any savings.

Myth 2: The Lower C Corporation Tax Rate

If eliminating all corporate income via deductions doesn't work (and it won't), the C corp promoter will try to convince you that because the C corp only has a 21-percent flat rate tax on all of its net profit (previously 15-percent on the first $50,000)—and thus possibly a lower rate than personal income tax rates—you will somehow experience savings. This is a shell game you can lose quickly if you aren't very, very careful.

To effectuate this savings, the guru will suggest you pay the corporate tax and leave the money in the C corp so you don't pay the double tax (your personal income tax) when you pull the money out. The problem with this plan is the ultimate outcome: Your money will be stuck in the corporation. You'll only be able to loan yourself the money, at best. Someday you'll want that income, pull it out of the corporation or zero out any loans, and then have to pay individual income tax on the retained earnings or distributions. Leaving the money only delays the inevitable.

Furthermore, when you consider the new 20-percent 199A pass-through deduction on S corp net income, the tax savings of an S corp is even greater compared to that of a C corp and savings that might exist between the corporate and personal tax rates.

Myth 3: The Higher Payroll Solution

Ultimately you plan to make money with this company, right? I hope so. After all these incredible C corp deductions, how are you going to take that profit out and *not* pay double tax? More salary? If you take a loan, the taxes will hit like a ton of bricks when you eventually shut the C corp. It's a ticking time bomb!

Where are you going to hide all the profit you plan on making? Invariably, when the C corp advocate is faced with the corporate income issue, they will suggest taking a greater payroll to wipe out the income.

Let's think about the salary strategy. If you take a larger salary to wipe out the net income of the corporation, what do you pay more of? Payroll tax! Remember that 15.3-percent SE tax we were trying to minimize by using the S-corp strategy? If we are required to take more payroll with a C corp, then what's the point? In the S corp we could take a lower salary and not have any corporate tax on the net, so obviously the S corp wins this argument as well.

Then comes the more aggressive and actually ineffective strategy of setting up multiple corporations or paying fees to other companies to try to move or hide your corporate income. The IRS has been very clear that taxpayers cannot shelter income in multiple corporations in an effort to hide income and lower tax rates. If you are ever presented with this strategy, run. However, if you truly feel the argument is compelling and you're about to sign on the dotted line, please get a second opinion from a licensed CPA.

Finding Trustworthy Advisors

Before you spend one dollar with someone advising you to start a C corp, make sure they run the numbers. Have them take your last year's business tax return/operations and your projected business revenue/expenses and calculate the savings as it ultimately "nets" onto your personal tax return. Then make sure you are actually going to undertake the strategies they are suggesting before the final step of comparing the savings with the administrative costs and headaches of the C corp. This also includes a comprehensive cost-benefit analysis of any other entities you may need to structure in conjunction with the C corp to save on SE tax and the double-taxation threat of the

C corp. Have them promise in writing that they will cover any penalties and interest for bad advice after they prepare and sign your tax return.

Game Plan Takeaway and Action Items

My clients in Seattle were relieved to learn we could salvage some of the entities they had set up. However, we would have to dissolve them in the unnecessary state and domesticate them in the proper state as well as convert the C corp to an S corp when the time was right. Unfortunately, most of the damage had already been done. Money was wasted and couldn't be recouped. They have shared their experience with many others, and I share it here as a warning to those considering an elaborate structure with outrageous promises of tax savings and asset protection.

- The C corp was primarily designed for and is used by public companies raising capital with thousands, if not millions, of shareholders.
- Be wary of those who suggest a C corp can give you additional tax write-offs or shelter income at a lower tax rate. Run the numbers, and get a second opinion based on your unique situation and income projections.
- If you are saddled with a C corp, it can be strategic to convert it to an S corp, but the timing is critical if you have been operating for a period of time as a C corp and have losses.
- C corps provide the same asset protection from the operations of a business that an LLC or an S corp would provide. Their differences are in raising capital and tax planning.

199A PASS-THROUGH DEDUCTION STRATEGIES

—— CASE STUDY ——

had two very interesting meetings early this year. They were consultations I had never before had in my career. They were discussions regarding the 199A pass-through deduction and what strategies to employ . . . if any.

My first meeting was with a client making approximately $150,000 as a realtor. She was a single mom and doing well, had an S corp, and was taking a reasonable salary. We had been working with her for years to maximize her FICA savings and other small business tax strategies, but then the question arose, "Am I entitled to the 199A deduction, and will I save any more taxes filing my tax return?" The answer was yes, with no major calculations or planning needed. The tax write-off was simple to calculate and no extra strategy was necessary.

My other meeting was much different. It was a married couple with a small manufacturing business. Now, although it was a relatively small business compared to most manufacturing operations, they were still expecting to net between $500,000 and $600,000. They, too, asked, "What about the 199A? Are we going to save any taxes and are there any strategies we need to be aware of?" The answer was yes AND yes. There were very important tax strategies that were CRITICAL to consider. Because they made more than $415,000, there was a much more elaborate equation that kicked in, and we needed to carefully consider their total payroll levels and other property and equipment investments.

Bottom line, the 199A can be very simple for many business owners, but for those over a certain threshold of income, the planning and complexities are significant.

Just like these business owners above, you may be wondering why understanding this law is so important. Well, if you make over a certain level of income and you don't implement some planning, you may be left out in the cold and miss out on this amazing tax strategy.

If you take the effort to read this chapter, I'll do my best to keep it simple, short, understandable, and to the point I will include a few key "takeaways" to discuss with your tax advisor as you strategize each year. As an important disclaimer, if you're a tax professional, please understand this is not a technical memorandum on all of the nuances, definitions, and strategies related to the 199A deduction. I'm writing this chapter for business owners to understand the *basic* principles of the tax law on this topic and some possible strategies they could employ. At the very least, as I stated above, my goal is to set forth some discussion points for a business owner to bring up with their tax advisor.

The Basics of the 199A Deduction

Plain and simple this is a deduction just for you, the small-business owner. Big corporations (essentially C corps) got a new *and* permanent 21-percent tax rate, but we, the small-business owner, receives a 20-percent *deduction* off our bottom line.

So, simply stated, if your business makes $100,000 in net profit, you get a 20-percent deduction or (in this example) a $20,000 deduction. The result: You only pay income taxes on $80,000. If you are in a 25-percent tax bracket (let's assume combined federal and state), that means you just saved $5,000. Not too bad.

The problem is that it's not that simple. If a business owner's "taxable income" (defined below) is above $157,500 if single, or $315,000 married filing jointly, then their type of business, wages paid, and business property value can reduce and/or eliminate the 199A pass-through deduction. Thus, there are a few key issues you want to be aware of when you do your planning and consider the 199A deduction. Let me summarize them in seven important planning points.

1. Definitions Matter

For purposes of the 199A deduction, there is an entire new set of definitions and terms unique to this deduction that need to be well understood in order to navigate the 199A phase-out rules and applicable equations.

Now, let me forewarn you . . . trying to understand these definitions is not for the lighthearted. I geek out on this because I'm an accountant, and I debated not including these definitions in this section of the book. However, as I explain the calculations for the 199A deduction below, even generally, I will be selling you short if I don't provide these definitions. So, you may choose to skip over them. However, if you try to make sense of the 199A calculation, you'll be interested in coming back to these definitions and understanding them. Sorry—it's a necessary evil to cover this important topic. And remember, don't hate the player; hate the game.

- *Taxable Income.* For purposes of qualifying for the 199A deduction, this is the taxable income you are used to seeing and calculating as the "taxable income" found on line 10, page 2 of your IRS 1040. This shouldn't be an unfamiliar term or concept and you would understand and refer to in the past. However, *this* is the figure that tells you if you start to phase out and/or limit or don't qualify for the 199A deduction.

- *Adjusted Taxable Income (ATI).* For the Section 199A deduction calculation, you reduce your taxable income by your net capital gain. The term *net capital gain* means the amount by which your net long-term capital gain for the year is more than your net short-term capital loss for the year. Essentially, your capital gains and losses are netted together. If there is a gain, it reduces your taxable income. This ATI is part of your calculated 199A deduction no matter what your income level is.

- *Qualified Business Income (QBI).* This is the big one and a new type of income and definition unique to the 199A deduction. Your QBI is the net income of the pass-through business, exclusive of any capital gains, dividends, or interest income. For example, if John and Mary operate an S corp with no other outside income, investments, or rental property, and the S corp has $100,000 of ordinary income after paying a salary to Mary of $50,000, and also has interest income of $20,000 from lending and $50,000 of capital gain from flipping a property, the QBI is still $100,000. However, the other income would be included in their taxable income, for a total of $220,000 taxable income on their 1040. Another example is that if you have a Schedule C or Schedule E on your 1040, your QBI is your net income at the bottom of either of those schedules.

- *Wages Paid by the Business.* For purposes of the 199A deduction, the wages paid is a big deal. Thus, it's important to understand what "wages" actually include. Gratefully, wages are defined as any and all W-2 wages paid by the pass-through business, including any W-2 wages paid by the business *to you*.

- *Qualified Property.* There is another part of the 199A calculation that may affect business owners and could indeed benefit them. The government wants to reward business owners who either pay wages or purchase equipment/property (essentially stimulating the economy). Qualified property is generally the unadjusted basis of property (or its original cost) that the business depreciated during the year that was either 1) purchased in the last ten years or 2) hasn't been fully depreciated yet. For example, if you bought a new server, printer, and set of computers for your business during the year totaling $15,000 and even fully wrote it off and depreciated it under Section 179, it would still be considered $15,000 worth of Qualified property for purposes of the 199A calculation.

I want to give the disclaimer that the 199A deduction also includes 20 percent of real estate investment trust (REIT) dividends and qualified publicly traded partnership income, but I frankly don't care or want to address it. 99.9 percent of Americans don't own these type of investments, nor will they ever, and they are creations of Wall Street that I would rarely, if ever, encourage an entrepreneur to consider. Both of these investment opportunities fly in the face of an independent entrepreneur who values, if not treasures, active control in their enterprises, including self-directing their retirement accounts.

Now that you have some basic definitions under your belt, let's jump into the concepts and basics of how the 199A deduction functionally plays out.

2. Equal Treatment Up to a Certain Income Level

All small-business owners receive the same 199A deduction under the application of a uniform equation up to a certain point. It's simple and easy to calculate, and frankly, there isn't much strategy involved, either (except noting the continued importance of controlling your salary and pass-through income with an S corp). Essentially, if your **taxable income** is less than $207,500 (single) or $315,000 (filing joint), the math is straightforward because you are *below* the phase-out range.

The calculation is:

> The lessor of:
> 20% of Qualified Business Income (QBI)
> 20% of Adjusted Taxable Income (ATI)

For example, let's continue with John and Mary's situation I set forth above in the definition of QBI.

S corp Ordinary Income	– $100,000
Mary's Salary	– $ 50,000
Interest Income	– $ 20,000
Capital Gain	– $ 50,000
Thus ..	
Qualified Business Income	– $100,000
Taxable Income	– $220,000
Adjusted Taxable Income	– $170,000
20% of QBI	– $ 20,000
20% of ATI	– $ 34,000
199A Deduction	– $ 20,000

3. Some "Phase Out" and Receive No Deduction

This problematic situation has generally come to be known as the "out-of-favor specified service trade or business group." If you are in the business of performing services in the fields of health, law, consulting, athletics, financial services and brokerage services, or the principle asset of your business is the reputation or skill of one or more of its employees, then you will ultimately lose out if you make too much money. Your deduction quickly fades away. Thus, these businesses are considered "out-of-favor."

Essentially, you and your deduction go "off a cliff" as some tax advisors have referred to it. The phase-out range (where the 199A deduction is limited for a range of income) begins at $157,500 if single or $315,000 filing jointly, and the cliff resides at $207,500 (single) or $415,000 (filing jointly). At the point of the cliff, for anyone on this "out-of-favor" list, the 20-percent deduction disappears, and they lose the deduction entirely. That's the bad news.

Here's the list of businesses that are at risk of losing the deduction:

- Physicians, pharmacists, dentists, veterinarians, physical therapists, or psychologists;
- Lawyers, paralegals, arbitrators, or mediators;
- Accountants, enrolled agents, tax preparers, actuaries, or auditors;
- Actors, actresses, singers, dancers, entertainers or directors;
- Athletes, coaches, or team managers;
- Consultants providing professional advice or counselors, financial advisors, wealth managers, or stock brokers.

Now keep in mind that if you are a W-2 employee serving in any of the capacities above, you don't get the deduction anyway. The 199A doesn't apply, and it doesn't matter. This deduction and the applicable rules only apply to those generating independent income as a business owner. More specifically, the deduction generally applies to their QBI or net income, not W-2 income.

It's also interesting to note that engineers, architects, and real estate agents and brokers (although many would argue they're *also* professional service businesses) are seemingly *excluded* from this list and the devastating phase-out rules.

This is also where things start to get really tricky, and strategies abound. If a business owner is on the precipice of going into the "phase-out range" or completely going off the cliff, it is *absolutely* critical they go over possible strategies with their tax advisor.

For example, here are some strategies to consider:

- *Contributing to a retirement account to reduce your taxable income.* This could be a 401(k) you establish before year-end, but contribute to the following year. It could also take the form of an SEP (simplified employee pension) created after the end of the year and before you file. Both of these contributions would reduce your taxable income and put the 199A deduction back into play. Not to mention it's not a bad idea for wealth building.

- *Harvest any capital losses.* Net capital gains add or subtract from your taxable income and thus determine your eligibility for the 199A deduction. Maybe it's time to sell a rental property, stock, or other asset that would reduce your taxable income and pay off with a 199A deduction.
- *Spin-off business income that qualifies for the 199A.* There is a tremendous amount of hope for future IRS regulations that allow for the 199A deduction on "in favor" types of business income. It may not be a bad idea to move that income into a separate entity for asset protection, exit strategies, and potential future 199A deductions.
- *Make charitable deductions.* Again, reducing your taxable income to avoid the phase-out range and/or the cliff could give you a nice tax break and add to the already tax-preferred benefit of giving money to charity. The goal is to get the deduction before that onerous $207,500 or $415,000.
- *Maximize* all *your business deductions.* More than ever, the 199A deduction is another motivation to renew your effort for better tax planning. Taxable income reduction planning couldn't be more important when you are in a professional service business and already taking it in the shorts under an arbitrary tax provision towards your industry and profession.

4. Limitations for Everyone Else at a Certain Income Level

If you thought you were home free and could breathe a sigh of relief because you weren't considered a professional service business, think again. The good news: Again, if your income is less than the threshold amount of $157,500 (single) or $315,000 (joint) you follow the same basic equation I set forth above taking the lesser of 20 percent of QBI or 20 percent of ATI.

The good news continues: You still get to take the 199A deduction in perpetuity and there isn't any cliff to fall off. Thus, restaurant owners, manufacturers, realtors, contractors, internet marketers, and *any* other business not on the "un-favored" list above should give three cheers for this great tax deduction!

However, the bad news: Once you hit that certain income level, there is a *second* calculation that comes into play that could limit your 199A deduction dramatically if you aren't careful.

What is that level? If you have taxable income greater than $157,500 (single) or $315,000 (filing jointly), you *must* follow a Phase 2 equation (as I have termed it), which is clearly more complicated and will more than likely limit your 199A deduction (although it's still something that could even be substantial depending on your situation).

Moreover, it is important to note that if you have income *between* $157,500 and $207,500 (single) or $315,000 and $415,000 (joint), then you are in a phase-in range before you get to the strict application of the Phase 2 equation. I'm not going to address the unique math and reduction during the phase-in period. It is simply too much for this chapter and would require multiple examples to do it justice, so check with your CPA for all of the finite details.

Allow me instead to focus on the Phase 2 equation and the importance of understanding the particulars. There are *truly* incredible opportunities for tax planning and strategies at these income levels, and their importance cannot be underestimated.

So, once income is above $207,500 (single) or $415,000 (joint), assuming you have a tax-favored business, the Phase 2 formula for the 199A deduction is:

The lesser of A or B:

A – 20% of QBI, or

B – The greater of

50 percent of the W-2 wages of the business, or

The sum of 25 percent of the W-2 wages of the business and

2.5 percent of the unadjusted basis immediately after acquisition of all qualified property.

So for example, assume Susan is a single taxpayer making $300,000 of net income in her online marketing business structured as an S corp. She then learns the strategies to take reasonable compensation under her entity and proceeds to take an $80,000 salary; therefore, the net-profit or QBI from the business is $220,000. However, her "Taxable Income" is $300,000 and she is subject to the Phase 2 formula or equation which would be as follows:

The lesser of:

    — $44,000 (20% of $220,000), or

    — $40,000 (50% of W-2 wages/$80,000)

    Susan can deduct $40,000 under the 199A deduction.

One would think that the 20-percent deduction would be $44,000 (.20 x $220,000). However, it is $40,000 (50 percent of $80,000— the salary). Thus, in Phase 2, the salary level becomes an important strategy issue, as I will discuss later.

Now, let's complicate it a little to understand the dynamic between "Taxable Income" and "Qualified Business Income" in the Phase 2 analysis. Assume Susan only had $100,000 of net-income from her S corp and $60,000 of salary, but also had $20,000 of taxable interest/dividend income, and $30,000 of net capital gain from the sale of a rental property. If you notice, here "Taxable Income" is $210,000. Thus, the Phase 2 formula or equation would be as follows:

The lesser of:

    — $20,000 (20% of $100,000), or

    — $30,000 (50% of W-2 wages/$60,000)

    — Susan can deduct $20,000 under the 199A deduction.

Notice the "Adjustable Taxable Income" figure only matters if she was below the phase-in range. A little tricky, I know.

Now, I'm sure you are also wondering what this qualified property figure has to do with Phase 2 equation. As I stated earlier, under TCJA legislation, the government was trying to give this deduction to business owners with big payroll or those that were buying equipment for their business, thus stimulating the economy (so was the plan). Because this property factor is such an integral part of the Phase 2 equation/formula, I want to give one example of how it may benefit a business.

Let's assume Mike and Monica file a joint tax return and operate a manufacturing company focusing on robotics and just-in-time inventory minimizing their dependence on labor with a very successful business generating $1,200,000 in profit. Further, assume their total wages paid in the business (including their own W-2s) is $300,000), and they also over the past ten years, including a significant purchase this year, have invested in $3,000,000 of robotics equipment for their business. Their 199A deduction would be calculated as follows:

The lesser of A or B:

A – $240,000 (20% of $800,000), or

B – The greater of:

– $150,000 (50% of W-2 wages), or

– $175,000 (25% of W-2 wages $100,000 + 2.5 of Qualified Equipment $75,000)

Mike and Monica would be entitled to a $175,000 deduction.

5. QBI and Those with Multiple Businesses

Remember, the business owner gets to take the 20-percent deduction against the net profit in their business, but that means ALL their businesses. Thus, if you have multiple businesses, there are careful calculations and decisions to be made. Essentially, you have two options, and there is also good news and bad news. First, the options to consider:

- *To Aggregate or Not to Aggregate.* If you meet the rules for aggregating your business operations (the threshold test being that you, or a group of people, directly or indirectly, own 50 percent or more of each business for a majority of the taxable year), then you can boost or take advantage of the 199A when you may have not been otherwise able to. For example, if you don't have wages in a particular business, and no real qualified property, but a bunch of in-favor QBI income, you may have received 199A deduction of zero. However, if you can aggregate that income with another business that has wages or property,

STRATEGIES FOR "IN-FAVOR" BUSINESS OWNERS

Just as I referenced above for the "out-of-favor" business owners, there are serious strategies to consider, especially after the phase-in period. First, staying below the taxable income levels of $157,500 (single) and $315,000 (joint) is priority number one if possible. I mentioned making contributions to a retirement account, considering more generous charitable contributions, and of course maximizing all possible business deductions.

But once a business owner hits the Phase 2 formula, planning gets even more creative and can have a significant impact on the 199A deduction. Consider the following:

- *Adjusting your personal salary.* Remember that one of the key figures is the total wages paid by the business. Thus, if you have a high QBI, first, congratulations! But then you may want to increase your salary, as a low salary could backfire for IRS requirements AND the 199A deduction. The 50 percent of wages could be exactly what you are allowed to take as it could be less than 20 percent of your QBI.

- *Buy more business assets.* This is the other factor in the equation when comparing the 20 percent of QBI to the wages and qualified business property. Remember, the government gives you a huge incentive to stimulate the economy by purchasing equipment, and it will have a direct impact on your 199A deduction. For example, you could purchase $40,000 of equipment for your construction business before year-end and depreciate the entire expense, but the fair market value is used in the calculation for the 199A deduction. In essence, if the math works out, the government could be paying you to purchase equipment that you will depreciate entirely in the first year anyway!

In sum, I can't emphasize enough that some planning during the year, and especially before year-end, is critical for successful business owners making over $207,500 (single) or $415,000 (joint).

you can utilize the Phase 2 formula to obtain a 199A deduction that is greater when you take all of your businesses together as a whole. Needless to say, this is a complicated analysis, but the time spent could pay off big-time! The drawback here is that if you have a business with a loss, you have to net that against your gains. Basically, you can't get the pleasure of taking the 199A deduction on the profitable businesses and ignore the losses in another business for purposes of the calculation (see more below on the dilemma real estate investors face).

• *Compute on a "business-by-business" basis.* If you don't choose to or can't aggregate your business wages, assets, and income from multiple businesses, you compute your QBI income on each business independently and add the results together before applying the applicable 199A deduction equation. But once again, if one or more businesses has a loss, you have to allocate the loss to your profitable businesses and thus reducing your 199A deduction.

6. Rental Property Owners Beware!

The benefits of rental property investment has been long celebrated and even explained and exploited by me personally for years as I have advised my clients. For example, an investor can be building appreciation, creating mortgage reduction and cash flow, and pushing rental losses through the tax return in the right situation and structure. Here's the good news: If you have positive net rental income from your property investments, your rental income will get the 20-percent 199A deduction.

However, most real estate investors, and certainly those using leverage, are going to always have a net loss because of depreciation and mortgage interest (paid by the tenant). The bad news: Under the 199A regulations, if you have a net loss, it has to be combined with your other positive QBI income and thus reduce your 199A deduction you might have otherwise received in a separate business. This stinks!

To illustrate this drawback, let's say you have $50,000 in rental losses and $50,000 in K-1 profit from your operational S corp business. You would think that the 20-percent deduction would give you a

$10,000 write-off ($50,000 of QBI x .20). However, the rental losses reduce the $50,000 in this example, and your QBI is now zero. Thus, no deduction!

If there's any silver lining or good news, it's important to note that even though the losses from your real estate may bite you in the butt for the total QBI and the 20-percent deduction, it still can reduce your income for income tax purposes as it always has for real estate professionals. For example, assume the same facts in the example above wherein the $50,000 of rental losses eliminated the $50,000 of business income. If you or your spouse are a real estate professional, the $50,000 can still reduce your Adjusted Gross Income and save you income taxes (see Chapter 13 for the benefits of rental real estate).

7. 199A Deduction Losses Carry Forward

Normally, the concept of a "carry forward loss" is a good thing. However, that's not the case under the 199A regulations. What this means is that any losses that may create a negative QBI in one year, whether from aggregating businesses or using a business-by-business analysis, the QBI loss must be carried forward to next year reducing any pass-through deduction will affect future years.

For example, let's assume you had a negative QBI of $20,000 this year. Next year, you would start $20,000 in the hole before adding in your QBI income. So if you had $100,000 of net profit from all your other businesses next year, you would reduce it by $20,000 because of the prior year, and the 20-percent deduction would be calculated on $80,000 ($100,000 minus the negative $20,000 carried forward).

The Deception to Maximize the 199A Deduction in an LLC vs. an S Corporation

You already read about choosing the correct entity for your business. However, let's look at it here with a specific focus on how it affects the way you can use the 199A pass-through deduction. There is a misconception that the LLC may be the better choice when considering the 199A deduction.

As you may assume, when you operate your business as a sole prop or LLC, you still get the 20-percent deduction. A sole prop or LLC is considered a "flow-through" entity, meaning that the income flows through to investors or owners. In fact, your 199A deduction will even be larger than that of an S corp owner because your net income will be larger. But don't be deceived into thinking that this is in your best interest. I have met with a number of business owners during the implementation of the TCJA that have been slow to implement an S corp (although it is a perfect fit for them) because they are fixated on the 199A deduction. Here is the real story.

When operating as a sole prop or LLC, the SE tax on the "net" is at its worst! As a business owner, you are paying both the employee and employer portions of Social Security and Medicare (otherwise known as FICA or the self-employment tax). But, if you register as an S corp, you're not only going to enjoy no corporate tax, no SE tax, no extra Medicare or ACA tax, you *also* get the 20-percent 199A deduction on the net.

Remember, the SE tax is a real dollar-for-dollar tax imposed at the bottom of your tax return, while the 199A deduction is simply that: a deduction. It only reduces your tax based on whatever bracket you are in.

For example, assume Joan is a caterer from home and operates a food truck in the summer. She will net $100,000 of profit this year. She has an LLC for asset protection from potential liability with patrons, but has *not* made an S-election. At the end of the day, she will pay $15,300 in SE tax (.153 x $100,000), but Joan will also receive a $20,000 199A deduction. But what does the deduction actually save her in tax? Let's further assume she is in a 25-percent combined federal and state tax rate, so with the 199A deduction she actually saves $5,000 in tax (.25 x $20,000). Joan's total out-of-pocket tax is $10,300.

Let's compare Joan to Timothy, an internet marketer. He also will net $100,000 this year in his business and operates as an S corp. However, Tim has made an S-election and learned the techniques and strategies that allow him to take a $40,000 salary in his S corp and take a net-income of $60,000. He still makes $100,000 but in the form of two types of income. With this strategy his SE tax is only $6,120 (.153 x $4,000), but his 199A deduction is only $12,000. So what is the net effect? If Tim's combined tax bracket is the same as Joan's at 25 percent, his 199A tax savings is actually $3,000 (.25 x $12,000). In the end, the total out-of-pocket tax cost to Tim is $3,120 compared to that of $10,300 for Joan.

In sum, it's significant to realize that the power of the S corp is even more impressive when combined with the synergy of the 199A deduction. I'm convinced that the S corp wins every time in this situation.

Game Plan Takeaway and Action Items

The 199A pass-through deduction can be a vital part of your playbook to help you realize a good amount of tax savings. The key is knowing where you stand in regard to income and business type.

- If your taxable income is less than $207,500 (single) or $315,000 (joint), the math is straightforward because you are *below* the phase-out range.
- If you are a professional service business owner and on the out-of-favor list of businesses, consider any strategy to reduce taxable income and avoid the phase-out range and/or cliff.
- If you are operating as a traditional "in-favor" business and your income is over $207,500 (single) or $315,000 (joint), it is critical to analyze the business owner's wages and any equipment acquisitions before year-end to assess the impact on the 199A deduction and Phase 2 formula or equation.
- If you own rental real estate, realize that your 199A deduction could be impacted as you maximize your rental depreciation and losses for federal tax savings.
- If you are operating as an LLC or sole prop, it's critical to not fixate on the 199A deduction alone, but consider the power of the S corp minimizing the SE tax while still maximizing the 199A deduction.

BUILDING PERSONAL AND CORPORATE CREDIT

CASE STUDY

Again and again, I have phone consultations with clients around the country regarding how *quickly* one can build corporate credit. In other words, they want to use their company's credit score and worthiness rather than their own to secure loans of various sorts.

Recently, I had one such call. The young couple wanted to do real estate deals with corporate credit because they didn't have any personal credit and couldn't get a loan. They presumed that their primary reason for setting up a corporation or LLC was to get the credit lines rolling (at least this is what they heard at a one-day seminar and were getting sold this strategy over the phone afterwards).

I told them that building corporate credit was only one benefit of having a company, coupled with creating legitimacy, asset protection, and tax/audit protection in order to truly utilize its full power.

However, I did assure them that corporate credit is real AND attainable.

Nonetheless, I explained that the reality is that it takes time, patience, and the coordination of multiple credit-building strategies; corporate and possibly personal. I literally encouraged them to read *this* chapter of my book and to not give up. I reminded them that we live in a quick-fix, fast-food, easy-solution culture and that it's truly an unhealthy and unrealistic perspective. Things worth working for take time, energy, and study. Corporate credit is one of those very pots of gold at the end of a rainbow if we are willing to work and wait for it.

Corporate credit *is* real. However, the half-truths and mysteries begin when one asks if a person with bad credit can really form a company and then, days later, borrow money under the company's name. Typically, promoters and websites promise thousands of dollars of unsecured credit lines. This kind of corporate credit does not exist and *is* typically a scam.

But with time, patience, and the implementation of specific steps in a proper order, corporate credit without the personal guarantee of the owner can eventually be obtained. Moreover, it can be done affordably, honestly, and legitimately.

What Is Corporate Credit?

Corporate credit is the ability of a company to obtain its own loans, lines, or trade accounts under its own credit score. Thus, a company (such as an S corp or LLC) can apply for credit and, without the owner's personal guarantee, use the money to expand its business. The owner of the company is not personally liable for the credit line, and their personal credit score has nothing to do with the company's ability to obtain credit. However, in some instances, having a good personal credit score can expedite the process of obtaining corporate credit.

The Relationship Between Your Personal Credit Score and Corporate Credit

Is it possible to obtain the corporate credit I describe above even if your personal credit score isn't great? Yes, but it takes time. A quality corporate credit-building strategy will typically include a plan to improve or repair your own credit score at the same time. The practical reality is that establishing your corporate credit without a personal guarantee means that you are going to start from the ground up. Much like the situation when you first established your personal credit, you will start with lower credit approvals and less expansive terms. The sooner you repair your own personal credit reports, the faster you will have access to capital based on both your corporate credit and personal credit, vastly opening the doors to capital for your business.

Now, don't be dismayed. Some of you reading this chapter may question your ability to succeed in this strategy because you have a low personal credit score. But there is hope! You truly can establish your corporate credit and improve your personal credit.

First, remember to be patient when building your corporate credit scores. I can't emphasize this enough. Rome wasn't built in a day, and the same adage applies here. Your quest to obtain credit to build your business is achievable; stay committed, and you'll see the benefits unfold over time.

Understand Your Personal Credit Score

Several factors are considered when the reporting companies create or change your credit score, also known as your FICO (named for the Fair Isaac Corporation) score. The FICO is a number ranging from 300 to 850 that ranks your credit risk and provides a predictive

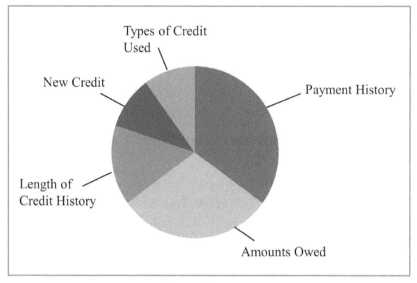

Figure 7.1 – **Understanding Your Credit Report**

analytic for how you'll manage credit in the future. It affects just about any major financial transaction you wish to secure, from getting a credit card to qualifying for a home mortgage. Getting to know what makes up your FICO is an important first step you should make when working to build both your personal and corporate credit. Five things are factored into the creation of your credit score: how you manage your payment history, how much you owe, the length of your credit history, types of credit used, and newly acquired credit. Let's break them down. See Figure 7.1 for a balanced look at how these factors work together.

How You Manage Payment History

You don't want to create a bad credit history, so don't be 30 days late, or more—ever. Pay the bill before the date, and credit card companies will report your balance. By doing so, you are creating a positive payment history over time that is reflected in your score. Why pay before the due date? Well, if the statement comes out with a really high balance on it, even if you pay it the very first day, it's still going to show you using a significant portion of your available limits. So, you want to make any payments before your due date in order to get your statement balance as low as possible and create a better credit score.

How Much You Owe

How much you owe is related to your payment history in the sense that 65 percent of your credit score is making sure you pay in a timely fashion and that you have balances that aren't too high. Speaking of magic numbers, another one that matters here is 30 percent. This is the percentage of available credit that you should not exceed if you want to maintain a positive credit score. If you use more than 30 percent of your available credit and carry that balance, it negatively affects your score.

HOLD A PERSONAL INVENTORY IMMEDIATELY!

Create a spreadsheet in Excel and list ALL of your debts. This won't be fun, but it is a critical starting point. We need to know how much we owe! When preparing the report, create a column showing the minimum monthly payment, and the interest rate. This will give you a clear picture as to where you are starting from and how much work may be in front of you.

If necessary, implement a "debt snowball." This is a tactical way to pay off your credit cards with a systemized approach that will amaze and shock you. It will astonish you how quickly you can in fact pay off your consumer debt and take control of your finances. Read more about this in my latest book *The Business Owner's Guide to Financial Freedom* (Entrepreneur Press, 2017), wherein I discuss the various types of good and bad debt and how to tackle this issue as you build your wealth. Also, if you email me at mark@markjkohler.com and request my Debt Snowball Spreadsheet and tutorial video, I will send it to you for free! It's something we have been doing for our clients for years in order to help them make significant progress in building their credit AND stabilizing their finances.

That said, you should use your credit to a small degree to maintain an active history. The banks want to see responsible and regular usage of your credit cards to show that you are a worthy candidate for a higher credit score and more loans if you so desire. If you're never using the cards, then there can't be a reward from lenders.

Length of Credit History

Keep your accounts open as long as you can because a healthy, long credit history proves that you are a stable, low-risk candidate for loans. Now, this advice may be surprising, but I advise you NOT to completely pay off accounts (and definitely do NOT close them). Sometimes, the best financial decision is not the best credit decision, at least in the short term. So, while it's a great way to save money by paying off an account early, doing so will lower your credit scores. Why? Because the longer and stronger the history, the better.

Don't close those old credit cards that you've been sitting on that you don't use anymore. In fact, use them every once in a while. Get that 1-percent balance on there. Buy a tank of gas and pay it off. Using those accounts and leaving them open can create a significant change, which accounts for roughly 15 percent of your score makeup. The longer you can draw those accounts out, the better that section of your credit will score.

Type of Credit Used

I spoke with my college-age daughter recently, and she said, "Dad, I'm at Target, and I save 10 percent if I get a credit card at the register. Should I do it?" I advised her to pay in cash as she always does and walk away from the credit card offer. Store credit and other consumer debt credit are not effective types of credit. Most lenders don't like to see those types of accounts on a person's profile. They want to see a well-paid mortgage, an auto loan or two, a couple of major credit cards, and maybe an installment loan through a bank. They want to see those long-term, value-based types of credit.

When you've got multiple types of credit, it's like being a basketball player. Imagine a basketball player who can hit every three shots he makes. Every three. But, he can't dribble, pass, play defense, make a layup, or shoot a free throw. If you're not well-rounded, it doesn't matter that you can do one thing really well. You're still going to be a negative contribution to the team overall. Instead, imagine that you can shoot threes pretty well, and you can shoot free throws pretty well, and you can shoot layups pretty well. That way, you're well-rounded. That's how it works with types of credit, too. You want to be well-rounded.

New Credit

Along the same lines, choose new credit sources wisely. Like having a well-rounded credit portfolio, you also want to be selective when adding to it. When you choose to secure credit on the fly, it shows on your credit report. So, as was the case with my daughter at Target, it's tempting—and store credit companies work overtime to entice you to sign up. But, when you act impulsively and get the card at the register at Nordstrom or Target, the credit reporting agencies hurt you, and you hurt yourself because they think you're being unwise with your credit. You shouldn't make an impulsive decision like that to get a new credit card at the register.

That said, don't be fearful of applying for new lines of credit when they make sense. If you're buying a new home or securing a college loan, feel confident. In fact, signing up for new credit (even if you don't get it) only factors into your credit score by 10 percent.

Eight Steps to Build and Improve Your Personal Credit Score

The following eight steps aren't an inclusive list of how you can improve your score, but they are recognized by many experts to be the most important steps in building your personal credit. Take them to heart when reviewing your personal credit score and credit-use habits.

1. *Employ a credit reporting service.* Signing up with a credit reporting service can be very important for repairing your credit and receiving identity theft alerts. The company will give you

constant updates regarding your credit and allow you to pull regular credit reports to observe any activity on your credit profile. They may even offer services to remove negative items from your credit. This work includes, among other things, the exhaustive follow-up and technical items that are a pain, like sending letters to credit-reporting agencies and creditors to remove items from your personal score. Bottom line, it's important to do your research and use a reputable, affordable company with a proven track record. Historically, this industry has been fraught with scam artists and frauds.

2. *Understand credit reporting.* As mentioned above, take the time to understand in detail how your credit score is determined so you can implement the proper strategy. Figure 7.1 on page 76 shows the average weight credit reporting agencies give to certain aspects of your credit when rating you.

3. *Manage your payments.* Don't be 30 days or later on any payments. Although being less than 30 days late may cost you in late fees and higher interest rates, it won't affect your credit score. If you are 30 days late, it can affect your credit score for up to nine months. Paying 60 days late can affect your score for up to three years, and being 90 days late can damage your credit for up to seven years.

4. *Know how much you owe.* Utilization ratios are very important to credit reporting agencies. "Utilization" refers to how much of the available credit a consumer is using on a credit card. Using more than 50 percent of your available credit on a card can negatively impact your credit score. Using less than 30 percent of your available credit can actually increase your credit score. Many experts caution consumers to never use more than 80 percent of the available credit on any particular card. This is considered the same as maxing out the card, and it will have an even greater negative impact on your score.

5. *Keep your accounts open and use them.* Don't close cards or accounts whenever possible. An older credit card has a very positive impact on your credit score. Reporting agencies want

to see that consumers have a good track record with credit card companies. Agencies will typically calculate the average age of accounts, which can have another major impact on your credit score. Moreover, it's important to regularly use the accounts, even minimally, to prevent a credit card company from arbitrarily closing the account and to show stability on the part of the consumer. Even if there are monthly or annual fees to keep a card open, it can be well worth the cost to increase your credit score.

6. *Use good types of credit.* Making timely payments on a mortgage or auto loan shows stability and a good payment history with "quality" types of loans. Experts generally recommend you stay away from department store cards because of their higher interest rates and the tendency they may show to make impetuous decisions at the register. Moreover, these types of credit cards aren't associated with wealth- or asset-building but rather consumer debt, detracting from your credit score rather than building it.

7. *Minimize new credit inquiries.* Only apply for credit when building credit or if you need it. Turn down point-of-purchase credit card offers. Too many of these types of cards will have a negative impact on your credit rating.

CRITICAL ALERT!
THE "SHELF CORPORATION"

Watch out for anyone who uses the term "shelf corporation" and promises unsecured credit lines in huge dollar amounts. Often, the promoters selling shelf corporations aren't licensed lawyers and charge $2,000 to $10,000 for the setup. I have never met anyone who paid for one of these shelf corporations and received what they were promised. However, I have unraveled plenty of these structures for new clients who were taken advantage of and had to create their entity again properly.

8. *Commingling spouses' credit.* Be careful when mixing your personal credit with your spouse's credit. It will expedite other steps down the road to *not* have your spouse's credit linked. For example, one spouse's credit rating may rebound more quickly, allowing you to use it in an overall plan sooner. Moreover, by using each of your credit scores independently, you can acquire more loans without them showing up on both of your credit scores. Finally, if there's a problem with a loan down the road, the creditor can only go after the individual spouse who guaranteed the loan, not both of you.

Eight Steps to Build Corporate Credit

At the same time you are working to build your personal credit (if necessary), it's time to start building your entity's credit. The following eight steps are straightforward and well-recognized, and they will get you on your way to accessing capital which can include lines, loans, credit cards, or trade accounts for your business. Please know that you aren't reinventing the wheel and there are no short cuts. If you follow the process, get support as needed, don't give up, and are patient, you'll obtain credit for your business. Here are the steps that legitimate industry experts advocate:

1. *Start and legitimize a business.* You need to have a moneymaking business—something that is truly a *business* and not just an entity. If you are going to work hard to build corporate credit, have a plan to use it. This is obviously a key to benefiting from tax strategies as well.

2. *Form an entity.* Form an S corp or an LLC that can evolve into an S corp and obtain an EIN. You will need a formal entity and will want to create a plan for longevity and success in building corporate credit. If you already have an entity, better still. You don't have to start with a fresh entity— unless, for some reason, you have tried to build corporate credit previously and your company has a poor payment history and bad credit.

3. *Get a D&B Number.* Often referred to as a D-U-N-S® Number, you will need this number as it becomes the basis for your Paydex score. Similar to a personal FICO score, a Paydex score is the rating system for your business credit report with D & B, a corporate credit bureau. To start this process, register your company and its EIN.

4. *Consider using a business credit coach and educate yourself.* There are honest and affordable services that can do the detailed work to educate you on the credit-building process. They can also provide resources and lists of companies and credit cards that are generally easier for your company to obtain. Finally, they will help you learn all you can and make sure you avoid any pitfalls.

5. *Open vendor and trade lines of credit.* Apply for lines of credit at Home Depot, Staples, Verizon, Office Depot, or other vendors under the name of your company, and then start using those cards and paying them on time. Start with the accounts that will approve a business with little to no corporate credit history and build from there. Relying on your credit coaching company during this process is crucial so you learn when to rely on your personal credit, but only when it makes sense strategically.

6. *Apply for business credit cards.* When the time is right, *after* building a history and credit score for the business via the previous steps, you can start applying for business Visa, MasterCard, and American Express cards.

7. *Ensure that your creditors are reporting to D&B Corporate Experian and Business Equifax, the business credit bureaus.* Track your business's credit score, and make sure your creditors are reporting to your business credit reports on a regular basis.

8. *Practice good habits.* Always make timely payments and use some of the same principles of good personal credit score building with your business credit score.

As you build business credit, creditors will look at the stability and earning potential of your business. Remember, your goal is to build a business and use the credit you are working so hard to get to impact your business in a positive way. Keep your eye on the ball and present a separate and distinct business from yourself. Have a business website, phone number, answering service (if necessary), and separate checking account. Complete your tax returns on time and focus on making legitimate income. Legitimate corporate credit will follow a legitimate business model.

Six Devastating Mistakes to Avoid When Building Corporate Credit

Although you may follow the steps above and employ the help of a coach and business credit reporting agency, there are still mistakes you might make during the process. Below are some pitfalls to avoid that could cost you big time.

1. *Using personal credit to build a business.* It's important to build and improve your personal credit score so you can then use it to co-sign and build your business credit—but ONLY when it makes sense strategically. Don't risk your personal credit score by racking up inquires, acquiring business credit that shows on personal credit reports, or not utilizing the corporate credit available for your business without using your personal credit.

2. *Pledging personal assets to build the business.* Unless it's absolutely necessary, stay away from pledging assets, like getting a second or third mortgage on your home. If you take your time and do it right, you can build your business credit with and without personal guarantees, not by pledging assets. Keep in mind that in lieu of pledging property or assets, personal guarantees are harder for a creditor to enforce and collect on, whereas a lien against an asset can be expedited through repossession or foreclosure.

3. *Not paying bills on time. 100 percent of the time.* Unlike a personal credit score, types of credit and usage do not matter when it comes to business credit. The only factor in rating your business credit and establishing your various business credit scores, such as a Paydex score, is your payment history.

4. *Falling for the shelf C-corp scam.* Nonlawyers overcharge and take advantage of business owners by promising to fast-track the process, and banks see right through the scam. It just doesn't work.

5. *Rushing the process.* Your business needs time and history to build corporate credit; it's just the nature of the beast. Follow a step-by-step process, and don't cut corners.

6. *Not following through.* If you don't stick with the steps, you'll be wasting your time and money. Many people don't follow through, and their business credit effort stalls or fails. Stay on a regimented plan.

Game Plan Takeaway and Action Items

Building corporate credit is not only possible but generally easy to do. However, there are no short cuts. It takes time and patience. To increase your business's access to capital, also work on your personal credit score at the same time. Don't try to complete the process on your own. Obtain ongoing education and support to help you reach your goals.

- Check your personal and business credit scores immediately and make a plan to improve them.
- Employ a credit reporting agency to monitor your personal credit score regularly and monitor your business credit reports with the three major business credit bureaus.
- Create an action plan with the steps in this chapter to start building corporate credit.
- Hire a coach from time to time to assist with your plan and repair your personal credit as necessary.
- Continue to learn about credit building and reporting strategies.

BATTLEFRONT ASSET PROTECTION FOR YOUR ENTITY

—— CASE STUDY ——

It was the "Awesome '80s" and Michael Kaplan owned and operated a Polaris dealership in Las Vegas. Despite this, Mr. Kaplan felt confident that if things didn't go well, he could simply claim bankruptcy and walk away because he was incorporated in Nevada. He believed that a Nevada corporation provided more asset protection, lessening the consequences if he mishandled the operations of his business. He could get away with almost anything . . . right?

Wrong. In fact, the Nevada Supreme Court had a very different opinion. Mr. Kaplan was the controlling shareholder and officer of his seemingly infallible

Nevada corporation. He had the sole control of the checkbook, and he didn't respect the procedures and corporate formalities for properly maintaining the company.

For the first time in Nevada history, the court explicitly stated that there isn't an all-inclusive rule for when a creditor is allowed to go after an owner, thus piercing the corporate veil. Rather, it depends on the circumstances of each case.

The court then pointed to Mr. Kaplan's use of corporate funds for his personal expenses and the overall lack of formal corporate protocol. It went on to hold that the corporation could have paid its debt to Polaris if Kaplan had not made numerous withdrawals of corporate funds for his own personal benefit.

Such actions caused injury to Polaris and were an injustice that allowed the plaintiff to pierce the corporate veil. From this, we learn that company maintenance and protocol *do* matter, and Nevada corporations don't protect you any better than another state's corporation if you don't follow the proper procedures. Thus, shareholder Kaplan was held personally liable, and the corporate veil was pierced.

Thousands of Americans each year are lulled into a false sense of security, thinking that by simply filing for a corporation or LLC, they have unlimited asset protection despite not following corporate protocols and procedures. Others are even further scammed into believing that their Nevada entity will protect them in *any and all circumstances* (see Chapter 3).

In fact, even more and more LLCs are being pierced around the country, and the owners being found personally liable, not because LLCs are bad, but because everybody thinks it only takes "one sheet of paper" to self-file and pay the filing fee to form an LLC. Wrong. More on that issue below.

The reality is that every business owner needs to make sure they are dutifully following specific procedures and taking special precautions to maintain their entity and protect their assets. ("Entities," as used in this chapter, include S corps, C corps, LLCs, and limited partnerships.) Those assets are at some form of risk, no matter what type of business structure you choose. There are two major types of liability that affect your assets: inside and outside. Let's start by assessing what happens in your business with inside liability.

Inside Liability vs. Outside Liability

Before we talk about protecting your entity OR protecting YOU from the operations of the business, we need to discuss the difference between inside liability and outside liability. This is so important!

Inside Liability

First, you want to protect your personal assets from the operations of your business. This is known as *inside liability*—liabilities that could occur inside your business and threaten your personal assets. For example, I once had a client call me frantically and explain they had a customer slip and fall on the way into their offices. It was due to some snow (from a late spring surprise snowfall) that had accumulated just enough on the sidewalk to make it slippery. Regrettably, the customer broke their hand in the fall. My client immediately wanted to review their asset protection plan as a result of the incident. This is a classic case of inside liability.

Luckily, my client in the situation above had implemented various asset protection strategies to maintain their entity and was able to avoid any personal liability. Protecting our personal assets from our business activities is the easier of the two types of liabilities, and simpler methods of asset protection tools exist for this objective.

Outside Liability

Liability can also happen outside the confines of our business, yet affect it all the same. *Outside liability* is exposure created outside our business that could allow a creditor to take our business from us.

While many consider this a unique approach to asset protection because they have never heard it explained in this manner, this is how courts and judges view asset protection.

Let's look at an example. Recently, a client of mine was in a car accident that was clearly his fault. Another driver and passengers were seriously injured, and the claims were going to be in the hundreds of thousands, if not millions. What makes the situation more precarious is that my client owns a successful business, a few rental properties, and a personal home with equity in it. Regrettably, he and his wife had not taken asset protection that seriously in the past. However, had he taken steps toward protecting his business against outside liability, he would not have been in danger of losing what he'd worked hard to achieve.

I explain more advanced asset protection techniques in Chapter 21. Outside liability protection is the core goal when it comes to advanced planning. Inside liability protection is all based on battlefront strategies to protect something called the "Corporate Veil."

GOOD TO KNOW:
WHAT IS THE CORPORATE VEIL?

One of the primary advantages of incorporating your business is that you are not held personally liable for the debts or liabilities of the entity. In other words, creditors can only pursue the entity's assets and cannot reach your personal assets. This layer of protection that separates the entity's liabilities from the business owner's assets is commonly known as the "corporate veil."

Four Ways the Corporate Veil Can Be Pierced

The corporate veil is such an important principle to understand and respect. This is really the battlefront of asset protection. The beauty is that it's cheap, easy, and simple to understand and maintain. It's just doing it. Think of the corporate veil as the shield that needs to be maintained and polished to give you maximum protection in a battle.

If you don't maintain this shield of protection, under some circumstances, a creditor can pierce the corporate veil and reach the assets of the business owner. While the law may differ slightly from state to state, here are four major reasons why or how a corporate veil might be pierced:

1. Failure to properly maintain separate corporate records, minutes, and status
2. Inadequate capitalization at the time of formation
3. Not using the company name in your operations or on documents
4. Commingling funds

These factors aren't the only ones courts generally apply, but they are certainly the most important. Essentially, the court is doing a balancing test to determine whether, in any given situation, the person

CRITICAL ALERT!
EXCESSIVE COMPANY MAINTENANCE FEES

It's not uncommon to see the same companies that sell online company formation services for Delaware, Nevada, New Mexico, or Wyoming also charging outrageous annual fees for "company maintenance."

Many times, these companies will claim their services provide "bulletproof asset protection," promising that as long as you employ their expensive maintenance service, your company will withstand any challenge. This is far from the truth.

In reality, you shouldn't pay more than a few hundred dollars for a service to make sure your annual corporation or LLC fees are paid to the state and to prepare your annual minutes. The same goes for fees to serve as a "registered agent" with an address in the state where your entity is organized. A registered agent is an individual or a company with a street address in the state where you are doing business. The agent will be on public record and receives mail and service of process if your company is ever involved in a lawsuit. You shouldn't pay more than $100 to $150 per year for this service. Shop around for both of these services if you are getting quotes above these ranges.

or shareholder is separate from the corporation and if the corporate veil has been maintained. Below, I'll go into more detail on each of these most important factors.

Failure to Properly Maintain Separate Corporate Records

Operating a business as a corporation is not the same thing as operating as a sole prop but instead requires strict adherence to corporate formalities, including holding annual meetings; documenting minutes and resolutions; appointing officers, directors, and managers; filing tax returns; and following the rules specified in the corporate documents.

How to avoid this: Hold annual meetings and prepare minutes outlining significant events or decisions made by the entity.

Inadequate Capitalization at the Time of Formation

This occurs when the entity is inadequately capitalized, such that at the time of formation there are not enough funds to reasonably cover prospective liabilities. This issue can and should be addressed by your attorney or CPA upon the formation of your company. This may also happen later in the life of a business when the owner proactively incurs a debt or liability for the entity without providing enough capital to pay for the liability. As such, the business owner cannot rely on the protection of the corporate veil to avoid payment for the liability.

How to avoid this: Don't proactively incur liabilities for your company that cannot be reasonably repaid.

Not Using the Company Name in Your Operations

It's possible to confuse customers and/or vendors if you don't place your company name or logo on all contracts and marketing materials. The public needs to know whom they are doing business with. If this is not made completely clear, you not only put your entity at risk, but you expose yourself personally as well. All contracts should be signed and entered into by the entity itself, and signatures by owners should be made as representatives (president, CEO, manager, etc.) of that entity, rather than the individual themselves (unless a personal guarantee is intended). Advertisements, business cards, stationery, websites, oral statements to customers, etc., should clearly and visibly indicate that the business is being operated under an entity with limited liability.

How to avoid this: Get in the habit of using the company name on everything business-related. You need only sign as the designated officer or manager of the company; indicate that on all documents.

Commingling Funds

This occurs when you use the company bank account for personal expenses. Remember, the corporation isn't your private piggy

---

CRITICAL ALERT!
FAKE STATE RENEWAL FORMS

At our law office, we regularly have clients anxiously email or fax copies of "notices" they receive demanding the business owner pay a nominal registration fee or their entity will be immediately dissolved.

These notices, which normally have a state insignia on the corner, can look very convincing. However, there are countless companies scamming business owners across the country with this ruse.

Often these notices come out within a few months of incorporation. Some of the red flags that these notices are fraudulent include:

- A date that isn't your annual renewal date (a year after incorporation)
- A fee that isn't the same as the required annual fee amount, which you should know
- No phone number to contact
- A blurry state symbol or just not looking as "official" as it should
- A return address that doesn't match the one for your state's Division of Corporations (or its equivalent)

Finally, if you have a law firm or maintenance service, they should be able to tell you if a notice is a scam and explain what you should be looking for.

---

bank. There needs to be a clear separation between the company's financial operations and your personal financial affairs. Different entities each have a separate legal existence, and this separation should include their assets. An asset of one entity—a company car, for example—should not be used for personal activities or for a different entity's business without proper documentation (e.g., a lease). Keep separate checking accounts for each business and for yourself personally, and do not pay for personal expenses out of business accounts or for the debts of one business entity out of another business entity's account.

How to avoid this: If you need to take out money from the entity, draw from the business account first, and then pay for your personal expenses from your draw. Don't pay for personal expenses with your business assets.

LLC Protection is Not Pierce Proof

When we use the term "corporate veil," we aren't just talking about S corps. It's really a general term that covers any business structure you use. Just because your entity isn't an S corp doesn't mean your corporate veil cannot be pierced. This is especially true for LLCs.

As I mentioned above, LLCs are being pierced around the country because business owners think that simply filing with the state is all they have to do. That is far from the truth. Asset protection is vital for any entity type, so doing your due diligence by setting up the entity properly (with all the pieces and parts) and conducting annual maintenance of your company is vital to protecting your assets.

If you have an LLC (or S corp, for that matter), you MUST do the following every year or face having no asset protection or even having your entity terminated by the state:

- Have a complete formation of the company with all the supporting documents.
- Hold annual meetings and record them in the corporate book.
- Renew your entity with the proper Secretary of State.

- File any necessary state and federal tax filings (including quarterly payroll reports).

Many clients tell me, "I don't have to do annual maintenance for my LLC because it's not required," and "My one page Articles of Organization from the state is all I need." They are sadly mistaken. Even the IRS is going to ask for these documents if you are under audit, for example. Banks, future partners, and even landlords will want to see your formation records.

Proper Formation Documents

Luckily, taking the extra steps to do it right doesn't have to be expensive. It starts with proper formation. When you set up an LLC, you should have the following pieces and parts:

- *Articles of Organization* (typically manager managed). Watch out for doing a Member Managed entity. It makes changes and modifications so much more difficult, time consuming, and expensive in the future.
- *Operating Agreement* (more than just two to three pages). You want a comprehensive operating agreement that deals with all sorts of issues in the LLC, even if you are the only owner. These are like the bylaws of a corporation. Did you establish a board of advisors? How will you add new members if you want? How will you add assets, remove them, and what bank provision might you need if you buy property in the name of the LLC? All of these items and more should be in an operating agreement. The ones we provide for our clients are at least 20 pages, single spaced!
- *Organizational Minutes*. This is the first "meeting of the members." You want to adopt important IRS provisions like an auto reimbursement plan, home office strategy, and more. These are called "accountable plans," which you need if you want the deduction on your tax return. Also, you should be listing your board of advisors.
- *Corporate Book*. Yes, that's right. A book with membership certificates and seal or seal(s). This will all be contained in a binder

with other important documents for your LLC. This could include deeds to properties, contracts and tax returns.

- *Application for Employer Identification Number* (EIN). You will want an EIN for your LLC, even if it's owned 100 percent by you. This can help with tax reporting, banking, and certainly building corporate credit. Yes, you can do that in an LLC too.

If you haven't properly set-up your LLC, don't feel all is lost. You can "tidy up" your records, for lack of a better word or phrase. For a few hundred dollars, your LLC can be completed, brought up to speed, and made as good as new. You can do it yourself or any law firm can assist. Just don't listen to anyone who wants to charge you north of $600— you may need to throw away your LLC and start over.

Annual Meetings and Records

The general purpose of meetings, minutes, and resolutions is to document and authorize acts taken by an entity. It also shows that you are "maintaining" the entity and respecting the separate nature of the entity. The business is separate from you!

These minutes can be typed up by the business owner themselves, even handwritten, but the important thing is to do them, create the documentation, and put them in your corporate book. At our office, we have a list of 25 questions the business owner can answer and talk about with their "board of advisors." We also charge approximately $150 a year to take care of the whole process.

It can be affordable AND easy to simply make sure you hold your annual member and manager meetings. Write down things like what the sales were for the prior year, what you purchased, what you sold, whom you hired, whom you fired, and then—most importantly—the plans for the future of the business.

Bottom line, when you have all of the sections to a properly set up LLC, *and* you maintain it, you will benefit not only with asset protection but also in the following ways:

- Increase your audit protection with the IRS
- Get you more tax write-offs

- Help you create a board of advisors for support
- Better build your business and increase sales
- And of course, give you the asset protection you THINK you have!

Dealing with State Cancellation or Termination

Every state is different, but the majority of states require an annual report and/or fee for a corporation or LLC to stay in good standing. If you don't do so, then the state automatically terminates your entity, oftentimes without even giving you notice they did so.

The result is that you no longer have the protection of the corporate veil, and owners and managers are open to lawsuits personally. When you have just been served with a lawsuit, it is a bad time to realize your entity has been cancelled as you are far too late to reestablish a cancelled entity. Also, the entity may no longer bring an action against another party in court. There is a growing body of case law where corporations or LLCs and other entities lack standing to bring any action against a party because they have been systematically dissolved.

Some other possible results of cancellation include entity contracts being deemed invalid and partners using dissolution as an excuse to bail on the partnership. The IRS may also require a tax return within three months of your entity being dissolved, and the tax result could be significant. This is why making sure you understand the rules about annual reporting and fees as set forth by your Secretary of State. Some states sends out notices, and others do not. Put it on your calendar or have a service to help you never forget to stay on top of this.

Protecting Yourself and the LLC as a Landlord

In Chapter 13, I discuss the importance of investing in rental properties for tax and wealth building purposes. Of course this strategy comes with asset protection concerns, but these risks can also be mitigated. Owning your rentals in an entity (typically an LLC) is just one of many strategies for protecting your personal assets from liability arising from your rental activities. However, you should not rely upon an entity alone as your sole asset protection strategy. Instead, use a multi-barrier approach that creates as many impediments as possible between you and any would-be litigant.

Below are the most critical steps to take in order to maintain MAXIMUM asset protection when investing in rental property.

Set Up an Entity for Your Rental or Rentals

You certainly don't have to set up an LLC for each rental you purchase, but at least have one as previously discussed in Chapter 3. You could even risk having multiple eggs in one basket—meaning that you have several valuable rentals in one entity, risking them with each other. However, don't risk your personal assets by owning rentals in your own name or trust. (I realize you have to think twice in expensive LLC states, but at least explore your options for an entity structure).

Act Like a Responsible Landlord

As a landlord, it is important to exercise due care and take reasonable precautions to prevent personal injuries from occurring on your property. You have an inherent duty to maintain the property in a safe condition, and the law does not generally permit a landlord to disclaim responsibility for his/her/its own negligence. This includes if you hire a property manager. Be careful whom you hire and make sure they are liable for any damages or negligence so you can include them in any lawsuit and hopefully mitigate any of your damages. On the other hand, the landlord is not required to be the "insurer" of the safety of tenants or others who come onto the property. There are limits, but make sure you are aware of your exposure.

Have a Quality Lease Agreement

Although a landlord cannot disclaim all responsibility for injuries, you can certainly take reasonably prudent steps to ensure that any foreseeable hazards and risks are abated or minimized as best as possible. Have a quality lease discussing these risks and do your best to mitigate them. Furthermore, have a comprehensive set of rules, guidelines, and policies that clearly set forth the obligations of the tenant with respect to the use and occupancy of property. While this may not completely protect the landlord, it may be effective in shifting at least some of this responsibility to the tenant and creating another barrier against liability. Finally, some of your biggest losses can be the result of a terrible lease agreement, damage to the property, and not being able to enforce collection. Review your lease agreement carefully.

Carry an Umbrella Insurance Policy

If you are just getting started and have just purchased your first rental, you can probably put this step on the back burner but not for long. An umbrella policy can provide a *significant* additional layer of protection at a relatively low cost. In fact, one policy could be structured to cover several rentals and even your personal assets/residence. Having proper liability, property, and maybe an umbrella insurance policy is critical for rental property owners. However, it isn't the fail-safe in every possible claim. Believe it or not, insurance companies don't always rush to your side to pay a claim and there are often exclusions, especially if it's found you are negligent in any way. Consider a consult with your insurance agent each year to explore your options with an umbrella policy. More on this later in the chapter.

Know What Risks Are You Liable For

When an owner/landlord is sued for personal injuries occurring on the property, the first question will be whether the owner/landlord knows or has reason to know about the dangerous condition that caused the injury. If a particular condition causing the injury was not known to the landlord and could not be reasonably anticipated, then chances are the landlord should not be held responsible. However, if an owner/landlord is aware of a particular risk of danger, then there is a greater likelihood that the law would hold the owner responsible for any injuries arising from that risk. Some typical examples include circumstances where the owner had reason to know of (this list is certainly not exhaustive):

- Dangerous animals or pets
- Hazardous conditions on the property due to faulty construction, lack of proper maintenance, serious or sustained water or moisture, risks caused by the surrounding environment, etc.
- Specific criminal activity creating a risk to personal safety
- Violations of state or local laws or building codes
- Misuse and/or misconduct of tenants and/or their guests

Asset protection exposure is a big deal, so be sure to call your attorney for assistance so that you leave no stone unturned when crafting a plan.

Is an Umbrella Insurance Policy the Silver Bullet?

I mentioned umbrella insurance earlier in this chapter, but let's unpack the concert a bit more. *Umbrella insurance* is exactly what it sounds like. It provides wide protection over other insurance policies you may hold by way of extra liability coverage. An umbrella insurance policy will cost an average of $300-$500 a year for $1 million to $2 million of coverage. Typically, umbrella insurance isn't going to cover fraudulent, criminal, reckless, or even negligent action. It's an extra policy above and beyond what you already have, which makes it seem at first glance to be a fool's purchase. You already have insurance, after all, so why do you need it? Is umbrella insurance inherently bad, a scam, or worthless? Is it a silver bullet that plugs all existing gaps in your coverage? Again, absolutely not!

You may want to use umbrella insurance to avoid the use of an LLC or corporation, even as your primary insurance because it's cheap. Don't do it! The reason why it's so affordable is because it rarely pays out. It's built for unlikely and catastrophic claims (as if normal insurance wasn't enough). I'm skeptical because in 2014 the average combined payout under auto insurance coverage, for property damage and bodily injury, was under $19,930—combined! Hence, if you carry a decent policy limit on your auto insurance policy (at least $250,000 or maybe $500,000), the chance of having an excess claim is less than .001 percent of all those that carry auto insurance.

Bottom line, the chances of ever having to make a claim under an umbrella policy and then it paying out after all the litigation is infinitesimal. Would you want to have umbrella insurance if you had a claim for seriously harming someone? Yes. But again, you need to carry it on *top* of your standard policy AND the use of an entity. It's a coordinated approach to a quality asset protection plan and basic battlefront strategies.

Game Plan Takeaway and Action Items

The corporate veil is the invisible wall that protects you personally from liability arising from the operations of your business. Other than maybe tax planning and raising capital, obtaining limited liability protection is one of the greatest benefits of incorporation.

Mr. Kaplan from our case study thought that he could flout the law by ignoring corporate formalities, perhaps because he was in Nevada. The point is that wherever you incorporate, you need to follow basic, time-tested corporate maintenance procedures if you want the personal asset protection of your entities.

- Make sure your entity has all the "pieces and parts" so you don't get caught without a complete entity formation.
- Don't commingle corporate funds with your personal funds. Use the company name on all documents, agreements, and advertisements.
- Mark your calendar to remind yourself to do annual company maintenance or hire a service to complete this procedure for you.
- Pay your annual fee to your state to keep your entity effective and in good compliance.

GAME-WINNING TAX STRATEGIES

Sometimes one aspect of your game plan can determine whether you win or lose. Taxes are simply that important. They are your single largest cost over your lifetime, and although they may seem boring or overly complex, you need to have a specific plan to address your taxes.

THE UNDERUTILIZED BUSINESS TAX DEDUCTIONS

—— CASE STUDY ——

A recent phone call with a new client started in the usual way. It was a husband and wife, one with a day job and one with a small business. They had children, a home, and typical family goals—hoping for a college fund for their kids and maybe even a retirement fund. However, they didn't see any light at the end of the tunnel.

Their CPA had prepped their tax return without any discussion. They looked at their tax forms in desperation and confusion, yearning for something to jump off the page and give them a solution to the large tax bill they were facing.

They knew owning a small business was critical to their success, and they had worked hard to create a legitimate business, which was helping to shelter some income and taxes.

Here was the problem: They believed there was one "big" thing they could do to save on their taxes, and they were hoping I could tell them what strategy they were missing. I explained there wasn't a single strategy but rather a comprehensive approach of small changes that could collectively save thousands of dollars.

Of course, the question immediately arose: "So then, what are the best small-business tax deductions? What are we missing?"

While there are many ways to save taxes, some involving complex strategic approaches, taking basic write-offs and maximizing deductions can save you thousands of dollars over the years. Believe me, it adds up. Building the right bookkeeping practices, like tracking expenses in programs like QuickBooks and saving receipts, can help you not miss any deductions. To get you started, I'll cover the most common and hottest tax deductions in this chapter.

Write-Offs and Being Too Aggressive

When I review a client's tax return, I always try to grab the low-hanging fruit first. These are simple, easy deductions that can quickly have a big impact on my clients' bottom lines.

Of course, with all of these expenses, remember the old adage: Pigs get fat and hogs get slaughtered. If you're not careful, you could end up in an audit. You need to consider your overall income, profit, and the size of your operations. Your deductions need to look realistic and common for your type of business. However, if they're legitimate and you can support them, don't be afraid to take them. Go for it; just have your records as backup if you ever need them to justify your expenses.

Keeping that in mind, here is my power list of the most underused write-offs and tax deduction strategies business owners should consider.

Technology, Electronic Equipment, and Supplies

Electronics, tech, and supplies can be big write-offs. You can write off your phones, computers, laptops, drones, cameras, iPads, speakers, video cameras, and any equipment or supplies used for your business. These expenditures can be absolutely critical to running a business, and most of them can be fully expensed. As long as you can show it's 100 percent for business use, it's a 100-percent write-off. On certain items, you might want to bring it down a notch if you also use it for personal reasons from time to time and say it's 80 percent or 50 percent for business use. Always be honest.

The more money you make in your business, the more you can write off. Now, if you're only going to make a few thousand dollars this year in your business, you may have a hard time writing off your new camera or your new drone, iPad, laptop, and Apple Watch. It's not going to happen. It's too aggressive. However, the more money you make, oftentimes the more you can justify and write off! Make sure you track the purchases and discuss with your tax advisor which expenses should be reduced by some percentage for personal use, if necessary.

Phone and Internet Service

In addition to writing off the cost of your phone and computer hardware, you can also write off your service for these devices. This is an ever-increasing expense as entrepreneurs use their phone and internet to do business day and night. Smartphones and in-home (or in-office) wifi and/or internet can dramatically increase productivity and are critical for social networking and other marketing-related strategies. Carefully track these expenses, and don't underestimate their deduction power. In fact, many taxpayers don't know that recent case law and IRS rulings allow business owners to write off 100 percent of their mobile phone service so long as they have at least one dedicated home phone line.

Make sure to include the cell phones and plans of your family members who work in the business if they legitimately need a cell phone for their job.

As for internet service, you can possibly deduct up to 100 percent of it. If the service is for your home office, you might not use the full 100 percent since your family may also be using it for streaming, the kids' homework, etc. But, you can at least claim some percentage of the service for business use.

Travel Expenses

In my opinion, this is one of the most underused tax deductions by small-business owners today. Unlike meals, which are limited to 50 percent, travel expenses are 100 percent deductible. These include airfare, hotel, house or room rentals through services like VRBO and Airbnb, rental cars, valet parking, taxis, rideshare trips through vendors like Uber or Lyft, trains, tolls, etc. You would be shocked to know how many new clients' tax returns come across my desk every year with zero travel deductions. Consider if any of your travels last year and your plans for the upcoming year were or are business-related.

Here are five ideas to make your travel a write-off:

1. *Meet with a client.* Find the opportunity to meet with a client every time you travel. This is another good reason to have multiple sources of income or several small businesses. More products or services mean more of a chance you could have a client or customer where you are traveling.
2. *Meet with a vendor.* Do you have a supplier or a support professional you could meet with when you're on the road?
3. *Attend a conference or training event.* In almost every major U.S. city, there are investment clubs, real estate clubs, professional organizations or conferences, and continuing education courses. These are great places to find educational and networking opportunities, as well as have a business purpose for your travels.
4. *Check on your rental property.* I am a consistent advocate of

buying rental property where you travel. Is there a good rental market where your siblings, grandparents, children, or grand-children live? Searching for new property isn't a write-off, but once you purchase it, trips to the area will always be a deduction if you are checking in with tenants or the property manager or working on the property.

5. *Hold your annual board of directors, shareholder, or member meeting.* Some people see their annual meeting as a burden, but I see it as a great opportunity for a tax-deductible trip. Moreover, it's an excellent chance to work on and update your game plan. Take good notes and document the minutes and results of your meetings.

These are five great ways you can deduct travel, and you should. However, be aware that things can get sticky if you try to combine business with too much pleasure. To protect yourself, you can only deduct expenses for travel days and days that you are doing actual business. "Doing business" may be a required meeting, but if you are on the road for more than a couple days, it's good to rely on the rule that doing business would be actual work for four hours or more. However, another added benefit is that weekends can be a write-off if it is sandwiched between work days. Here's how that works.

For example, say you travel on Thursday, you do business on Friday, you're stuck there on Saturday and Sunday, and then you do business on Monday. This whole trip would be a write-off because you had business bookending the personal dates. Again, personal days, those are generally not a write-off on a business trip unless they're sandwiched between business and you couldn't prevent it.

But, if you're going to be trying to write off seven days in Hawaii or the Bahamas or somewhere exotic or even Thanksgiving with grandma, it's going to be tough. You want to make sure you can justify the trip, that you're doing business every day, and if you're going to spend seven days in Hawaii and only one day is doing your corporate meeting, you can write your flight off and a couple nights hotel, but that's probably going to be it. You can't write off all seven days unless you're doing business the entire time while you're there. Be cautious and stay honest in your reporting for travel.

TRAVELING WITH SPOUSES

What if you are traveling with a spouse and you want to deduct their airfare and other travel expenses? You can—as long as your spouse is an employee or board member.

If you are headed out of town for the weekend to check out a rental property and you want your spouse to tag along, do it! The reason why is that your spouse should and will be working by your side on the property with you. This is a write-off in the business because at the very least they are a part-owner and serve on the board of directors or board of advisors. This is why with every LLC we make sure that you have a board of advisors that you should be serving on. So even if your spouse isn't getting a paycheck, you want to make sure that you're getting a deduction for your travel while you're on the business trip.

A Note About Per Diem

If you are not a "receipts person," you can use a tool called a *per diem* rate to help calculate what you can deduct for travel *meals* expenses. This is a fancy way of saying you can deduct a rough per-day estimate of your travel costs.

Per diem rates are produced by the government. You can find the most up-to-date rates at www.gsa.gov/travel/plan-book/per-diem-rates where you'll find a search feature for every city and state. Rates vary by location. Let's look at an example in Las Vegas. Say the *per diem* rate for a hotel in January in Las Vegas is $134. Now, if you go cheaper than that and get a great deal off the Strip for $65, you can still deduct the full per diem of $134. If you opted for a fancy hotel right in the heart of the action and spent $400, you could only apply the $134 for a deduction, leaving you with a big hotel bill that has no tax benefit. But (and here's why receipts are important), if you spend that $400 and keep your receipt, you get to deduct the greater of the two between the actual cost and the per diem. I know which one I'd choose.

Should you pay for the travel expenses personally and then reimburse yourself, or employees, the *per diem* rate? That's two separate issues. Here's what I recommend you do: Let your business pay for your travel. So, if you're traveling to a convention this weekend, let your business pay all the bills and make a note on your calendar of times when the *per diem* rate was better. Then, tell your accountant to do a journal entry at the end of the year and take out what you did spend and replace it with the higher amount.

TRAVELER BEWARE

There are a couple of things you should be especially mindful of when trying to deduct travel expenses: cruising and dining.

Be careful of cruises. Cruises are very dangerous from a tax standpoint because they have a *per diem* daily limit. So you can spend $10,000 on a cruise but your daily *per diem* is only around $120 a person. And you have to also show you're doing business every day on that cruise ship when, if you've been on a cruise ship, that's the last thing you want to do. Don't plan on taking your entire team for a four-day booze cruise to Cabo and think it's all on Uncle Sam's dime. Uncle Sam will have something to say about that.

Another caveat emptor category is dining while traveling. Now, dining gets a 50-percent deduction, as you will read in the section below, and that holds true for travel dining as well. Don't think you're pulling a fast one if you bury your dining costs in the 100-percent-deductible hotel bill (looking at you, people who love room service). You must separate out those costs for reporting, and they are only worth a 50-percent deduction—even if you ate them while wearing a cushy hotel robe and watching HBO in your room.

Dining and Entertainment

Meals are a highly underutilized expense and should really constitute a healthy line item on a small-business owner's tax return. So much business is completed over food, and it's important to track these expenses. However, the TCJA legislation that went into effect in 2018 contained significant changes with dining and entertainment.

There used to be types of meals/food/dining experiences that could be 100 percent deductible, but most dining deductions are now restricted to 50 percent. The IRS feels strongly that everyone needs to eat, whether at work or not, and a 50-percent deduction is fair and sufficient. Oh well!

Now with that said, keep a thorough calendar of all your meetings, and do your best to track and write off all your meals even if you don't have the receipt. I realize that many folks aren't the best at keeping receipts, but for future audit protection, do your best to save, take photos of, or scan all your receipts. So that brings us to the types of meal experiences and how they are deductible. These are *very important* for business owners to understand and to track.

1. *Meals discussing business with someone else.* Dining expenses are always a write-off (limited to 50 percent) when discussing business with a partner, client, potential client, or vendor. Make sure to record all expenses, including tips, food, and the bar tab. If you opt to only turn in your portion of the meal (say you decide to split the check), you would deduct 50 percent of your portion only. Your accountant will make this adjustment when preparing your tax return.

2. *Meals by yourself while traveling.* Another overlooked savings strategy is to write off dining by yourself when you are traveling. This "traveling/dining" deduction has been defined as times when the taxpayer is doing business outside their normal commute or where they operate their business. Again, this is limited to 50 percent.

3. *Food provided in the workplace.* All are now limited to 50 percent. This typically included food items like donuts on Wednesday, bagels on Friday, the coffee maker, and even a

company cafeteria. These types of expenses use to be 100 per-cent deductible; yet that is no longer the case under the TCJA in 2018 and until 2023.

4. *Food with an event or presentation for customers.* This 100-percent-deductible food would include things like wine and cheese at a Realtor's open house, a training workshop for customers that included lunch, or even a booth with food at a county fair or at the mall to attract customers. Track this separately so it doesn't get cut in half by your accountant thinking it is typical dining limited by 50 percent.

5. *Special company events for employees.* There are still a few limited circumstances in which you can get a 100-percent deduction when providing food for your employees. The most common example would be a company holiday party, a training activ-ity with food to build a team mentality, or an experience as a reward for employees. However, keep in mind the majority of those attending that need to be legitimate employees or vendors and cannot be the owners of the business or their family.

Entertainment is a different story. Before the 2018 tax code change, you could have deducted entertainment with your partners,

CRITICAL ALERT!

Although there is no longer an entertainment deduction whatsoever, the IRS issued Notice 2018-195 in the fall of 2018 providing clarity between meals and entertainment when they occur at the same time. The rule essentially provides that you can still write off the food at an entertainment experience so long as you are discussing business (just like any other dining deduction requirement). For example, say you want to take a client to dinner followed by a football game. You can deduct 50 percent of the business dinner prior to the game, and even 50 percent of the snacks and food at the game. But you cannot write off the tickets to the game or any perks or benefits that come with it (except 50 percent of the food).

employees, board members, vendors, and even customers at the same rate of 50 percent. Now, however, that is no longer the case.

Essentially, although the TCJA included a number of tax breaks, they had to make it meet balanced budget requirements, and the IRS felt like this was their chance to get to get the ear of Congress and finally get rid of the entertainment deduction (something they felt was being abused for years). The good news is that it's only a temporary provision until 2023. Hopefully, we as business owners will get this important deduction back in the future.

Home Office Deduction

Don't be afraid of this deduction! It astonishes me how many tax advisors discourage their clients from taking this helpful tax break. Frankly, it only becomes an issue when taxpayers are abusing the deduction or clearly don't qualify. As long as you are entitled to take it, aren't too aggressive, and use the proper method/strategy there is nothing to worry about. Even if you are audited, you shouldn't shy away from taking a deduction when you are legally able to do so.

The Requirements to Claim the Deduction

Before you can talk about how you take the deduction, you want to make sure you can. There are two basic requirements for your home to qualify as a deduction:

1. *Regular and Exclusive Use.* You must regularly use part of your home exclusively for conducting business. Don't be concerned by the word "exclusive." As long as it isn't your bedroom or the kitchen, even a portion of a studio apartment will qualify. Just make sure you have a desk and a computer reflecting the business use.

2. *Principal Place of Your Business.* This is the more serious qualification, in that you must show that you use your home as your principal place of business. Thus, if you have another office in town or use a co-working space for your business, your home office may be off limits. However, the "administrative office"

has evolved in various tax court cases over the past two years. This gives an option to the business owner that meets clients/customers at a main office but then comes home to return email, return calls, do the books, and various other administrative tasks.

Also, keep in mind that if you have multiple businesses (i.e., a rental property business), you can use the home office deduction for *one* business and leave it alone for your primary or operational business.

Home Office Deduction Options

Generally, deductions for a home office are based on the percentage of your home devoted to business use. So, if you use a whole room or part of a room for conducting your business, you need to figure out the percentage of your home devoted to your business activities. However, the IRS has now come up with another option for completing the actual calculation. Here are the three main ways to tackle this deduction:

1. *Simplified Option.* Since 2014, there is now a simpler option for computing the business use of your home. This new simplified option can significantly reduce your record keeping burden by allowing a qualified taxpayer to multiply a prescribed rate by the allowable square footage of the office in lieu of determining actual expenses. (The standard method has some calculation, allocation, and substantiation requirements that are complex and burdensome for small-business owners.) There are several principal benefits of this new option:

   • The maximum deduction is $5 per square foot of the home used for business, up to 300 square feet (so $1,500 a year).
   • Allowable home-related itemized deductions are still claimed in full on Schedule A (e.g., mortgage interest and real estate taxes).
   • No home depreciation deduction or later recapture of depreciation can be claimed for the years the simplified option is used.

2. *Regular Method.* Now you can probably get a higher deduction with the Regular Method. In many instances, however, you will

have to worry about a more technical calculation AND have the issue of depreciation recapture in the future. Moreover, you will be stealing deductions from your Schedule A in order to maximize the deduction. However, in some instances, this could be a better route to take. Essentially, taxpayers using the regular method must determine the actual expenses of their home office. These expenses may include mortgage interest, insurance, utilities, repairs, and depreciation. Generally, when using the regular method, deductions for a home office are based on the percentage of your home devoted to business use.

3. *S Corp Home Office Reimbursement.* For those operating as S corps, a standard industry practice is to calculate a fair home office reimbursement amount and take a deduction for rent in the S corp (and receive it as a tax-free reimbursement for the use of your home). As long as the amount would be similar to that taken with the home office worksheet for a sole prop, this is a great way to take the deduction in a much less visible manner and further reduce your chances of an IRS audit or interest in you taking the deduction.

Bottom line, the home office deduction is a legitimate write-off. Don't be afraid to take it and also be creative and think outside the box on which business to take the deduction.

Hobby Loss Rules

Like many, you've probably dreamed of turning your favorite pastime into a regular business. What better way to be passionate about your business and make money at the same time? In fact, you won't have any unusual tax headaches if your new business is profitable.

However, if the new enterprise consistently generates losses (deductions exceed income), beware of the "hobby loss" provisions. This involves the IRS and an audit where they may claim it's *not* an activity engaged in for profit, but rather a hobby.

What are the practical consequences? Under the so-called "hobby loss" rules, you'll only be able to claim deductions up to the amount of the income generated by the enterprise (meaning no loss is deductible against other income). This is a terrible tax planning result. The losses are essentially . . . lost.

By contrast, if the new enterprise isn't affected by the hobby loss rules, all otherwise-allowable expenses would be deductible on Schedule C, even if they exceeded income from the enterprise. This is obviously the goal.

There are two ways to avoid the hobby loss rules:

1. Show a profit in at least three out of five consecutive years (two out of seven years for breeding, training, showing, or racing horses).
2. Run the venture in such a way as to show that you intend to turn it into a profit maker, rather than operate it as a mere hobby. The IRS regulations state that the hobby loss rules won't apply if the facts and circumstances show that you have a profit-making objective.

How can you prove that you have a profit-making objective? In general, you can do so by running the new venture in a businesslike manner. More specifically, IRS and the courts will look to the following factors:

- How you run the activity
- Your expertise in the area (and your advisors' expertise)
- The time and effort you expend in the enterprise
- Whether there's an expectation that the assets used in the activity will rise in value
- Your success in carrying on other similar or dissimilar activities
- Your history of income or loss in the activity
- The amount of occasional profits (if any) that are earned
- Your financial status
- Whether the activity involves elements of personal pleasure or recreation

The classic hobby loss situation involves a successful business-person or professional who starts something that looks like an obvious hobby and then has consecutive losses. Avoid this at all costs by making sure you have a true business structure and profit motive involved.

Game Plan Takeaway and Action Items

Track everything, and don't believe there is a single silver bullet for saving on taxes. With quality bookkeeping, regular consultations with your CPA or tax advisor, and a commitment to tracking your expenses carefully, you'll save more on taxes than you can imagine.

Are you going to pay some taxes? Sure. But as I consulted with the family in my case study and went through their tax return, they were truly shocked by how much we added up in savings by just reviewing line items and thinking outside the box.

Be cautiously aggressive and align your risk tolerance with a tax professional who will discuss your ideas and present options for you to consider as well. And there are options! Don't feel trapped. A tax return just isn't "what it is." It can be an honest, well-planned work of art that will stand up under audit and review by any IRS agent.

- Review your tax return with your tax professional based on the ideas and deductions in this chapter.
- Get a second opinion if your CPA shoots down your ideas and won't come up with creative options to consider.
- Recognize that you will certainly file a tax return and pay taxes but you are entitled to write off every legitimate expense.
- Maintain good records and log any and all expenses so they can be considered during the tax-prep process.

THE NEW AND IMPROVED VEHICLE DEDUCTION

--- CASE STUDY ---

John and Mary owned a craft business in northern California. They maintained a personal residence and John worked for the sheriff's department. They also had purchased a 5th-wheel RV that they used to drive around the western states in the spring picking up supplies for their craft products. They would also attend trade shows and visit boutiques and shops that they would ultimately wholesale or consign their products with later in the year. (Ironically, many of the locations they visited were close to children and grandchildren's residences.) Then, they would spend the summer in their garage building their craft product enjoying their time together, not as a hobby, but with a true intent to make some profit to supplement their retirement savings.

In the fall, they would load up the RV with their product and drive around to the same towns and cities (and national parks on occasion that just happened to be right in their route) and place their products for sale with the same boutiques and shops they had visited in the spring. Their RV was used 90 percent of the time for their business. So, they legitimately wrote off 90 percent of the purchase price, 90 percent of the fuel, repairs, licensing, and maintenance—and all the while making a profit of over $30,000 a year after expenses.

Not only did they score some amazing auto (RV) deductions, they also found a way to let their lifestyle pay for itself—and then some. They discovered, as you likely will, that you can write off many of your automotive expenses and do it in a way that enhances your lifestyle. **With the TCJA legislation, the tax code has dramatically improved the write-offs for vehicles across the board and especially for autos.**

Cashing in on the Vehicle Deduction

I use the word "vehicle" because this just isn't about cars and autos. It includes SUVs, trucks, RVs, motorcycles, and more.

With that said, in the past the auto/car deduction has been something of a dud for small-business owners. The best they could do was to typically use the "mileage deduction." However, if you had an SUV, truck, or RV you could use the depreciation or Actual Method and really get some huge tax breaks while integrating these larger vehicles into your business.

Things have changed, however, and for the better! You are *now* able to cash in on far more than the mileage deduction. It's a wide-reaching write-off that you can truly maximize—no matter how much you drive.

Now, with that said, the mileage deduction can still be the perfect fit for millions of small-business owners. But now we have options, which I love. We can strategize! In this chapter, I'll walk you through the basics as well as show you how you can turn your vehicles—even your recreational ones—into significant tax savings (cash) at tax time.

First and foremost, remember the auto deduction isn't the same thing as the travel deduction. The auto deduction refers to expenses for your car, truck, or SUV. Also, remember this includes ALL your vehicles as long as they have some sort of business use. So, even an RV, van, delivery truck, or motorcycle used in your business is fair game for the auto deduction.

The Auto Deduction: Mileage vs. Actual

As I said above, things have gotten a lot better for business owners with cars and autos in 2018 (and the law will hold until 2023). This is because you can calculate and compare the mileage or Actual Methods. By considering both of these options, you may be able to write off your vehicle a lot faster and with bigger deductions.

Mileage

The mileage deduction is still an excellent method to expense the business use of any vehicle and could be the best choice in certain instances. As of 2019, mileage deductions are as follows:

- Business—58 cents per mile
- Charity—14 cents per mile
- Medical and Moving—20 cents per mile
- Personal or Commuting—NO DEDUCTION

This method makes the most sense when a client is putting on A LOT of mileage, in fact even better when a client plans to buy a used vehicle or a little more economical *on top* of a lot of miles. Take it to another level if you get good gas mileage!

Consider this. If you buy a lower-cost vehicle with great gas mileage, why take the Actual Method? The depreciation will be lower, and you're saving gas to boot. So your fuel expense won't be as high, either. Hence, the mileage method could be fantastic.

For example, assume you drive 20,000 business miles. That's an $11,600 mileage deduction. If your vehicle gets 30 miles to the gallon, and assuming a $2.50 per gallon rate for gas, that's only an actual fuel expense of $1,666. Depreciation on a cheaper car isn't going to make up for that over time.

Actual Expenses

The second method in deducting automobile expenses is by using the actual expenses for the vehicle. When you use this method, you CANNOT use mileage. Essentially, you track your fuel, repairs, maintenance, insurance, tires and then also "depreciate" the vehicle or a portion of the lease payment if leasing.

Now this method makes the most sense if you buy a more expensive car (even new or used), and don't plan to put on a terribly high number of miles. Then throw in a not-great gas mileage; the Actual Method starts to look amazing!

The problem in the past was that because of limits imposed back in the 1980s, your depreciation deduction was ridiculously low. For example, if you bought a $40,000 car and drove it 100 percent for business, your maximum deductions for the first five years would only be $15,060. To fully depreciate the car would take 19 years! Are you kidding me? That's not a good ROI for your bottom line, and it's a terribly long time to wait for it. Thus, most people would choose mileage.

Under the TCJA, if you were to buy that same $40,000 car today, you can actually write off approximately 89 percent of the car in the first three years, in addition, to writing off fuel, repairs, maintenance, etc. That's equivalent to using the mileage method and driving over 80,000 in miles in the same period. Thus, if you don't plan on putting on that many miles, you can see how the Actual Method could really pay off.

Depreciation Is the Key

Under the TCJA, tax laws have enhanced the depreciation write-off for not only cars and autos, but also the SUV, truck, and RV. Essentially, all large vehicles also benefited from enhancement to depreciation.

If you are wondering what the policy is behind these increased write-offs, it should be pretty obvious. If the government can reward business owners on their tax return for buying a new or used vehicle for business operations, the government has now arguably stimulated the economy in multiple ways.

Under the TCJA, the rules were enhanced in two significant ways:

1. Higher annual depreciation limits
2. Bonus depreciation

The limits for depreciation have been dramatically increased whether you buy a new or used vehicle. In fact, you can convert a personal car to a business vehicle and take the same depreciation amounts. However, if you have already started the mileage method for a vehicle, you can't change to actual. The entire policy is, again, to encourage investment and a purchase. The new annual limits for a business vehicle are:

- Year 1—$10,000
- Year 2—$16,000
- Year 3—$9,600
- Year 4 and each subsequent year—$5,760

The Bonus of "Bonus Depreciation"

If increasing the regular or standard depreciation wasn't enough, Congress then threw gas on the fire by taking the bonus depreciation deduction to a whole new level. For an auto/car, the bonus depreciation amount is now $8,000 in the first year, whether you buy new *or* used (also a major change to the law). This means that in the first year of buying a car, a business owner can get up to an $18,000 deduction before even fuel expenses. For SUVs, trucks, and RVs (vehicles that weigh more than 6,000 lbs.), there is no limit to bonus depreciation. More on this below.

General Rules for Choosing Actual or Mileage

This is where it gets tricky. As a small-business owner, you have to weigh the value of either going with your mileage or actual expenses.

It's definitely a choice you should make once you have taken a wide view of the benefits of each. There are lots of issues to consider:

- The miles per gallon (MPG) on the vehicle
- Bonus depreciation if a new purchase
- Total repairs or expected repairs and maintenance
- How many miles you expect to put on the vehicle
- Vehicle cost

There are also some general rules and guidelines that can at least be helpful as a starting point in your decision-making process:

- *Rule #1.* If you are going to put on *a lot* of business miles, and the car is generally a lower purchase cost, then the *Mileage Method* is going to win.
- *Rule #2.* If you're NOT going to have a lot of business miles, and it's an average cost vehicle used exclusively or primarily for business, then you will lean towards the *Actual Method*.
- *Rule #3.* If you're NOT going to have a lot of business miles, and it's a more expensive car used exclusively or primarily for business, you should consider leasing and the *Actual Method*. You'll have lower monthly payments making a better economic decision.
- *Rule #4.* If you are going to have low miles and it's a lower cost vehicle used primarily or exclusively for business, I would still lean towards the *Actual Method* because the miles won't give you the benefit compared to at least some type of depreciation.
- *Rule #5.* If you are going to use your car part-time for business because you have a day job, you will typically use *Mileage Method*. The reason being is that you have to show at least 50-percent business use in order to utilize the Actual Method.
- *Rule #6.* If you are going to buy a 6,000-pound or more SUV or truck, you will generally lean towards the *Actual Method* because you are going to have a lower MPG pushing up your actual costs and bonus depreciation is 100 percent. In other words, you can possibly write off entire vehicle in the first year.

- *Rule #7.* If you have a high MPG (think hybrid or electric), but still have average use and miles, you will lean towards the *Mileage Method* because your operating costs are going to be much lower.

Again, keep in mind these are just general observations and considerations; you need to consider all the facts of your situation with your tax advisor before choosing a method.

Tracking Mileage

No matter what method you choose for writing off your vehicle, the IRS needs you to be able to verify the actual business use percentage. This is obvious for the mileage method, but even for the Actual Method, how else are you going to be able to verify the amount allowed for bonus or actual depreciation?

Thus, it's important that you always track your mileage (or at least estimate it as best as you honestly and ethically can). It can be as simple as a written record in a notebook you keep in the glove box, using an Excel spreadsheet, or adopting a GPS phone application (getting more and more affordable each year).

SUV and Truck Deduction

Remember the good old days when you could write off 100 percent of your new SUV or truck under the 179 deduction? That was the Wild West (pre-2006 and well before the Great Recession of 2008). Then, we all became quickly familiar with the $25,000 cap on writing off these gas guzzling vehicles.

The rule for SUVs and trucks with less than a 6-foot bed that we have been operating under for over ten years was that of the Section 179 deduction. This provision allows certain assets to be deducted in one year if a Section 179 election is made, but it places a maximum deduction of $25,000 on what it classifies as a sport utility vehicle (SUV). For tax purposes, an SUV is defined as any four-wheeled passenger automobile between 6,000 and 14,000 pounds (this includes trucks with less than a 6-foot bed).

However, the game has changed with possibly an unintended loophole under the new tax code, and it's that silver bullet called bonus depreciation. As I stated above, the bonus deprecation rule passed under TCJA is unlimited. So with the combination of the 179 deduction and bonus deprecation, a business owner can now again deduct 100 percent of their SUV (assuming 100-percent business use), in the first year of purchase, whether the vehicle is new or used!

For example, in 2018 and until 2023, if you were to purchase a Tesla Model X (weighing over 6,000 pounds), a loaded Range Rover, or truck for $80,000 (used 100 percent for business), the first year deprecation would indeed be $80,000. Under the TCJA, a taxpayer can use a combination of IRC Section 179 and 168(k)(6) (A), which allows a write-off for 100 percent of the SUV or truck purchase. See the calculations below in Figure 10.1 to see how this works:

Vehicle Cost	$80,000
179 Expense	$25,000
Bonus Depreciation	$55,000
Remaining basis under MACRS	zero
Total 1st Year write-off	$80,000 + actual expenses

Figure 10.1 – **2019 SUV/Truck Purchase (new or used)**

This means that a business owner can deduct 100 percent of the cost of a new SUV or truck (with a bed under six feet long), including larger trucks and RVs! They all fall under the same rule, as long as they weigh 6,000 pounds or more. It's all through this "back door" of bonus deprecation.

Leased Vehicles

Leasing is also a phenomenal strategy and can be the perfect fit for certain types of business owners, First, the tax benefits are excellent. For example, you can take all the actual expenses as you would for a purchased vehicle, including the lease payment (based on your business use percentage). The other benefits include the ability to drive a luxury car without making a higher monthly payment and a bumper-to-bumper warranty during the leasing period.

However, leasing isn't a perfect fit for everyone. The drawback isn't a surprise for those who have leased a vehicle before—the mileage limitations by the manufacturer/dealer can really bite you in the end. For example, if you are only allowed 15,000 miles annually under the lease, when you turn in the vehicle at the end of the leasing period, you have to pay for every mile you went over. If you are driving this leased vehicle for work, those miles add up quickly, and the amount you have to pay in the end may offset any savings you would have otherwise gained.

In the end, leasing is a good choice for those who want a second car and maybe something a little nicer to take clients and customers out to lunch in and make sales calls. Also, when you have another vehicle for personal or business use in which you can be indiscriminate with miles and rack them up when needed, and NOT on the leased vehicle, then leasing may be a perfect fit for that second vehicle.

RVs for Business

Let's get real: most people don't buy an RV for a tax write-off. They are a utility vehicle in some rare circumstances, but they are certainly by far more of a lifestyle choice and just what they are called: a "recreational" vehicle. But that doesn't mean that you can't find a few tax perks in your RV if you do it right.

As with most tax situations, there is good news and bad news. Like a bitter pill, let's start with the bad news: the RV no longer qualifies as a second home for a mortgage interest deduction. Under the new tax law, the only deductible mortgage interest is that of your primary residence. Furthermore, it's only interest on acquisition indebtedness. That means you can't deduct the interest for the RV even if you use a home equity line of credit (HELOC) or second mortgage to pay it. What this boils down to is that any interest on your RV loan is NOT going to be deductible on your personal tax return as an itemized deduction.

But the good news is that if your RV can qualify as a business vehicle, you can either use the mileage or the Actual Method to write it off. To some, simply bringing up the idea of using an RV for business is preposterous. After all, you bought your RV for recreation, for personal use, for fun—not for making sales calls. Well, don't jump to conclusions; there might be a scenario where it could be a perfect fit.

As a part-time RV user, you may find a huge opportunity to write-off your RV as a small-business owner. While you won't be able to rid yourself of the cost of a personal residence or seek greener pastures for your domicile in a no-tax state, you can easily reap the benefits of the RV life. Your RV may become a huge write-off as you utilize its storage capacity and its ability to be an office or workshop on wheels for your business.

You might even be able to rent your RV out while you aren't using it in the style of a home vacation rental (just think of it as Airbnb on wheels). This is another major way to justify its expense and generate extra income. By turning it into a rental property, the ability to write off the expense got even better because not only are you able to claim auto deductions aplenty, you can also claim the business deductions on the business you run by renting it. There are plenty of brokers out there to help you navigate the RV rental waters. One such business that helps owners rent their RVs is RVshare.

The bottom line is, think outside of the box. Realize that the RV becomes a method or a tool for you to better live your American Dream. It can be a way to make money, save money, get out of debt, and live a better lifestyle. If you feel your RV is a financial burden, rethink your ownership strategy. Do some study on the possibilities, and you might be pleasantly surprised.

Game Plan Takeaways and Action Items

The vehicle deduction involves far more than just cars and can include SUVs, trucks, and even RVs. The right strategy can pay you great tax-year benefits if you do it right. The key is to remember that you need to substantiate the business-use percentage any time you are taking auto-related deductions. Follow these tips to get the most bang for your automotive buck:

- Historically, the best method to prove your business use is through a mileage log. Many business owners think that when they use the Actual Method, they can roll down the window and throw out the mileage log. Nope. Not a chance. That mileage log is your key to proving "business use." Make sure you can prove the business use versus the personal use of your car, SUV, truck, or RV.
- New rules under the TCJA give more options for writing off an auto/car. The Mileage Method was generally the best way to go for years. Now the Actual Method could give you a lot more bang for your buck. This gives you bigger annual deprecation and even bonus depreciation write-offs. Run the numbers both ways from the outset of putting a vehicle into business use.
- It also even got better for SUVs and trucks of all sizes! Bonus deprecation is unlimited, literally allowing you to write off 100 percent of the vehicle (assuming 100-percent business use), plus the other actual expenses like fuel, repairs, and maintenance.
- Finally, if you are an RV owner, don't forget to consider making the RV part of your business model—especially if you plan to live life on the open road.

WISE HEALTH-CARE STRATEGIES

—— CASE STUDY ——

'm always excited to have a meeting where I'm able to make an immediate and major impact on my client's life. This was one of those times. It took place a short time after the Affordable Care Act (ACA) became the law of the land.

I sat down with a young man in his 20s who was doing really well in the internet marketing industry. The purpose of our meeting was to create a health-care strategy, and more specifically, a way to avoid the health-care penalty. He was infuriated that he would have to pay a penalty if he didn't buy insurance, which he didn't feel was necessary because he was young and healthy.

After I explained to him that he didn't meet any exceptions and he was going to have to get insurance or pay the penalty, I was able to give him the unexpected silver lining.

Because he was healthy, I suggested getting low-cost, high-deductible insurance and contributing to a Health Savings Account (HSA). When he grasped the concept of self-insuring himself with an HSA while still having the backup of catastrophic high-deductible insurance, getting tax deductions, and building a tax-free account for health care that can grow with creative investments and carry forward from year to year, he was absolutely blown away. He said emphatically, "You mean I can quit paying for insurance I don't use, take the savings on the premiums and sock them away for the future, *and* get a tax deduction for the whole thing?!"

As small-business owners, we have more options than any other group of Americans to save on health-care costs. The tax-saving strategies combined with the cost-saving ideas can have phenomenal results. It simply takes a little investigation and perhaps consulting with several professionals to create the perfect plan for yourself.

I won't get into the pros and cons of the ACA. Both exist. I don't care if you are a Republican, Democrat, or Independent. You can find provisions of the legislation that will help you *and* provisions that will cost you. A little proactive planning can help you take advantage of the pros and avoid the cons.

The KohlerCare Strategy

Over the past few years, I have created and implemented a comprehensive health-care strategy with hundreds of clients. The results have been incredible. It's called "KohlerCare." That's a little bold, but my goal is to make health-care savings great again. (Two political puns in one plan—amazing!) Now keep in mind that with the passing of the TCJA, starting in 2019 there is no longer a "penalty" for not carrying insurance. With that said, my suggestion to use a coordinated attack of maximizing your health-care benefits, reducing costs, and getting tax benefits to boot. It consists of seven steps:

1. Minimize or avoid ACA taxes.
2. Choose the right type of insurance policy.
3. Deduct your health insurance correctly.
4. Use the Small Business Health Care Tax Credit.
5. Deduct your medical expenses strategically.
6. Start a Health Savings Account (HSA).
7. Understand Health Reimbursement Arrangements (HRAs).

Whether you are young or old, healthy or unhealthy, single or married with children, there are options that can save or even make you money. I'll go into each of these options with some degree of detail. After reading, continue your research to see which options can apply in your situation.

Minimize or Avoid Affordable Care Act Taxes

There are two taxes you should be aware of that can have a significant impact: The Net Investment Tax and the additional Medicare Tax. Here is the Cliffs Notes version: If you are single and make less than $200,000, or are married and collectively make less than $250,000, neither of these taxes will affect you. But if you make more than these respective amounts, it's important to know the strategies for getting around the rules pertaining to them.

The net investment tax is a 3.8-percent income tax most people don't see coming. Essentially, you owe this tax calculated on the lesser of your net investment income or your modified adjusted gross income exceeding $200,000 for single taxpayers and $250,000 for married taxpayers.

The Medicare tax of .09 percent also kicks in on single individuals with wages or self-employment income of more than $200,000 and married couples with the same type of income over

$250,000. Frankly, if you have a big W-2 at a corporate job, enjoy the perks, but you won't be able to get around the Medicare tax.

The best way to avoid the net investment tax is to create, transform, or manufacture income that isn't subject to the tax. The types of income that aren't subject to this tax include:

- S corp pass-through income
- Sale of property if you or your spouse are a real estate professional
- Self-employment income (the additional Medicare tax provision still applies)
- Retirement income

For those of you who own a business, this again is where the S corp and controlling your payroll is absolutely critical. Not only do you want to keep your salary down to avoid high FICA taxes (see Chapter 4), but you also want to keep it below the $250,000 threshold in combination with your spouse (if married) to make sure you don't pay the additional Medicare tax.

In Chapter 16, I discuss ways to save on taxes when selling property, and in Chapter 25, I offer the strategy of "opportunity shifting," wherein you can use retirement plans to invest in what you know best and more rapidly build your investments while coming out ahead on tax savings. Several of these strategies have the ancillary benefit of avoiding the Affordable Care Act's net investment tax.

The strategies for avoiding the net investment tax are all in line with what I have been teaching and implementing with clients for years. Some of the strategies you will learn throughout the rest of the book to avoid this tax include the following:

- S corps to reduce salary and funnel K-1 income (Chapter 4)
- 1031 Exchanges to exchange properties without incurring taxes (Chapter 16)
- Installment sales of property (Chapter 16)
- Charitable remainder trusts for receiving income on property that you will donate after you die (Chapter 16)

- Self-directing your retirement investments and using Roth IRAs and 401(k)s (Chapter 25)

Choose the Right Health Insurance Policy

Some might find it odd to get insurance advice from a tax attorney. I'm not licensed to sell insurance and won't be any time soon. However, throughout this ACA roller coaster ride over the past few years, I have attended countless seminars, read hundreds of articles, worked through the health-care websites, and consulted hundreds of clients on health-care and insurance topics. Moreover, I have shared the stage and my weekly radio show with some of the best insurance experts in the country. I have learned some critical tips that will help you weave your way through this maze.

- *Be aware of what enrollment options are available in your area.*
- *Understand the "metal" health insurance plans and the differences between each one.* Essentially, you will have to choose between a Platinum, Gold, Silver, or Bronze plan with different benefits, deductibles, and, of course, premiums.
- *Know your network.* Who is the doctor you want to use? What hospital? As you look closer, you may be surprised to see a wide range in premiums between the different types of plans based on the network. The savings under certain policies are because the insurance company provides a smaller network of doctors under

---

GOOD TO KNOW:
PROVIDING INSURANCE FOR EMPLOYEES

Under the Affordable Care Act, if you have more than 50 employees (or the equivalent in part-time employees), then you are required to provide health insurance for your employees. However, many small-business owners with fewer employees choose to offer health insurance voluntarily, finding it critical to provide insurance to attract and retain the right type of employees.

---

the plan, which may also be stripped of benefits like dental or vision care.

- *Bet on your health.* If you're healthy and want to self-insure yourself in the future, you can often get a lower premium with a higher deductible and fund a Health Savings Account (more on this below).
- *Cash in on your business.* Rely on your status as a small-business owner whenever possible. Don't forget that you have an edge when shopping for policies. You can possibly shop for an individual policy or a business policy if you are going to provide insurance for two or more employees. (Your spouse, however, does *not* qualify as that second employee.)

Deduct Your Health Insurance Correctly

Health insurance is 100 percent deductible for the small-business owner, a huge benefit the average American can't take advantage of. A nonbusiness owner would have to try and itemize these costs, more than likely to no avail. Make sure your CPA is aware of all health insurance premiums you are paying and that they are properly accounted for. For example, if you have an S or C corp, you need to separately state the insurance premiums you have paid for out of the business on your W-2. This is critical to get the tax deduction, and it can trigger an audit if you skip this procedure.

Use the Small-Business Health Care Tax Credit

This little gem is a literal dollar-for-dollar tax credit against any taxes you owe and up to 50 percent of any health-care premiums you pay for on behalf of your employees. There are a number of simple, very manageable rules. For example, you are required to cover at least 50 percent of the cost of single (not family) health-care coverage, you must have fewer than 25 full-time-equivalent employees, and those employees must have average wages of less than $50,000 a year. If you have employees, look into it and run the numbers. It's a great way to provide a perk for employees that *also* gives you a tax credit.

Deduct Your Medical Expenses Strategically

Surprisingly, writing off your medical expenses (not insurance) has gotten increasingly difficult for the average American. It can be done, but it takes a little more creativity; again, being a small-business owner gives you a strategic advantage.

The first problem is that medical expenses are an itemized deduction and, as such, are limited by your adjusted gross income (AGI). Specifically, this means that your medical expenses are only deductible above 10 percent of your AGI. For example, if you make $100,000, your first $10,000 of medical expenses are nondeductible. Ninety-seven percent of Americans who try to deduct medical expenses either are better off with the "new and improved" standard deduction or phase out completely. **Bottom line, itemizing your medical expenses on Schedule A is a joke.**

Next, the benefit of Flexible Savings Accounts (FSAs) have also been decreased. These are the "use it or lose it" plans many of us have come to know through our employers. Contributions are now limited to $2,700 in 2019 and adjusted for inflation each year. I still recommend clients take advantage of them if they have a day job where they or their spouses can contribute. However, this is NOT a small-business tax strategy. It's a big corporate/employee strategy and a before-tax deduction from your paycheck; just remember to use it and *not* lose it.

So what, you may ask, *is the KohlerCare trick?* Essentially, I suggest my clients consider *either* a Health Savings Account (HSA), a Health Reimbursement Arrangement (HRA), or a *combination* of the two. I discuss these more fully below.

Disclaimer: These are huge topics, and if you truly think they might work for you or your family, I strongly encourage you to take some additional time studying their benefits and learning how to implement them before you dive in.

Start a Health Savings Account (HSA)

Essentially, HSAs are for the healthy and don't require that you have a small business. However, you *must* have a high deductible/qualifying health insurance plan. The reason I like these for business owners is because, as an entrepreneur, you will typically have much more control over your health insurance plan and can use creative strategies to acquire the right type of insurance. This is in contrast to W-2 employees, who are at the mercy of whether their employers offer a qualifying plan that allows the employee to open an HSA. But, W-2 earners can still have an HSA in addition to their regular plans, so if that's you, be sure to check with your employer.

To hit the highlights, HSAs are pretax accounts, contributions are deductible on the front page of your tax return (regardless of your income level), and the monies in the accounts grow tax-free. It's *not* a "use it or lose it" plan. Money stays in the plan from year to year and will continue to grow from investments and additional contributions. Tax-free withdrawals can be made at any time for a host of health-care expenses like copays, deductibles, prescriptions, dental, chiropractic, massage therapy, etc. Deductible contributions in 2019 are $3,500 for individuals and $7,000 for families (adjusted for inflation each year).

This is a fantastic tax deduction on the front page of your tax return. There are NO phase outs for making too much money. Boom! Right off the top. How great is that?

One other unique strategy (a seemingly unknown fact in the world of mainstream accounting) is that HSA owners can self-direct the funds into real estate or alternative investments like cryptocurrency, gold, silver, or other small businesses. You can self-direct your HSA account like an IRA and dramatically increase its value to levels that could cover your health-care expenses for the rest of your life with tax-free withdrawals. And, should you die and leave money in the account, the funds will go to any beneficiary you name and then continue to grow tax-free for them. It basically ends up turning into something akin to an IRA in that case.

In order to qualify for an HSA, the taxpayer as an individual or family must purchase a high-deductible HSA-qualifying health plan. The deductible amounts, which are regularly adjusted for inflation, are currently in 2019 at $1,350 for a single individual and $2,700 for a family. Once you have the right type of insurance policy, you can open an HSA at almost any bank or credit union, or you can self-direct your HSA. You can even make contributions up until April 15 for the prior year and still be able to deduct them. That's a great benefit!

If you feel an HSA could benefit you or your family, I encourage you to do additional research and speak with your tax advisor, CPA, and insurance advisor to formulate a game plan. Maybe you won't implement it this year, but you could plan for future years when your health insurance needs a change.

Understand Health Reimbursement Arrangements

A Health Reimbursement Arrangement (HRA), sometimes referred to as a Section 105 Plan, is a strategy for the unhealthy. When I say "unhealthy," I simply mean those with higher-than-average medical expenses; HRAs work for those whose insurance plans may not cover everything they need—for example, dental costs, copays, prescription medications, or chiropractic or acupuncture services.

However, this strategy is exclusive to small-business owners, and the average American shouldn't consider this strategy unless they have a legitimate business-generated income. The HRA essentially allows you to set up your own "benefit plan" for health care and reimburse yourself for all your health-care expenses, thereby getting a 100-percent write-off for all medical expenses. The only challenge can be putting the right structure in place to allow the plan to work. Sometimes it takes a little extra business planning and some attention to bookkeeping to make it happen, but it can be very lucrative and worth the time spent.

Regrettably, if you are operating as an S corp, you cannot adopt an HRA for yourself. Moreover, if you simply have rental property held by an LLC, you can't use an HRA. There are very specific methods for implementing an HRA, which differ depending on whether you are single or married.

HRA Implementation for a Single Person

If you are single and have multiple businesses or an S corp for your operations, you must form a C corp and provide a payroll and HRA plan for yourself as an employee under this new C corp. Your other businesses can "lease" you from the C corp. If you have an S corp, your payroll requirement is now satisfied by leasing you from your C corp. Yes, this procedure requires you to form a new company and prepare tax returns for it; thus, it's essential to do a cost-benefit analysis and make sure the procedure pays for itself. See Figure 11.1 for a visual representation.

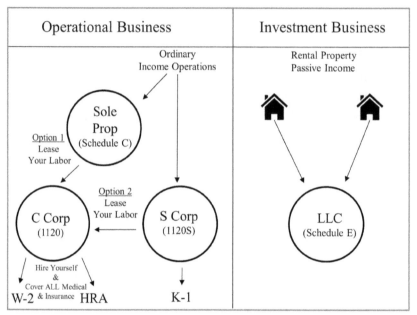

Figure 11.1 – **Single HRA Plan**

HRA Implementation for Married Persons

If you are married, you will typically create a sole prop support company for your other businesses, including S corp(s), and hire your spouse. As part of your spouse's compensation, he or she will receive an HRA covering all of their medical expenses *and* those of their dependents—including you! Therefore, you "back door" yourself into an HRA through your spouse. Of course, there are a few details and particulars to implementing the plan, but they can be simple and affordable to put into place. On a cautionary note, keep in mind that if

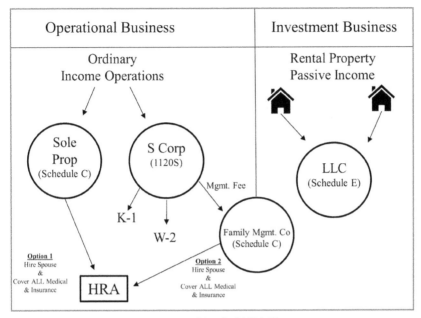

Figure 11.2 – **Married HRA Plan**

you have other employees in your business(es), you'll have to carefully determine if you must cover those employees with the same plan.

See Figure 11.2 for a visual representation.

HRA Pros and Cons

Remember a few quick pros and cons of the HRA. The pros include:

- Deduct 100 percent of medical expenses in a solo entrepreneur plan
- Self-administered with no health insurance requirement
- Great for the "unhealthy" (i.e., you have more than $4,000 in medical expenses per year and the tax benefits exceed the cost of implementing and maintaining the plan)

The cons of the HRA include:

- No insurance with an HRA if your health gets worse (get insurance separately)
- Requires a family management company (sole prop) if married

- Requires a C corp if you are single
- No savings account option

In either case, whether married or single, add up how much you are spending on medical expenses annually (not including insurance), and see what the tax benefit would be on your return if you could legitimately deduct those expenses. That's a great starting point to see if you should consider an HRA.

Game Plan Takeaway and Action Items

I understand that my case study client represents only a small cross-section of the American public. There are the healthy, the unhealthy, single, married, families, young, and old. In fact, premiums and options can change dramatically from state to state, but the important point I want to emphasize is that there are choices and strategies for everyone. With a little work, you can find better health care, better insurance, and more tax savings. Don't give up.

- Determine if you are subject to Affordable Care Act taxes and plan accordingly.
- Take a more active role in shopping for health insurance and review multiple options.
- Consult your CPA on your strategy for health insurance deductions and credits.
- Make a strategic plan to deduct all your health-care costs.
- Consider a Health Savings Account (HSA).
- Determine if a Health Reimbursement Arrangement (HRA) would make sense financially.

HIRING FAMILY MEMBERS FOR TAX SAVINGS

—— CASE STUDY ——

I have four children, and I think many parents would agree that being a parent isn't easy; in fact, it might be one of the greatest challenges in life. The teenage years are especially difficult. Don't get me wrong—I love my children and wouldn't trade them or the experience of raising them for anything. But helping them become productive and successful adults sometimes seems an elusive goal.

The biggest impact my business and career have had on me and my family is helping my children become financially independent, better students, and entrepreneurs.

My youngest daughter helps in the office: She cleans, stuffs envelopes, shreds paper, recycles cans, and takes out the garbage. She has her own debit card, has learned the value of a dollar, and understands bank and ATM fees. She started learning these principles when she was 7 years old.

My teenagers have all started their own businesses, with varying degrees of success, but the important thing is that they have tried. They all worked in my business through high school and in the summers and learned how to manage their money and save for large purchases.

If I didn't have a small business, I don't know how I could have ever taught these principles to my family. In fact, I think my advice to hire children in the business may have had the greatest impact of any of my strategies for families. I've actually had parents in tears, thanking me for showing them ways to teach their kids about money and business ownership. You can do the same.

Hiring your children and family members is one of the most powerful tax strategies used (and sadly underused) by entrepreneurs today. Many people don't realize that paying their children or grandchildren, whether they're under 18 or adults, is an excellent strategy to minimize tax liability and enjoy a host of other ancillary benefits.

The days of hard work on the family farm are rapidly disappearing, and more and more children are leaving home without a work ethic, money management skills, or a concept of entrepreneurship. Moreover, many business owners forget that some of their most affordable labor is sitting right across from them at the dinner table. Get your family involved in the business! The beauty of this strategy is that it has multiple benefits:

- Save on taxes
- Help children become self-reliant
- Teach small-business ownership skills

- Instill the concept of a job well done
- Save money in the business by not hiring outside help—it's money you were going to give them anyway
- Teach them how to complete a hard day's work

In this chapter, I'll walk you through the benefits (and some of the pitfalls) of hiring your children and other family members.

Paying Children Who Are Under 18

It's important you follow the right procedure when paying your kids who are under 18, or this strategy could backfire on you. Here are the pertinent facts and rules to follow when putting your minor children to work in the business.

First, you don't have to withhold any income taxes or payroll taxes. This also applies to workers' comp as well as state and federal unemployment insurance. The reasoning is that the government and insurance carriers assume your children won't sue you if they are hurt on the job—at least we hope not. Your children are also probably on your health insurance plan; you'll end up paying the bill one way or another. Moreover, they are unlikely to file for unemployment insurance since they are dependents and you are providing for their care. Again, this is only for children under 18. Still, I recommend you review the laws in your jurisdiction to ensure you are operating legally regarding workers' comp and other payroll taxes as well as work permits and other regulations.

Second, all of us, including our children, don't pay taxes on the first $12,200 they earn in 2019. It's the standard deduction which is adjusted for inflation each year. Interestingly, you can still claim your children as dependents on your tax return and take the child tax credit if you qualify. However, they don't pay taxes on their earned income up to the standard deduction. Stated another way, your children get their own "standard deduction" for their earned income even if they are a dependent of yours on your tax return.

Therefore, when you pay your children for services they perform in your business, you can generate an expense for your income taxes by pushing income to your children. Of course, I'm not advocating you pay your children as a "sham" operation. They must be legitimately involved in the business; you will want to keep records of their time worked as well as pay them a reasonable wage. This could include having a clear job title and description for the child and keeping track of their tasks.

The IRS allows any sole prop or partnership (LLC) that is wholly owned by a child's parents to pay wages to children under 18 without having to withhold payroll taxes.

However, if you have an S or C corp, be careful of this strategy. You do not receive the benefit of avoiding FICA when paying your children *unless* you pay them through a sole prop or an LLC owned solely by mom and dad. Bottom line: Don't pay your children out of a corporation or you have to withhold payroll taxes.

Thus, we recommend you pay children out of a family management company, structured as a sole prop or LLC with independent income and operations and paid a management fee from the corporation. Figure 12.1 gives an illustration of this structure.

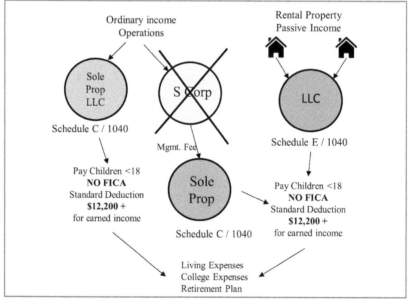

Figure 12.1 – **Children and/or Dependents Under Age 18**

Paying Children 18 and Older

If you are paying children 18 or older, you have the option of treating them as subcontractors or as employees. If you pay them as a subcontractor, then you simply issue them a 1099 in January. They file a small-business Schedule C, get to take small-business tax deductions, take a standard deduction of $12,200 in 2019 (adjusted for inflation each year), and will probably be in a lower tax bracket than you. If done properly, the savings you get as a family can be phenomenal. I love to see older children serving on the board of directors in a corporation or board of advisors in an LLC, providing advisory services, marketing support, research, consulting, etc.

However, if your adult child works in your business alongside your other employees and looks like and acts like an employee, then you need to treat them as an employee. Thus, you will have to withhold FICA and other typical payroll fees. Again, with overall family tax planning there is nothing wrong with this and a little tax strategy with your kids can go a long way. Figure 12.2 illustrates this arrangement. If you plan on helping them financially, anyway, at least make them earn it.

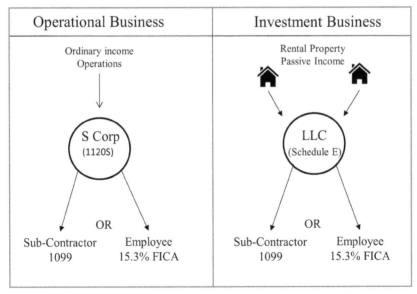

Figure 12.2 — **Children 18 or Older, Parents, Nieces, and Nephews**

Paying Grandchildren

Don't think I forgot about you, grandparents! Certainly we also want to teach our grandkids the importance of hard work and entrepreneurship. Again, why not try to integrate them into the business with legitimate services you need and were going to outsource or do yourself anyway?

The tax strategy for paying grandchildren, however, is not by direct payment but to 1099 your children and the support company they establish to supervise and hire their children, i.e., your grandkids. This way they can pay the kids under the "children under 18" strategy and save you from giving the grandkids a W-2 or 1099. Your children won't pay taxes either because on their Schedule C reporting the support company operations, they will claim the income you 1099'd them and deduct the payments to your grandkids, thus zeroing out the income of their business supporting *your* business. Figure 12.3 shows how this company structure works.

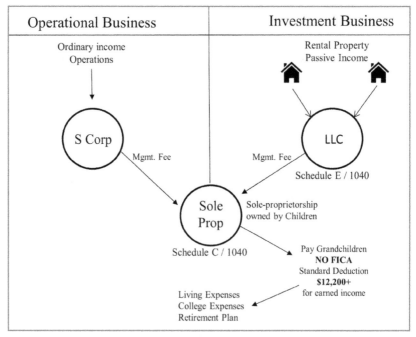

Figure 12.3 – **Hiring Grandchildren**

Do Family Chores Count?

Hiring your children to do family chores will not qualify as a valid deduction and will certainly set you up for an audit. Legitimate tasks include cleaning the business office, shredding papers, stuffing envelopes, providing social media support, entering bookkeeping items, or even working on rental properties. Just keep good records of their hours and the work they do.

How Young Can My Children Be When I Hire Them?

It depends. I know professional artists and photographers who legitimately use their younger children as models, pay them a modest amount, and deduct the expense. In this situation, they could easily be under age five. However, they are serving a legitimate role in the operations of a substantive business.

The most important thing is to be able to show a bona fide job description, duties, and log of work performed. Teenage kids are obviously the best fit for this strategy because of their ability to make a legitimate contribution to the business activity. Again, make sure you review any local laws regarding work permits, wage laws, and allowable hours for minors, even if the minors in question are your children.

Will the Kiddie Tax Apply?

The "kiddie tax" is a tax on children's unearned income imposed at the parents' tax rate and exists to prevent parents from moving assets with passive income into children's names. Some parents ask: "When I pay my kids, won't they end up paying taxes on their income at our rates anyway?" The answer is no. The kiddie tax only applies to unearned or "portfolio" income, not earned income from a job.

Game Plan Takeaway and Action Items

Don't miss out on the opportunity to involve your family members of all ages in your business. I have seen this strategy not only save clients thousands of dollars in taxes, but also literally change the lives of their families as well. If your children want money, tell them you need help in your business and they need to earn the money they want. They can start at any age with any level of service. Share your passion about your business with them and help them cultivate that same passion for a business idea of their own.

- Open bank accounts with and for your children.
- Talk about the service they can provide in the business.
- Create a job description and empower them to help you in your business.
- Discuss your tax and legal structure with your CPA to make sure you pay your children properly and in the correct amount.
- Keep good records on your children's and family members' employment and follow proper structure and procedures without cutting corners.

BUYING RENTAL PROPERTIES

I'll always remember one of the most emotional and moving consultations of my career. I was still relatively young, and I often felt awkward and inadequate when consulting older clients who clearly had more life experience than I did. However, I have learned time and again that my older clients look to me for advice not because of my age but because of my education and experience. As Indiana Jones said in *Raiders of the Lost Ark*, "It's not the years . . . it's the mileage."

In this particular instance, my clients were in their mid-60s at the end of their W-2 careers with a meager retirement account and looking down the barrel at Social Security as their primary source of retirement income. They were meeting with me about their retirement savings, desperate to find the best and quickest way to build more retirement income and cash flow.

I searched my heart and mind for inspiration after reviewing their affairs and believed rental real estate was the answer. They had strong credit scores but would need to partner with others for capital. However, if they were wise and careful, they could build a decent real estate portfolio over the next five years.

Their reaction shocked me, and I'll never forget it. With tears in their eyes, they said, "Mark, we knew you were going to say this. We've felt we should buy rental property, no matter how small, for years and years, but never found the time or courage to get involved." They explained that they wished they would have started years earlier and knew they were in this mess because they hadn't heeded those promptings earlier.

They begged me to tell their story to my other clients and everyone I could— how it's important to start by buying just one rental property a year as soon as possible. This chapter is dedicated to them.

It was because of this experience and several others like it early in my career that I started recommending that *all* my clients purchase at least one rental property a year—no matter how inexpensive—for its tax planning and wealth-building benefits.

I'm not saying you should *only* buy real estate. Certainly you should diversify your investment dollars. Having stocks, bonds, mutual funds, notes, and a whole host of other investments is very important as well.

I also understand that real estate isn't for everyone. Age, personality type, and financial resources are just a few of many good reasons why your real estate potential may be limited. However, your reasons for not buying real estate shouldn't be lack of capital, credit, or know-how. Each of these things can be acquired through time, energy, and partnerships with others who are stronger in the areas where you are weak.

Let's go through a checklist of reasons why buying rental real estate can be life-changing:

- The tax write-offs are incredible when you treat your rental property as a small business. You may get to use those deductions against your ordinary income, but if not, they will carry forward until you sell the property.
- The value of the property will grow tax-free until you sell, and you may be able to use other strategies to delay or avoid the gain entirely.
- The vast majority of rental properties allow investors to create tax-free cash flow based on the number of write-offs related to the property.
- You can leverage your money to buy more investment properties and thus increase your return on investment (ROI), something you can't do with stocks, bonds, or mutual funds.
- You can involve family members as employees and travel to check on your rentals and take these expenses as valid business deductions.
- You can enjoy average appreciation and growth that outperform Wall Street and a variety of other benefits.

Most important, it's like a forced retirement plan. I say this because Americans are generally terrible at saving money. We may try to save a few dollars in our IRA or 401(k), or even in an after-tax account, but let's face it: On average, our savings rate is pretty pathetic. Rental properties, for whatever reason, give us a greater sense of commitment. We feel an urgency to maintain the property, and we're even motivated to push through the bad cash flow times.

Is Real Estate for Everyone?

I certainly want to acknowledge the risks of buying real estate; this type of investment requires commitment and isn't for everyone. It's important that investors get properly educated and not rush into the process. However, despite these risks, I still feel strongly that buying real estate can be one of the most secure paths to creating tax-free cash flow in today's economy and a major reserve of equity for retirement.

With the power of leverage and responsibly using the bank's or other people's money, you can increase your net worth dramatically. Don't rush; take your time and realize it's not a sprint, but a marathon. Recognize the risks and minimize them with calculated decisions.

This may seem bold coming from a CPA or attorney, but I'm not a realtor selling you real estate. I'm an advisor trying to help you save taxes and build wealth.

Ten Steps to Purchasing Your First Rental Property

Thinking of buying rental property can be daunting and overwhelming. Where does one start? Over the years, I have developed and created the following ten steps as a guide for my clients who are new investors. I hope this list serves as a starting point in your venture into owning and operating rental real estate.

1. *Make a goal.* Set a deadline to purchase your first rental and stay committed. Let friends and family know your goal. Write it down and set short, concise deadlines for conducting a property search and deciding, rather than having vague, open goals like, "Buy rental by X date." However, make sure you set manageable goals that you can meet.

2. *Start shopping.* Just get out and start looking at rental properties. Hire two or more real estate agents or work with other investors to send you leads in the markets you're considering. Once you start looking, you'll get more motivated.

3. *Develop a spreadsheet.* A coherent spreadsheet for analyzing your prospective properties is crucial. You should set forth criteria to rank the properties by rent rates, operating costs, debt service, property management, etc., and create an ultimate annual ROI calculation for each of the properties you're considering. By determining this ROI, you can then compare it against the other properties and options in your investment portfolio.

4. *Look at lots of property.* Take your time and look at plenty of properties. There is no rush. I tell clients again and again: There will always be a deal next week. Follow your gut and don't get sucked into a deal you don't feel good about.

5. *Make an offer and start due diligence.* Once you find a property that fits the bill, make an offer contingent on due diligence. If you don't like the deal, *get out.* Don't get emotionally attached to a transaction you aren't positive about.

6. *Do* more *due diligence.* Look at the property from every angle. Read books and talk to others about nightmare experiences so you can look for similarities and spot any possible problems in your own transactions. Be patient and don't get discouraged.

7. *Open escrow.* Once you're happy with your due diligence and the property looks like a winner, start reviewing documents and move toward closing. Begin forming an LLC, which I recommend to hold rental(s) because asset protection is critical (see Chapter 3). Certainly don't do your first deal on your own; set up a consultation with your CPA or tax attorney so you can discuss the matter and get help reviewing your documents if necessary.

8. *Close and deed the property to an LLC.* Don't stress about closing in your own name if you don't have the LLC finished before closing. There are only a few states where this is important to consider. Also, don't worry about the "due on sale clause" when deeding to your own LLC. The bank is worried if you transfer the property to someone else after closing, not if you simply transfer it to your own entity or trust.

9. *Track expenses.* Keep track of everything for tax purposes. This includes the costs you incurred before you closed, the closing statements, and expenses afterward. Everything related to the purchase and management of the property is a tax write-off. Consider Chapter 9 as a good starting point for understanding write-offs and review the list at the end of my book, *What Your CPA Isn't Telling You: Life-Changing Tax Strategies* (Entrepreneur Press, 2011), if you need more ideas for deductions.

10. *Manage the property, tenant(s), and your property manager.* In summary, this property won't run itself. Stay involved. Take lots of pictures regularly. Keep good records on your tenants and your property manager, if you are using one. Visit the property regularly. There are excellent books, online education, in-person training, and consultants and coaches who can help you learn how to properly manage your property without having to learn the hard way by making unnecessary mistakes.

Four Benefits of Owning Rental Property

As previously mentioned, a good rental property strategy will not only build immediate cash flow and provide a long-term retirement strategy, but it can also create some incredible tax benefits if you plan wisely.

Below is Figure 13.1, which I have used countless times in presentations and lectures around the country to help identify the following benefits.

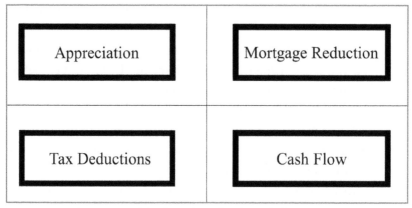

Figure 13.1 – **The Four Benefits to Rental Property**

1. Property Appreciation

I'm not advising a "fix and flip" strategy. You should plan on keeping your rental property for at least seven to ten years. As such, appreciation is one of the key benefits in your ROI. In fact, the

National Association of Realtors (NAR) has reported that real estate nationwide has averaged more than 6.74-percent appreciation annually during the past 50 years.

This rate of return outperforms the S&P 500 and most Wall Street investments. I realize that not all property in every market experiences this type of growth, but this average is definitely something to consider. Don't discount the power of property appreciation.

2. Mortgage Reduction

This is an oft-overlooked benefit to owning rental property. If you purchase wisely, the property should be at least breaking even in cash flow if you have tenants. The renter is essentially paying the mortgage for you.

This principal reduction within the mortgage is an ongoing tax-free benefit, along with appreciation, that you can calculate and count on over time. Keep this in your spreadsheet as you calculate your total ROI.

3. Tax Savings and Deductions

It's no secret that rental properties lose money on paper. But with the power of depreciation, the fact that you get to deduct the mortgage interest your renter is essentially paying for you and the additional deductions you can take for travel, property taxes, HOA fees, repairs, maintenance, home office, supplies, cell phone, etc., the tax benefits add up very quickly!

However, how you are classified as a real estate investor is absolutely critical. The IRS may classify you as passive, active, or professional unless you take proactive steps to understand and elect the best classification for your situation on your tax return. The benefits vary widely. Here are the basics:

- *Passive investors.* Anyone qualifies, but losses are only deductible against other passive income.
- *Active investors.* To qualify, you simply need to make decisions— buying or selling property or hiring a property manager— regarding your properties and check the proper box on your

tax return. However, losses are limited annually to $25,000 and phase out completely at $150,000 of adjusted gross income (AGI).

• *Real estate professionals.* All real estate losses are deductible against any type of income. However, you must meet a two-part test (your primary occupation is real estate and you spend 750 hours per year working on it) *and* materially participate in the management of the property under one of another seven tests.

It's very important to understand these options and discuss them with your CPA. My clients all qualify as active investors and can carry losses forward indefinitely to write off against future property sales. Remember, even if you aren't able to deduct losses immediately against your other income, you will eventually realize the write-offs, and the tax benefits can be phenomenal.

4. Cash Flow

Simply stated, good rental property creates cash flow; bad property does not. Purchasing good cash-flow property causes the other benefits to fall right into place. If the economic downturn and the drop in real estate values have taught us anything, it's that we *must* analyze and purchase property based on cash flow above all.

Cash flow is also a part of your ROI when you analyze a property. You will consider all of your cash expenses to determine what your cash-on-cash rate of return is as you try to minimize cash expenses related to the property. Conversely, you'll want to maximize your tax write-offs for the tax benefits I discussed previously.

In summary, many savvy investors realize these four quadrants or benefits work together and can produce double- if not triple-digit rates of return on their leveraged rental properties. Your overall ROI analysis of any property will include cash flow, the mortgage principal pay-down, property appreciation, and tax benefits. With these benefits and the substantial ROI, it's no surprise that the wealthiest and most successful people in America hold rental property as a large part of their portfolios.

So many people ask me, "What are *your* successful clients doing, Mark? How are they surviving the economy?" And I tell them: Almost every one of my wealthy clients owns rental real estate. Granted, rental real estate is not *all* it takes, but it's certainly a key factor in the equation. If you want to build wealth, give your CPA something to work with on your tax return, and feel like you are more in control of your retirement money, please consider rental real estate.

Consider Buying a Rental Property Before Contributing to Your IRA or 401(k)

Sounds like a crazy idea to some, but I always encourage everyone to consider buying a rental property before contributing to a savings plan. Go ahead and set aside a predetermined percentage or amount of income each month for savings and investments. Then, as soon as possible and before choosing stocks, bonds, and mutual funds as your primary retirement investment, I think you should consider a rental property.

First, a disclaimer; if you work for a company that offers a 401(k) and any matching, then obviously participate. You are simply doubling your money with a match from your employer. That's an excellent investment return you can't turn down. But after that, maybe think twice.

Why? Real estate really acts as a "forced retirement plan," and in the long run, you won't regret it. We as Americans are typically poor savers. Staying committed to regular contributions to a 401(k) or IRA can be very difficult for some. However, once you buy that rental, you will be far more dedicated to keeping it going than you would a simple savings account.

Next, although over time rental properties will have ups and downs, every financial statistic shows that on average, real estate will outperform the stock market while building more wealth and tax-free cash flow along the way.

Finally, the ability to use leverage to build rental properties is a unique characteristic only available to real estate, at least for the average American. (We can't all set up margin accounts with our broker to day trade our IRA). Essentially, the opportunity to borrow from the bank and leverage a down payment is a huge opportunity to build wealth.

In the end, we should be using BOTH financial instruments AND real estate to build wealth. Don't get hyper focused on one versus the other. Stay balanced. I just like the real estate idea from the outset when and where possible.

Don't Oversimplify and Disregard the Risks of Rentals

Is there risk involved in buying rental property? Certainly! Is it sometimes hard to manage rental property, both locally and from a distance? Yes! Can you buy bad property at times? Absolutely! Should *all* of us buy rentals? Not necessarily! But there are solutions. Knowledge is power and will reduce fear. I encourage all my clients to find inspiration and guidance from other successful real estate investors, while making sure they are cautious, careful, and conservative. I also urge them to focus on cash flow and the numbers, never just appreciation.

Game Plan Takeaway and Action Items

Don't make the mistake of thinking Social Security or a few hundred bucks in savings a month will allow you to retire in the lap of luxury. It will not. Real estate is an alternative!

With my older clients who came to my office with their retirement income dilemma, time will only tell. They have purchased several rentals and are on a fast learning curve to master the system of purchasing and managing their rentals. They aren't out of the woods yet, but they are grateful they now have a plan where they can see the light at the end of the tunnel and only wished they had started sooner.

- Make a goal with a timeline to buy your first rental.
- Start shopping for rentals, and build a spreadsheet to analyze properties.

- Get educated! Keep learning and get support when necessary.
- Find a system for identifying and analyzing quality properties.
- Don't give up. Follow my ten steps to buying your first rental.
- If you currently own rentals, maximize your write-offs and create an entity for asset protection.

THE IMPORTANCE OF BASIC BOOKKEEPING

—— CASE STUDY ——

I was looking out my office window when a client pulled up in his pickup truck with the bed full of bankers' boxes. I wondered what they could be.

Minutes later, he was wheeling a dolly down the hall outside my office, rolling in the first round of boxes. We began our meeting and he confessed: Those boxes contained three years of accounting records for his business, and he hadn't done a lick of bookkeeping. He needed me to give him an intervention and tell him how bad this was for tax reduction, planning, and decision-making. He already knew this, of course, but he wanted it to sink in hard so he wouldn't let it happen again.

> I didn't think anything I could say would sufficiently emphasize the crisis he
> was facing, so I gave him a fee estimate for working through the mess. That
> did the trick, and he pulled out his checkbook to start the process of cleaning
> up his "books."
>
> Years later, he is one of my best clients, and he has never let his bookkeeping
> and accounting get behind since. He has saved on accounting fees, saved on
> taxes, and made better business decisions in the process.
>
> Those three years of poor bookkeeping certainly cost him financially, but
> he later admitted that the biggest toll was on his health and peace of mind.
> Feeling overwhelmed by the pressure and stress led to some of the darkest
> years of his business career.

It alarms me to see how many clients don't maintain their checkbooks and records properly or don't even keep separate books for each of the companies they own and operate.

Maintaining your books is not something I advocate solely as a tax-savings strategy; it can also prevent you from losing your sanity and getting dragged into a potential lawsuit over commingling your funds. In this chapter, we'll walk through some bookkeeping plays that will keep you in the black.

Start with Separate Accounting

It's critical that business owners have a separate checkbook for every business enterprise they own. Some feel it creates more work to have separate checkbooks, but I guarantee you the extra effort will actually be well worth it in the long run.

Here are five significant reasons for maintaining a separate checkbook and set of books for each of your businesses:

1. *Corporate veil.* First and foremost, maintaining a separate check-book substantiates the corporate veil, one of the primary reasons for forming a new corporation. Having a separate checkbook

shows you recognize the company is its own distinct entity. Furthermore, separate checkbooks will hopefully encourage you not to commingle personal and business funds.

2. *Tax savings.* Separate banking will improve bookkeeping procedures, prevent payments from being missed, and provide better records to improve your tax return.

3. *Audit protection.* Having a separate checkbook will improve your chances in the event of an IRS audit. The IRS will often disallow a number of expenses when personal and business expenses are commingled in a single checkbook.

4. *Less stress and more sanity.* One might think having separate checking and bookkeeping for a new company is cumbersome, unnecessary, and possibly even a waste of time. In fact, this procedure saves time and money in the long run. When your books are disorganized, you'll feel constant stress to take care of it, and this ultimately can cause you to feel undone.

5. *Improved decision making.* Having a separate checkbook starts the process of better bookkeeping, expense tracking, and budgeting, which leads to quality decision making. How can you expect to be a successful business owner without accurate records? You owe it to yourself and your business to keep good books.

Adopt an Accounting System

Once you have separate checking accounts, the next step is implementing a system for tracking income and expenses.

It's absolutely critical for small-business owners to at least consider QuickBooks as their primary accounting software system. Yes, there are a few alternatives to QuickBooks, but not many and even fewer worth considering.

QuickBooks is the most affordable, user-friendly, efficient, and effective accounting software ever written. That may sound a little cheesy or over the top, but it's true. Here are just a few things that QuickBooks can do to help you become a better, smarter business owner:

- *Keep essential information at your fingertips.* QuickBooks generates amazing reports that will allow you to easily stay abreast of your business's most important financial information, like profit and loss by product or property, accounts receivable by customer, sales reports, or expense reports. The list is tremendous. By having a quality set of books, you will inevitably be a better decision maker.

- *Better use your online banking system.* QuickBooks allows you to harness the online benefits that many banks offer. It coordinates with most banks, even lesser-known ones, to provide instantaneous information so you can download transactions and reconcile your data with ease.

- *Collect more of your accounts receivable.* QuickBooks allows you to generate professional-looking invoices that can be delivered via email and offer your customers the option to make online payments using several methods. You can also generate regular statements and create various reports to determine who your high-risk customers are for collection purposes and to help you make better decisions regarding your accounts receivable.

- *Delegate your accounting services with ease.* If you are the type that hates bookkeeping, QuickBooks will still make your life easier. Once you understand the basics—and I recommend that every business owner at least master the basics—you can delegate tasks, from reconciling to overseeing financial reporting. QuickBooks will even allow your CPA to log in online to access your financial data while doing your accounting.

- *Pay your business bills efficiently.* Let QuickBooks track your accounts payable so you can better manage your cash flow and pay bills when it is most convenient for you. Ultimately you will save on past-due fees and interest, and you'll be able to interact with your vendors in a more professional manner.

- *Receive payments immediately.* Accept credit card payments online and have the funds recorded directly in your QuickBooks file. You can even upgrade your QuickBooks software and tech supplies to integrate a point-of-sale (POS) system with your cash register and merchant/credit card machine.

- *Access your financial information anywhere.* The online version of QuickBooks allows you to access your books anywhere you have an internet connection. Moreover, your accountant can access them online with you for consultations and to look for training and reporting issues.
- *Use scanning software to track receipts.* Scan in receipts through a service like NeatReceipts, which immediately records and categorizes the information in QuickBooks. You can then keep a copy in your "cloud" storage of all receipts and contracts for audit and legal protection.

The list goes on and on. Please take this suggestion seriously; the sooner you integrate this system into your business, the sooner you'll see money savings, greater revenue, and more profit. Don't be afraid of QuickBooks—embrace it, and it will set you free! OK, that was a little much, but I can promise you this: It *will* save you money, and you'll also get addicted to the little "ping" you hear every time you enter a check or item in the register.

Get Help Implementing Your Accounting System

Be honest with yourself: Do you want to do the bookkeeping for your business? If so, great. But if not, who is going to do it? Have a plan! Yes, this is my best attempt at giving you an "intervention." Look at yourself in the mirror and assess your level of dedication, knowledge, and available time to implement and maintain your books. However, while it's fine if you have someone else do the dirty work, you still need a general understanding of the process and accounting system so that you, as the captain of your team, can oversee the process.

The following are five options to consider when it comes to divvying up the accounting duties.

Option 1: Learn QuickBooks and Input Items Yourself

I know this strikes fear in some of your hearts. In fact, this may be why your books currently aren't getting done. But you still may want to hold off delegating any part of the process until you put in a few hours a week to learn the basics, like inputting figures. At the bare minimum, you need to be able to view and print reports and check the accuracy of the work.

Option 2: Hire a Family Member to Keep Up the Books

I love this idea when you have teenagers or young adults you are supporting financially. This is a great way to make them earn their keep and teach them about entrepreneurship in the process. They will learn about the heart and soul of small business by doing the books. Adding them to the payroll is also a great tax write-off.

Option 3: Engage a Local Bookkeeper

This could be a local college student wanting internship/externship hours or a seasoned bookkeeper with affordable rates. It can free up a lot of your time so you can do what you do best: Make money for the business. This is also a natural step in the growth of a business before choosing the next option. Remember, this person will probably not prepare your taxes or do significant planning for you; she will simply maintain your books affordably so you can focus on more pressing tasks.

**GOOD TO KNOW:
DELEGATION PITFALL**

Remember that just because you hire someone who can do daily QuickBooks tasks, it doesn't mean you can ignore learning the software altogether. It's important you have at least a cursory knowledge and don't give away critical control. A wonderful feature of QuickBooks is that you can have different admin levels and passwords in order to delegate different tasks to individuals without giving them complete control of your books. Embezzlement is a constant threat, and you need to be able to access and double-check your books periodically.

Option 4: Hire Someone "In House"

You would be amazed at how quickly you can find a local college student or bookkeeper wanting to pick up some part- or full-time work for an hourly wage. This person could come in daily or a few days each week to input data and print reports. You might need to provide some supervision (thus learning the basics, as I previously advised), or you could have your outside CPA train and supervise your in-house bookkeeper. It can be extremely convenient to have an employee available to keep things in order. You can also hire someone who can wear different hats and help with other tasks, like answering phones, scanning, doing collections, shipping, or running errands.

Option 5: Use Your CPA or Tax Professional Throughout the Year

Many business owners like the comfort and security of knowing they not only have highly skilled accountants doing their books daily, but the benefit of one-stop shopping for tax planning and quarterly and annual reports as well. It may seem more expensive, but the value of better long-term planning and a higher quality of books can far exceed the cost. More mature and seasoned business owners may naturally "graduate" to a more experienced bookkeeper when the time is right. We have many clients who use my firm for this role and have been pleased with our accounting services department. At most firms, you can get an accounting support package tailored to your budget and needs.

Can I Use My Smartphone for Bookkeeping?

A smartphone is one of your greatest assets nowadays. You can photograph receipts, track mileage, and record your itinerary and expenses while traveling. Search for bookkeeping apps on the App Store or Google Play Store to find applications that may assist you in record keeping, helping you save more taxes and time and reduce stress. (I have my own branded app—brilliantly called the "Mark Kohler App," of course, and supported by Deductr—which you can find at www.markjkohler.com and test out for free for 30 days.) And since I mentioned QuickBooks earlier, note that you can link the app to your online portal as well for on-the-go invoicing and other tasks.

What Do I Do with Receipts?

Receipts provide protection from an audit, but that doesn't mean your accountant wants to see them. Frankly, you don't need to organize them either. You can photograph receipts with your smartphone or toss them in a box until you can scan them. Once they are scanned, you can throw away the paper. In fact, I suggest you just scan and save them in a folder each year, back up the data, and simply forget about them. Keep them at least six years. If the fateful day arises when the IRS wants to review or audit your return, you can open that electronic folder, print your receipts, and finally organize them.

Again, your receipts are just audit protection. The accounting information should have already been inputted into QuickBooks through your bank statements, credit card statements, or even your online banking system. This is another reason not to use cash for business expenses—you don't want to be inputting information from receipts by hand.

Game Plan Takeaway and Action Items

If you want to throw caution to the wind regarding corporate veil protection, commingle revenue, and wind up with an auditing nightmare, that's fine. But keep in mind the dollars and cents. Good bookkeeping is also about tax deductions—capturing write-offs you would otherwise miss and having the power of better information to make informed decisions quickly and effectively.

A better bookkeeping strategy is not an elusive goal. Trust me when I say you can do it! I recently had a client bounce into my office in an uncharacteristically good mood, excited to drop off their information for us to prepare their taxes. They could see I was visibly surprised at their positive attitude, and I quickly asked what the reason was. (Believe it or not, most people don't approach their tax planning with such enthusiasm.)

My client explained that they had struggled with bookkeeping for years, but this particular year they were able to implement an affordable system and were amazed at the benefits. I remembered my past client with the truck bed full of boxes and saw the same change and excitement in this client's eyes. Good bookkeeping can change your life.

- Adopt a software program, probably QuickBooks.
- Determine who is going to maintain the books and delegate the duties.
- Do your books on a regular basis. Don't wait until the end of the year.
- Scan and store your receipts.

DEALING WITH THE IRS

CASE STUDY

was astonished when I received the call. A potential new client wanted to see if I could be of service. He said he was getting audited and was looking for a CPA who could help him fight the IRS.

The surprising part of the call was that the client felt he had a case. He had started a new business during the prior tax year, and in that same period, he had paid a large amount for education and coaching. He didn't make any money that year but proceeded to deduct the entire amount of his education expenses.

When I say he didn't make any money, he literally didn't have any sales. Thus, he didn't realize that he was in startup mode, which was going to come back to haunt him as well. So with zero sales, he deducted close to $30,000 in various expenses against his W-2 income, received a huge refund, and was now infuriated that he was getting audited and might have to return the refund.

Regrettably, I told him, if you don't have sales, you are in startup mode and need to amortize the write-offs over time, but since he didn't file a special election to do that amortization, he probably wouldn't be able to take the deduction in the future either. He told me his tax software hadn't alerted him to that rule. Moreover, he had described the line item as "education" for a business that hadn't even started yet—this abnormal item was a red flag.

Given all these errors, he wasn't going to win the case, and I had to suggest a different approach rather than fighting the IRS.

An audit can be an expensive, time-consuming, and emotionally draining experience. However, most audits can be avoided with good business practices, including getting the support of a professional when you are in unknown territory. Using self-service tax software is fine when you have a very simple return, but when you are venturing into a new business, it's time to upgrade to a professional.

12 Ways to Stay on the Good Side of the IRS

Here are a number of tried-and-true tips and procedures for keeping taxpayers out of hot water with the IRS. Please take these to heart when planning your taxes and preparing your returns.

1. File Tax Returns Even if You Owe and Can't Pay

One of the quickest ways to find yourself audited is to not file your tax return. It's better to extend if you must—extending doesn't increase your chances of an audit and gives you more time to prepare your information and file a more accurate tax return.

Moreover, if you can't pay the taxes you owe, it's still critical to file your return. Out of fear or frustration, many people choose to stick their head in the sand if they cannot pay and decide not to file their tax return. The reality is that that approach will increase your penalties and interest, and **the penalties for not filing are worse than just not being able to pay**.

Even if you don't owe anything or don't have any income, I still highly encourage you to file. The IRS is like a boyfriend or girlfriend: If you don't stay in touch, they will assume the worst. They'll also say bad things about you to their friends.

2. Be Aware of Your Industry Averages and Common Expenses

When you file a tax return, you must also indicate the industry in which you work. The IRS has a computer system (Discriminant Function System) that compares your tax return data with other taxpayers in the same occupations, geography, and/or industry (if a business). This allows the IRS to categorize your expenses and look for abnormal expense levels compared to your income and industry. Obviously you would never increase an expense because it wouldn't be noticed, but you certainly *should* consider reducing an expense if it's far too high and will stand out. Carefully review your expenses, deductions, and credits to make sure none of them are above average. Your accountant should be able to complete a quick analysis before the tax return is filed and inform you of any dollar amounts that are out of the ordinary. Make sure to inquire about this review with your accountant before signing your tax return.

3. File as the Proper Entity

Having a small business is a great tax-saving strategy, but reporting it as a sole prop can dramatically increase your chances of an audit. Many people realize that if they operate as a sole prop, they are unnecessarily exposing themselves to liability; however, they may not realize that they are also exposing themselves to a greater chance of an audit. Statistics from the IRS show that a Schedule C/E/F small-business return (Schedule C, E, or F) is typically audited 12 times more frequently than that of an S or C corp. (A Schedule C is for operational small businesses; a Schedule E is for rental property, and a Schedule F is for farming operations.) Thus, your chances of an audit in a sole prop vs. an S corp is 1,200 percent higher. For this reason, beware of sole props and choose to file as a partnership or corporation when economically feasible.

4. Issue Your 1099s

This is a huge area of concern for the IRS. When you are claiming deductions for paying subcontractors, you need to issue the proper 1099s in January. If you already missed the deadline this year, don't let it happen again. And request W–9s from all subcontractors *before* you pay them.

5. File Payroll Reports and Remit Your Payroll Withholding

If you own and operate an S corp, filing payroll reports and making the necessary deposits are critical tasks. This is sacred money in the eyes of the IRS, and you must never fall behind. This will save you not only from an audit but also from possible *jail time*.

6. Use Exact Numbers

Avoid round numbers. I'm not talking about line items or above average numbers; I'm talking about rounding numbers to even dollar amounts, whether up or down. You don't want figures that seem too nice and neat. For example, if you are reporting a mortgage interest deduction, it would look odd to report $15,000, as opposed to $14,931. Please make sure you are reporting the actual numbers. Rounding can work against you in the long run.

7. Avoid Excessive Auto, Dining, and Travel Expenses

I'm the first one to advocate taking a healthy deduction for auto, dining, and travel. However, these expenses should look normal and well-balanced for your income level and industry. For example, if you run an eBay business out of your basement in the evenings, I don't think daily dining and golfing expenses are going to fly with the IRS. However, if you are a sales rep peddling products on the road, those type of expenses will appear to be standard.

It's OK to take any expense related to your business so long as you don't get too greedy. Remember the adage: "Pigs get fat, and hogs get slaughtered." This couldn't apply more than it does in the arena of deductions. Be sure to consult with your tax planner on what types of expenses and amounts will keep you out of hot water with the IRS, and make sure you are reporting these expenses legitimately.

8. Avoid Suspicious Numbers and Abnormal Items

Beware of descriptions of expenses and line items that appear odd or are for large amounts that draw attention because they don't make sense based on your type of business or industry. For example, in the case study at the beginning of this chapter, the client had put a large dollar amount on their business tax return under the line item "education." This is the type of abnormal item that would draw the attention of the IRS. Again, this is why it makes sense *not* to file your own tax return when your situation is more complicated; a seasoned tax professional will recognize and alert you to these types of items.

9. Beware of Continual Losses in Your Operational Business

If you have a business that routinely takes losses, you could be in for an audit. Remember, the IRS's hobby loss rules require a business to show a profit on a regular basis. The IRS also has a specific list of subjective criteria they use to help taxpayers determine if a business is legitimate or just a hobby. Search irs.gov for "Section 183" or "hobby loss rules" to see this list. The "years of profit in relationship to the years in business" section is generally a good guideline to consult as well.

10. Don't Be Part of the "Dirty Dozen"

The IRS consistently announces new scams and tax avoidance strategies to watch out for. Please make sure that none of your business activities fall into any of these categories. To view the most recent list, go to irs.gov and search for "Dirty Dozen."

11. Observe Good and Honest Tax Practices

Report all of your income, and don't plug in numbers unless you can support them. If you own a small business, consider having a tax advisor prepare your return, and always know your own numbers. Review your tax return, and discuss it with your planner.

Don't be afraid to take an expense you're entitled to, especially if you have kept good records. But also make sure you're filing your reports correctly and that your tax return doesn't stand out. This isn't your high school prom—you *want* to stand in the corner and *not* get asked to dance.

12. Receipts and Audits

Does keeping receipts help you avoid an audit? They may not prevent an audit, but they can certainly minimize the severity of one and even reduce the extent and time it may take. Keep the best accounting records you can. It will help you produce a better tax return and more accurate figures, ultimately reducing your chances of an audit.

How to Respond to an IRS Notice

Sometimes, despite your best efforts, an audit can still happen. And, when you DO get that dreaded letter from the IRS, you should respond to it promptly.

The IRS tends to send a fair amount of correspondence once tax season has closed, so you might be on the lookout for letters of inquiry or notices of payment due in the summer months. That said, this is also prime time for scammers to send fake IRS notices to bilk you out of your hard-earned money, so be sure to confirm that your IRS notice is legit. **Remember: The IRS will never ask you for immediate payment, demand a specific payment method, or threaten you with law enforcement, and they will never, let me repeat never, call you on the phone.** If the person contacting you mentions any of these things, it's a scam. Wait for the mail from the IRS and respond in writing, or *you* call the IRS.

The most common kinds of legit notices you might receive include a CP2000, which is the IRS's way of saying they would pretty please like you to pony up a different amount of tax than what you reported on your return. Another biggie is the CP3219, which is a "notice of deficiency" and typically a follow-up to the CP2000.

You have options for how you respond to these (or any other) notices from the IRS. Typically, you have a set amount of time to respond (often 30 days). You may agree with the changes, sign, and send back the notice along with payment. Or, if you disagree, you have the option to write a letter of explanation and return it along with corresponding documentation to support your case. The IRS will review and respond.

How to Handle an Audit

In the event that the IRS auditor does come knocking on your door, there are several plays you can make to help the process go as smoothly as possible. Let's break them down.

First, just like when it comes to notices, respond in a timely fashion. Communication is key to succeeding in an audit and greasing wheels at the beginning. Ignoring notices or IRS requests for information isn't going to help and will certainly make things worse. So once you've received the IRS notice of audit, provide a written response and consider getting professional help. Watch out for flat-fee national services advertising on the radio or TV. Find a trusted advisor that can bill you as they go and keep you aware of progress in the process of the audit.

Next, build your case with any supporting documentation you need to explain errors or appeal. This also means helping a professional whom you have hired. They can't do it on their own. They are going to need information from you to prepare and deliver to the IRS if you employed them to help you. However, no matter what, it's not a good idea to flood the IRS agent (or your professional) with irrelevant paperwork. Keep it focused on documents that will help you build a case and substantiate your point of view. Also, know your rights. As a taxpayer, you have specific legal rights during the process, and you shouldn't be afraid to exercise them. For a complete list of taxpayer rights, visit https://www.irs.gov/taxpayer-bill-of-rights.

Finally, breathe and stay calm. An audit is not a referendum on your character or business acumen. Sometimes, your number just comes up, and you get randomly selected. Other times, it may boil down to a simple accounting error or forgotten piece of documentation.

Game Plan Takeaway and Action Items

Avoiding an audit is very different from preparing for one. Avoiding an audit means having a tax return that makes sense, is well-balanced, and generally falls in line with industry averages. However, one shouldn't be afraid to be cautiously aggressive. If you are entitled to the deduction and can support it, take it!

With my new client trying to deduct his large education expenses, his best option was to have it classified as a startup cost. It wasn't ideal, and it was still a precarious situation because he didn't fill out the "startup election" form and attach it to his tax return. Bottom line, he quickly realized that easy-to-use tax software may not be the best for a new business owner or one with a lot of transactions or a complex situation.

Preparing for an audit starts now by implementing good habits and business practices. If and when you get audited, you want to have your books in order and receipts stored in a file ready to go. Typically, you will not organize your receipts at all; just scan and file them for safekeeping. However, if you do get audited, then it's time to print them out, organize them, and prepare for battle.

- Review the 12 ways to stay on the good side of the IRS that I detailed in this chapter and follow wise practices in preparing and reporting your taxes.

- Step back and look at your tax return at the end of the process. Make sure you feel comfortable with the deductions you are taking.
- Keep good books and save records of your receipts.
- Use a professional to prepare or at least advise you on preparing your tax return when you have a small business, rental properties, and/or a more complicated tax return.

TAX-SAVING STRATEGIES FOR SELLING PROPERTY

——— CASE STUDY ———

A telephone consultation with clients from Washington state's farm country ended up being one of the most creative real estate transactions I have ever worked on. We were able to combine multiple tax strategies to the maximum benefit of my clients.

These clients owned three parcels of land. Two parcels, one larger than the other, were used for farming. The third, still several acres, surrounded the family home. Their plan was to sell all of the properties and house and retire in another state. My clients were the quintessential farmers: land rich and cash poor.

Of course, they didn't want to pay too much in taxes, but they also needed to create cash flow, do some creative investing, and even give some money to charity.

First, we maximized the home sale tax exclusion, protecting $500,000 of the profits from the sale of the home and its surrounding land from taxes. They gained enough money to downsize and buy a home in a town they loved, and they still had extra cash to pay down debt, finance the move, and start fresh in a new area of the country.

Next, we took the large parcel of land and completed a 1031 exchange (which means that you can sell one property, buy another, and defer the tax indefinitely or until the second property is sold) into some commercial rental properties in another state. The rentals created excellent cash flow and write-offs and gave the family a small business to manage in their spare time.

Finally, the smaller parcel of land was contributed to a charitable remainder trust. This provided my clients a tax-free sale, a large pool of cash, and a tax write-off for the ultimate gift that would land in the lap of their favorite charity after they both passed away.

Everyone won except the IRS—the transaction was completely tax-free. I can't remember who was more excited, my clients or me, to see such a creative and exciting transaction come together.

Of course, there were a lot of moving parts, including appraisals, title companies, legal documents, and a 1031 exchange accommodator. However, with a relatively small amount of work, we saved substantially on taxes and brought the American Dream to life for a retiring couple.

As the real estate market continues to bounce back from the 2008 crash, I find myself having more and more consultations like the one above, and I constantly get asked: "What can I do to save on taxes when

I sell my property?" Few realize that so many creative options exist when selling appreciated property.

In my accounting firm, we consistently discuss four options with clients each time they are faced with this question. These options are strategies you can "hang your hat on," and most CPAs can help you navigate the steps to implement them.

However, the key is proactive planning. When clients talk to us at tax time, a year after their property sale, the damage is often already done, and the only option left is to pay a hefty tax bill.

In this chapter, I'll give you some useful plays for saving on tax when selling your property. Check out these options and run the numbers when you have a property to sell with a potentially big profit.

Option 1: Pay the Capital Gains Tax

The first strategy is to simply pay the capital gains tax. Some may think this is crazy talk, but there are certainly some benefits to doing so. First, you are "ripping the bandage off"—the tax is now paid, and

---

GOOD TO KNOW:
RULES FOR SELLING A PERSONAL RESIDENCE

The tax rules for selling your residence have remained the same since 1997 and are pretty straightforward. You can sell your home and are exempt from being taxed for up to $250,000 of gain if you are single and $500,000 if married. You simply have to have lived in and owned the home for two out of the five years preceding the sale. You can also sell your home and receive the same tax benefit every two years. It's important to note that there are also a few exceptions to the rules: If you sell before you have two years of ownership and residence in your home, you may prorate the exemption amount if you are moving more than 50 miles for job relocation, are being called to military active duty, have had multiple children born closely together, etc.

---

you don't have to worry about it anymore. The money isn't locked into any other property or tax strategy, and the remaining money is yours to spend however you like. This freedom can be a big benefit.

Moreover, capital gains rates may be much better than your ordinary income tax rate. Over the past few years, rates have ranged from 0 to 20 percent, depending on your income level. These rates are a far cry from the highest marginal federal income tax rate of 37 percent, not to mention state tax rates.

Keep in mind that you may also be facing ordinary income rates if it's a short-term gain, meaning you held the property less than one year before sale. Those wonderful long-term capital gains rates are for properties that have been held for more than one year.

Even if you don't jump on this first option, it's important to at least run the numbers. Don't just estimate. Determine specifically what the federal, state, and Affordable Care Act net investment tax would be. This will establish a baseline for comparison with your other options.

Option 2: Installment Sale

This strategy involves receiving and spreading out income over time, typically including an interest payment from the buyer. This can be a very powerful long-term tax strategy if it allows you to keep your income out of higher tax brackets.

Of course, installment sales also involve some important investment and legal strategies that have nothing to do with tax planning and need to be carefully considered. For example: What is your security as the lender over time? Is there another loan involved and assumed by the buyer? What position as a lien holder do you have against the property? What is the interest rate you are receiving on the note? These questions and issues vary depending on your circumstances. Though complex, installment sales can be a great tax strategy to consider when selling a property.

Finally, you want to make sure you qualify for the installment sale under IRS rules and understand how the installments will play out on your tax return over time. You might spread it over 5, 10, or 15 years—whatever you desire.

Option 3: Like-Kind/1031 Exchange

The 1031 exchange (which you briefly read about earlier), also referred to as the like-kind exchange, allows a taxpayer to sell one property and buy another of equal or greater value, deferring the tax indefinitely or until the second property is sold. A property obtained via a 1031 can be exchanged again and again. Moreover, you can exchange one property for multiple properties or vice versa. There are timing and exchange rules, but they are quite flexible.

A myth regarding this type of exchange is that you have to exchange a duplex for a duplex or a single-family home for a single-family home in order to qualify. However, in reality, the rules are much more lenient. As long as it's a "titled" property, you can trade it for any other titled property. You can trade Mississippi swamp land for a downtown Los Angeles high-rise, for example.

One other important consideration is that an accommodator or qualified mediator must be involved to facilitate the exchange. This is necessary because, as you can imagine, it can be very difficult to find someone who wants your property and owns some property you want. The accommodator brings the parties together and acts as an escrow service so that all parties stay at arm's length and don't touch the proceeds until they are allowed to under IRS rules.

Moreover, the reason you need an accommodator is because there will always be at least one other party to the transaction. As Figure 16.1 shows below, typically the person you are selling the property

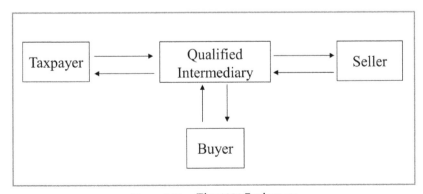

Figure 16.1 – **The 1031 Exchange**

to doesn't own the property you want to buy. Thus, there is a second seller in the mix who will receive the proceeds from the sale of your property to the buyer. Of course, these roles can vary as well as the dollar amounts, loans, and even down payments.

Despite the seeming complexity of the 1031 exchange, if you are looking to sell one property and purchase more real estate with the proceeds, learning more and getting a consultation about the exchanges is certainly in your best interest.

Here are a few of the property requirements to qualify for a valid 1031 exchange:

- Both the property traded and the property received must be held for business or investment purposes and not as your personal residence.
- The property traded must *not* be held primarily for sale, such as an inventory of properties held by a real estate developer.
- The properties must be tangible real estate. They cannot be stocks, notes, securities, or evidences of debt, for example.
- You must use an accommodator or qualified intermediary if it is a delayed exchange.

Some of the important timing rules are as follows:

- Within 45 days of sale, you must identify replacement property(ies). This is called the 45-day exchange period.
- Within 180 days of sale, you must close on all purchases of replacement property. This is called the 180-day replacement period.
- On the 45th day, you may identify three properties of any value, and close on any or all of the three, or you can identify as many properties as you want, so long as the aggregate value of the properties does not exceed 200 percent of the value of the exchange property. Under either option you need to close on the property or properties within 180-day replacement period.
- You can violate the 200 percent rule, so long as you close on 90 percent of the properties identified within the 180-day replacement period.

- Finally, you can replace the exchange property with as many replacement properties as you choose, at any value, so long as you close within the first 45 days.

Option 4: Opportunity Zones

Opportunity Zone (OZ) investments were created under the passage of the TCJA and designed to jumpstart communities that struggle economically, and allow investors to reduce taxable gains and possibly obtain tax-free growth if they reinvest capital gains into real estate within designated zones. Tax incentives are available to corporations and partnerships holding at least 90 percent of their assets in OZs and must be established after December 31, 2017. Each state has designated approximately fifty tracts of land as OZs. A map of these zones can be found on the U.S. Department of Treasury site: www.cdfifund.gov.

ANY capital gain amount a taxpayer wants to defer can be invested. The capital gain can be from the sale of stock, real, or personal property and only the gain amount needs to be re-invested, not the entire sales proceeds (like a 1031 exchange). In order to qualify, a taxpayer must invest in an OZ property within 180 days of recognizing a capital gain from the sale or disposition of property. The capital gain proceeds, whichever amount the taxpayer wishes to defer, must be invested into the purchase of a rental property new to the investor, or an already existing property owned by the taxpayer to be rehabbed and used as a rental property. If it's a rehab, the investment needs to be "substantial," which the IRS defines as improvements equal in dollar amount to the basis of the building to be rehabbed (excluding the land value).

Once the investment in the OZ property is made, there are four benefits a taxpayer could take advantage of:

1. The gain on the sale is deferred until the taxpayer divests of the OZ property, or until December 31, 2026, whichever comes first. Basically, it's an interest-free loan from the IRS. You don't have to pay the tax for possibly several years!

2. If the taxpayer holds the OZ investment for 5 years, there is a 10 percent exclusion of the deferred gain.

3. If the taxpayer holds the OZ investment for 7 years, they receive an additional 5 percent increase basis on the deferred gain, which means you only pay tax on 85 percent of the gain, which means you get to another decrease the taxable gain amount, AND you defer the tax bill to boot.

4. The biggest benefit is that if you hold the OZ investment for 10 years, you never pay any capital gains on the OZ investment.

If investors play their cards right they will certainly see tax savings and can easily tax the benefit now and into the future.

Option 5: Charitable Remainder Trust

The charitable remainder trust is a common structure in this area of planning. Essentially, it is an eight-step process that allows a property to not only be sold tax-free, but the seller even gets a tax deduction as well. With the right type of plan, the seller retains a steady stream of income for the rest of their life, a charity of their choice gets a big chunk of cash, and the seller's family still has a nest egg through life insurance.

Many taxpayers are surprised to learn that this strategy is allowed by the IRS and has been for many years. There are so many reasons why the parties involved benefit and why the IRS effectively loses. The reason the government allows it is because of its beneficial impact on charities and thus society as a whole.

I should first point out there are several variations on selling property with the charitable trust strategy. There are charitable lead trusts, net income charitable remainder trusts, and charitable remainder annuity trusts, just to name a few. Each one provides various tax, charitable, and income benefits to the donor.

Here are the basic steps involved in creating a charitable remainder trust. Keep in mind that there can be a lot of variations on this basic plan, and charities are more than willing to get creative to meet a donor/property seller's needs.

1. Create the trust, designate the charity, and define the terms of the trust. For example, what amount of income from the trust will be paid to the donor and when and how it will be disbursed.
2. Donate/transfer property to the trust. This needs to take place before the property is put under contract; other IRS rules apply as to the timing of the trust and the transfer and sale of the property.
3. The trustee sells the property to a third party tax-free. All proceeds from the sale of the property donated to the trust go into a trust account controlled by the trustee.
4. The donor takes a tax deduction over the next five years. The deduction will be based on the property value, typically determined by the sale to the third party or an appraisal.
5. The trust pays income or an annuity to the donor for life. Again, the terms of the trust will direct the trustee as to how to invest the trust assets and when and how to distribute funds.
6. The donor may fund life insurance. The income paid to the donor can then fund a separate irrevocable life insurance trust on the life of the donor and/or their spouse. This is the final piece of the equation, as you can see in Figure 16.2.

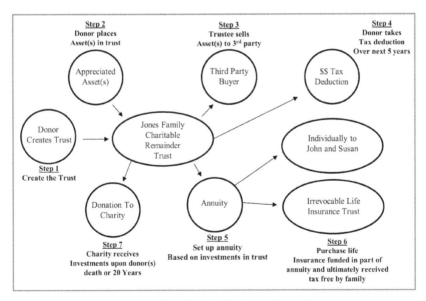

Figure 16.2 – **The Charitable Remainder Trust**

7. The charity gets the remaining money in the trust in 20 years or upon the donor's death, whichever is longer. This is typically the incentive for the charity to pay for preparing and implementing the entire charitable trust strategy.

8. The family gets life insurance tax-free upon the donor's death. As I mentioned in number 6, this is the life insurance policy that will be paid tax-free to the beneficiaries upon the donor's passing and, in effect, replace the value of the assets that were donated to the charity.

Game Plan Takeaway and Action Items

Any of these strategies can be used independently or in combination, as I demonstrated in the case study at the beginning of this chapter. I understand some taxpayers will want to rip the bandage off, pay the taxes, and be done with it. However, if you carefully analyze your long-term goals, a creative tax strategy can often put more money in your pocket and provide some asset protection for that cash flow to boot.

- Run the numbers on any property you own and determine the baseline of the taxes owed if you simply sold the property.
- Compare the various options for selling a property available to you against the baseline of simply selling and paying taxes.
- Get a second opinion if something sounds too good to be true, or if someone says you can't do it.
- Always consider the "time value" of money and the present value of saving taxes over time. The key factor in determining if a charitable trust is right for you is the real impact of a steady stream of income and tax savings over a period of time.

PROTECTING YOUR ASSETS

In an athletic organization, there are valuable assets that can make the difference in whether the team has long-term success. It can take years to build your assets, and it's vital that you implement strategies to protect them so they can play a role in your overall game plans.

AFFORDABLE ASSET PROTECTION STRATEGIES

―――― CASE STUDY ――――

I literally fielded a call from a client while I was making final edits to this chapter and had a classic conversation I've had countless times in my career.

The client was doing well and making money but was relatively new to financial success. The whole experience was unnerving to him, and he was justifiably concerned about asset protection. However, rather than asking the basic steps he should implement, his questions centered around the exotic, expensive, and uncommon.

We talked about irrevocable trusts, moving assets offshore, hiding income and assets in other people's names, and even hidden forms of ownership. I didn't mind the conversation. I enjoy the topic, and there wasn't discussion of hiding income from the IRS but simply making it harder for creditors to find or collect on assets in the future if something went wrong.

But the reality was, all those sexy and unique strategies were overkill. The cost and lack of control far outweighed the benefits. After I explained the pros and cons of these strategies, my client agreed to focus on the basics—the many procedures and structures he didn't yet have in place that provide excellent and affordable protection.

If things continue to go well for my client, someday in the future we will certainly implement more advanced strategies, but this wasn't the time. We spent the rest of our meeting working on the basics and making incredible progress with a great asset protection plan.

To help people avoid overdoing it, I advise the clients and groups I speak to on a regular basis to keep costs down, be cautious of those selling elaborate plans, and start with the basics.

In my opinion, there are two primary approaches to asset protection that consistently save my clients time and money as well as provide them with the protection they really need without overkill: 1) avoid asset protection scams and myths, and 2) get into the habit of basic, affordable asset protection practices. In this chapter, I'll discuss both with you.

Asset Protection Myths

First and foremost, it's shocking how many new business owners and investors get sucked into the scams and myths that run rampant in the world of asset protection. These scams can cost well-intentioned Americans thousands of dollars and are often not even worth the paper they are printed on. Remember, if it sounds too good to be true, it probably is.

Here are the most common asset protection myths:

- *Asset protection is an all-or-nothing proposition.* Wrong. You can start now by taking small steps to protect your assets and add more protective barriers as your income, assets, and needs change and grow. Small steps help us take bigger financial steps. Ultimately, you will tailor systems, structures, and strategies to your particular situation as your assets and businesses grow.

- *Asset protection is expensive, and I must use an attorney for a complete plan.* Wrong again. Asset protection can be as simple as taking advantage of certain statutory exemptions in your state, refinancing your personal residence, buying additional insurance, or placing your assets and businesses in a more advantageous structure or business entity. I'll list several strategies later in this chapter that you can start implementing on your own today.

- *I don't have anything to protect, so I don't need to worry about asset protection yet.* Not true. Wealth is relative, and you don't have to have millions of dollars to need asset protection planning. The equity in your home might be only $50,000 to $100,000, but that could represent years of working hard to make a house payment every month. Moreover, in a lawsuit, someone could get a judgment or lien against you that could affect your credit or even end up as a garnishment on your paycheck or business income.

- *I have an insurance policy, so I'm already covered.* This is completely false. Do you really want to risk all of your assets on a one-inch-thick insurance policy full of exclusions and claim provisions? Don't misunderstand me; insurance is an important part of protecting your assets. However, I also think it is foolish to put all of your eggs in one basket. Insurance is not the be-all and end-all to a properly conceived and implemented asset protection plan.

- *I can protect my assets simply by hiding them.* Not so. As I discuss in Chapter 18, secrecy and privacy protection are an important part of asset protection, but they can by no means replace it. We can't assume that people with enough resources won't pursue us until they find all our assets. If your assets are on your tax return or you control them, more than likely someone will find them. That's when real asset protection needs to take over.

Basic Asset Protection that Works

Every year I'm in practice, I am further convinced that fundamental asset protection begins with implementing affordable, tried-and-true strategies and simple habits. There's no need to reinvent the wheel. There are already laws on the books you can easily implement that will provide you with incredible protection in the event of a claim or lawsuit.

Here are the critical strategies to consider as part of your personal asset protection plan.

Choose the Right Business Entity

There will certainly be multiple tax-planning considerations, but operating as a sole prop definitely isn't your best choice for asset protection. As a sole prop, your personal assets are completely exposed to a potential lawsuit. Setting up an entity, such as an S corp or LLC, is an important step in the development of your business and protection of your assets.

Maintain Your Corporate Veil

If you have set up an entity, don't think that just having the entity's articles of incorporation in your drawer will save you when a lawsuit comes. You need to maintain a separate bank account and checkbook for your business; use the company name on all documents; title the property in the name of the company if necessary; and, most important, maintain corporate records and log the minutes at your annual meeting. Moreover, LLCs are not exempt from performing this type of annual maintenance. I discuss the procedures for proper corporate maintenance and how to protect the corporate veil in detail in Chapter 8.

Use Proper Contracts and Procedures

One of the easiest ways for creditors to pierce the corporate veil and attack your personal assets is if you act negligently or fraudulently. This can be avoided by having good lease agreements for your rentals, placing property and equipment titles in the company name, having subcontractor agreements and contracts on every project, not relying on emails for terms in an important relationship, and never hiring people to work under the table. Only use licensed, bonded, and/or insured professionals to help you in your business. This includes but is not limited to asset protection specialists, legal and tax advisors, contractors, and repairmen.

Purchase Appropriate Business Insurance

Insurance is an important part of your business and should be included in your startup budget. Insurance gives you the ability to take care of an incident in your business and gives plaintiffs another target. Moreover, make sure you get the correct insurance policy. Owning a rental property vs. a professional practice or retail store requires very different types of insurance.

Umbrella Insurance

This type of insurance can be personal or business, and it functions as an "umbrella" over any other type of insurance you may carry. It costs an average of $300 to $500 a year for $1 million to $2 million in coverage. That said, don't assume you can throw caution to the wind because it will protect you in every instance. As a rule, umbrella insurance won't cover fraudulent, criminal, reckless, or negligent action.

Place Certain Assets in Your Spouse's Name

If one spouse has a riskier occupation or lifestyle, it can be extremely strategic to place assets in the other spouse's name. Generally, the creditors of one spouse cannot reach the separate assets of the other. Therefore, asset protection in the context of marriage requires a strategy whereby valuable assets are held as the separate property of the spouse with the least exposure to risk. This is where a prenuptial or postnuptial marital property agreement can be beneficial.

For example, in most states, if the husband is a business owner who incurs liabilities, the couple can enter into an agreement that certain valuable assets will be the wife's separate property, thereby shielding those assets from the husband's creditors. Obviously, if both spouses agree to be co-debtors on a loan, such as when spouses both sign the family home mortgage, then both spouses would be jointly liable.

To provide maximum asset protection with this strategy, the marital agreement or a memorandum thereof should be recorded in the county where the property is located. The property you are moving to the low-risk spouse should actually be titled in their name and/or their trust, as well. This will often entail updating the estate plans for each spouse so they have separate trusts for the ownership of assets. Upon either passing, the trusts can be coordinated with each other to ensure that the proper beneficiaries inherit.

A word of caution with this planning strategy: In Chapter 20, I discuss the impact divorce can have on your assets. Thus, when conducting marital or estate planning, you should carefully consider the implications of deeding property into one or the other spouse's name. By protecting your assets from a creditor in this way, you could be seriously affecting the division of your assets if you divorce.

The Homestead Exemption

One of the most powerful exemptions available is the protection afforded to our individual personal residence, commonly referred to as the homestead exemption. This is a statutory exemption available in most states that protects a certain amount of the value of a person's home from a creditor or bankruptcy. For a more thorough discussion of this topic, see Chapter 19 regarding asset protection strategies for your home.

Tenancy by the Entirety

This is another strategy for protecting your personal residence that I discuss in more detail in Chapter 19. If your state allows it, you can title your personal residence as "tenancy by the entirety," which means if one spouse is sued, the property cannot be attached or bifurcated by the lawsuit. The beauty of this strategy is that it is also statutorily based, meaning you don't have to pay big bucks to implement or maintain the designation. Just make sure your property is titled properly, and you can protect your home in this way if your state allows for such a provision.

Life Insurance

Life insurance can be used for asset protection as well as for investing and estate planning. Honestly, however, I don't think the primary reason to purchase life insurance should be for asset protection. It can be expensive, and you should have other important goals you want to accomplish if you are going to make such an investment. Therefore, I don't recommend that anyone rush out and buy life insurance just to protect their cash in the bank. Rather, I encourage my clients to make the wisest possible decision for the investment of their liquid assets and real property.

CRITICAL ALERT!
FRAUDULENT TRANSFERS

I would be remiss if I didn't mention fraudulent transfers. Inherent in virtually every asset protection plan is the potential that an asset transfer could violate fraudulent transfer laws.

Generally, a transfer of property may be deemed fraudulent and reversed if it was made with the intent to place the property out of reach of actual or potential creditors. Some people try to move assets quickly or hide them after a cause of action arises. In these instances, the transfer will most certainly be deemed fraudulent. Therefore, it is important that you consider asset protection strategies *before* the need arises. Otherwise, you run the risk that any asset protection strategy could be unwound by a court as a fraudulent transfer.

Essentially, life insurance is afforded some protection under federal bankruptcy exemptions, but protection across the states varies drastically. Some states give blanket protection of all the accrued cash value inside an insurance policy. Others may give just a limited dollar amount of protection. There are even limitations on the IRS's ability to collect against the cash value or the proceeds of life insurance.

Of course, if you have term life insurance, which does not build up liquidity inside the policy but simply pays out a death benefit upon your passing, there is no cash value to worry about protecting.

In sum, be cautious about being oversold insurance for the purposes of asset protection.

Game Plan Takeaway and Action Items

Everyone can start with asset protection immediately and on a budget. Many strategies just take a little time and study to implement. Believe it or not, our legislators, judges, and insurance agents also own assets, and they use time-tested, court-tested, usable, and affordable asset protection strategies. We don't have to look under rocks to uncover incredible methods when they are posted right on the tree trunk in front of us.

- If anyone suggests something that sounds too good to be true in the asset protection world, get a second opinion.
- Be aware of the myths in asset protection and avoid them like the plague.
- Start with an entity if you have a business or hold assets.
- Keep a separate checking account for your entity and do your annual corporate maintenance.
- Use your company name on all your agreements.
- Have your company hold title to your assets and equipment.
- Always carry the appropriate type and level of insurance and undergo regular reviews with your insurance agent.
- Consider implementing umbrella insurance when the time is right.

- Know what your state's rules are for tenancy by the entirety and homestead exemption amounts.
- Consider putting the title to property in your spouse's name if appropriate.
- Understand what a fraudulent transfer is and start building your asset protection strategy *before* a cause of action arises.

PRIVACY MEASURES VS. HIDING ASSETS

Those from the Twin Cities in Minnesota know this case all too well: the story of Denny Hecker.

At his peak, Hecker had 26 auto dealerships and claimed annual sales of nearly $7 billion. He was accused of fraudulently soliciting and using inventory loans from Chrysler Financial and others to the tune of half a billion dollars during 2007 and 2008.

The interesting aspect of this case to me—and there are many fascinating details—is that it wasn't the cases from Chrysler, Ford, the creditors, or the bankers that ultimately landed Hecker in jail. True, some had an impact, but the slam dunk was his bankruptcy and fraudulent transfers, including his attempts at hiding assets.

His lawyers told him to file bankruptcy to help rid him of the more than $767 million he owed Chrysler Financial and other creditors. They didn't know he had previously entered into creative asset protection schemes and moved money to try to hide assets. Federal prosecutors and the trustee handling the bankruptcy case said Hecker committed bankruptcy fraud by not disclosing all his assets, repeatedly lied, and "chose to put his own financial interests above all else, including the rule of law and our system of justice."

Hecker's asset protection plan—hiding his assets and then lying to the court about them—didn't protect his assets at all. In fact, it got him got him into hot water. His life spiraled out of control. In early 2010, he was indicted on fraud charges. A month later, Hecker's father-in-law committed suicide after he was accused of helping Hecker hide about $81,000 from creditors. Hecker's wife pled guilty to charges that she helped Hecker hide assets and lied on a credit application, and she received four years of prison time.

After serving more than seven years for fraud, Hecker was released in July 2018. Because of the bankruptcy fraud, Hecker will still owe more than $31 million in restitution after his assets are liquidated.

While there can be valid reasons for shrouding your assets and business activities from the public eye, hiding your assets from creditors and the law is not one of them. One of Hecker's many, many mistakes that made it easy for the court to put him in prison was trying to hide his assets from and deceive his creditors.

Regrettably, there is a serious misconception in America that asset protection means "hiding." People will go to great lengths to be mysterious or secretive with their entities or the titling of their assets, thinking they are working toward asset protection. Yes, to some degree that can help when someone is searching for your assets. However, protecting your privacy is a completely separate issue from protecting your assets, and there is room for both. Coordinating your privacy protection tactics with your asset protection strategies is the key. That is the theme of this chapter.

There are many reasons to protect your privacy, a primary one being identity theft. The Federal Trade Commission (FTC) has reported that identity theft is America's fastest-growing crime. According to The Harris Poll, over 15 million American consumers were victims of identity theft in 2017.

One of my favorite books on protecting your identity is *How to Be Invisible* by J. J. Luna. I have corresponded with J.J. over the years via email, quoted him repeatedly in prior publications, and interviewed his attorney, John Clark, on my radio show.

J. J.'s teachings have inspired me to write this chapter. It provides important strategies for improving your privacy that can save you thousands of dollars and hours of wasted time and heartache if your identity is stolen. Moreover, it can add a layer to your overall asset protection plan, making it more difficult for a plaintiff or creditor to pursue and attack your assets in a lawsuit.

Reasons to Implement a Privacy Plan

The three primary goals when creating a privacy plan are:

1. Preventing identity theft and mistaken identity cases
2. Increasing your privacy
3. Enhancing your asset protection structure

Let's go through each one.

Preventing Identity Theft

As I mentioned above, the FTC has reported that identity theft is one of the fastest-growing crimes in America. However, many of us think this is simply someone stealing our credit card, when in reality there are many types of identity theft. In fact, identity theft can be far worse than having your credit card stolen, and it can be financially and emotionally devastating to the victims.

Here are just a few types of identity theft:

- *Financial.* Someone accesses your banking information and credit card(s) and/or obtains loans in your name, stealing money and negatively affecting your credit.
- *Insurance or medical.* Someone uses your medical insurance, which can lead to your policy being cancelled and false information entered on your record.
- *Criminal.* Someone gives police your information instead of their own, leading to a false criminal record, arrest warrants issued in your name, and other serious legal problems.
- *Driver's license.* Someone steals your driver's license to use for other forms of identity theft, especially criminal identity theft.
- *Social Security Number (SSN).* Someone steals your SSN so an undocumented immigrant can use it to work, filling out W-4 and I-9 forms in your name and wreaking havoc for you with the IRS.

Increasing Your Privacy

Good privacy protection practices are at the core of identity theft prevention, but these habits can also help you avoid other unwanted situations. For example, do you own low-income rental properties in high-risk areas or have potentially unstable or litigious tenants like rowdy college students? Do you want your tenants to be able to find your home address online and then show up at your door one night? Such an encounter could be unnerving and even dangerous.

Do you travel a lot on business or for pleasure? Maybe you post photos of yourself and your family on a cruise on Facebook or Twitter. You just announced to the world that your home is unattended; with a simple search, a thief is at your back door breaking in. What if you post on Twitter that you are at a business conference? Now you just announced that your loved ones are home alone and unprotected by your presence.

GET STARTED NOW
PLUG IMMEDIATE SECURITY LOOPHOLES

Be more aware than ever before you give out your SSN, home address, or date of birth to anyone other than a government agency. Shred everything, open a P.O. Box, get a home safe for important documents, go paperless, and have a system to store and regularly change your electronic passwords. Make it so expensive and difficult to steal your identity or trace you and/or your assets that the bad guys or gals will give up before they achieve their goals.

Sometimes protecting your privacy can be critical if you are dealing with a stalker or a radical ex-spouse or because you are a witness to a crime or even serving on jury duty.

Enhancing Your Asset Protection Plan

With today's technology, it's very hard to hide your assets if someone is mad enough or has deep enough pockets to investigate you—not to mention the little process called "discovery" in lawsuits. A plaintiff will eventually find your assets if they have the resources to do so; at that point, your real asset protection needs to kick in.

As such, good asset protection is a barrier that will come into effect when someone has a legitimate claim against you. In Chapter 17, I discuss the basic asset protection strategies that all people should consider, and in Chapter 21, I discuss the more advanced and cutting-edge asset strategies that planners are implementing around the country.

However, privacy planning can enhance your asset protection by making you less attractive as a defendant when a cause of action arises. For example, say you get into a minor car accident with someone who is fairly litigious. A good privacy plan will make it look like you aren't worth going after in a lawsuit. For those who still try, it will make it more expensive and challenging to determine how much you are really worth and what and where your assets may be.

As you can see, privacy protection strategies play an important role early on by dissuading a potential plaintiff from pursuing you or by making it more expensive for the plaintiff's attorney to figure out what

---

CRITICAL ALERT!
KIM KARDASHIAN'S STOLEN IDENTITY

In early 2014, a 19-year-old man stole the identity of Kim Kardashian and others and transferred thousands of dollars from their bank accounts into his own. Luis Flores Jr., will be spending the next three and a half years in federal prison for this identity theft scheme, and the facts sound all too familiar.

According to federal court records, someone phoned American Express claiming to be Kardashian who knew the star's private information. The person then changed the primary SSN on the account to Flores' and the mailing address to the Florida apartment Flores shared with his mother, Kyah Green. They requested a replacement card to be mailed.

Luckily, Kardashian's representatives alerted the authorities, who staked out the Flores home. When UPS delivered the replacement cards, agents confronted Green. She feigned ignorance and refused to cooperate.

During the investigation, agents learned that SunTrust Bank also suspected fraud because two wire transfers totaling more than $71,000 had been made from the account of Kris Jenner, Kardashian's mother. SunTrust investigators had nearly a dozen surveillance video pictures depicting Green withdrawing cash from that account at ATMs. Flores was sentenced to prison, and Green was sentenced to probation.

Most of us don't have the resources of Kim Kardashian and a financial team looking out for our well-being. However, there are simple things we can do to protect against such a situation happening to us—or at least catch it before it gets out of control.

---

your assets are worth, which could encourage a settlement or prompt the plaintiff to give up entirely.

Four Stages of Privacy Protection

J. J. Luna created a four-stage approach to removing your name and overall identity from the public eye. I love his approach, and through additional research and experience helping clients with these strategies over the years, I have enhanced and expanded on the steps in these stages.

- *Level One.* The first stage calls for simple and economical moves that will give you more privacy than most of the general population.
- *Level Two.* At this point, you will place your home, vehicles, and rental properties in anonymous LLCs or trusts, adding to your pre-established asset protection or estate plans. Accounts for utilities, smartphones, and other electronic devices will be in alternate names. You will use a P.O. Box or a service like The UPS Store for all correspondence.
- *Level Three.* You will probably move to reset your personal information in all databases, and only your closest relatives and friends will know your address. It will no longer appear on your tax return, other government documents, *or anywhere else.* All email and internet activities will be undercover, and you will adopt several aliases to use when necessary.
- *Level Four.* At this level, you are duplicating the Federal Witness Protection Program. When the feds do it for a witness or felon, it's completely legal. When you do it for yourself, it's not. All bridges are now ashes, and friends and relatives are a distant memory. These extreme measures may be worth taking if a bounty is on your head, for example. However, someone with enough money could eventually find you.

Given the illegality of Level Four, in this chapter I will focus on the first two levels, as well as provide the basics of Level Three. However, if you are interested in learning more, I recommend J. J. Luna's *How to Be Invisible.*

Level One Security: Basic Habits

There are many small ways we can change our habits and daily activities to better protect our privacy. Here are the 13 easiest and most important items that almost everyone can implement *right now*:

1. Pay for a credit bureau tracking service and carefully monitor any activity they find.
2. Keep the following critical data, for both you and your family members, under a watchful eye and in secure areas:
   - SSNs
   - Driver's licenses, including the numbers
   - Credit cards
   - Bank account numbers
   - Business tax ID numbers
   - Insurance policy numbers
   - Tax information
   - Birth certificates
   - Firearm licenses
3. Invest in a safe deposit box, or a carefully hidden fireproof safe for the house, and place important papers in it.
4. Go paperless with an encrypted cloud hosting service to store all your data.
5. Copy all contents of your wallet and keep in an encrypted cloud service, a safe, or a safety deposit box.
6. Confirm that all firearms are properly registered and that the licenses are protected from theft.
7. Move the contents of the glove compartment in your car to a locked box in the trunk.
8. Consider the significance of the content you share on social media.
9. Protect your incoming and outgoing mail, which might have sensitive information in it.
10. Shred important documents and sensitive information with a quality cross-cut shredder at home and in your office.
11. Install antivirus software on all business and family computers.

12. Don't keep sensitive information on laptops or smartphones.
13. Remember to log out of your computer at home and at work and use a security measure like a password or pass code on your mobile phone.

As you can see, Level One strategies don't take a lot of time or money. In fact, you aren't really taking your assets off the grid or implementing serious privacy strategies that would help in a lawsuit. However, by simply implementing these easy measures, you'll be doing far more to protect your important data and your identity than most other Americans, thus making yourself a difficult target for the average criminal.

CRITICAL ALERT!
WHAT'S IN YOUR GLOVE COMPARTMENT?

Many of us don't realize what sensitive information we keep in our car's glove compartment. Typically there will be an insurance card and vehicle registration paperwork with your legal name and home address just sitting there.

When I interviewed John Clark, J. J. Luna's attorney, on my radio show, he said he's frequently seen questions on privacy and security blogs from people who had their car broken into but their expensive items left alone. Only their registration documents were stolen. Perplexed, the victims asked why this was happening.

Apparently, Clark explained, this type of crime is happening more and more. Savvy criminals can use them to obtain your credit report and SSN. But even if the break-in doesn't lead to full-blown identity theft, the thief could also steal your license plate or just order new plates from the Department of Motor Vehicles (DMV) using your identity, and then attach the plates to another vehicle. If they use that car in a crime and the plate is reported, your name will pop up and you become a possible suspect, which could complicate your life enormously.

Level Two Security: Trusts and Privacy LLCs

Certainly this next level takes more effort, funds, and commitment, but it may be an important step to take depending on your assets, lifestyle, public presence, or liability exposure. At this stage, it is often critical to form a trust in which you don't personally serve as a trustee or a privacy LLC, which is an LLC in a state that doesn't disclose the LLC manager, its members, or its owners. These are sometimes referred to as Ghost Trusts or Ghost LLCs. Once you have this type of trust or privacy LLC set up, it can serve as the owners, managers, or trustees for other trusts, entities holding assets in creative ways.

Keep in mind that you are not using this trust or LLC for tax purposes; everything is fully disclosed to the IRS. Moreover, if you get into a lawsuit, the purpose of this trust or LLC is not to hide from a court or bankruptcy trustee or from opposing counsel in a deposition. If you own the assets, you need to disclose this information at the proper time and then rely on your asset protection procedures.

This is what Danny Hecker *didn't* do in the case study at the beginning of this chapter. Among his other mistakes and lies, he thought his "hiding" strategies gave him the right to not disclose the assets he owned. Remember, our goal is to remove assets from the public eye, not to fraudulently hide them from a legitimate court action.

After setting up one or more of these more private structures or entities, here is a list of four more aggressive steps you can implement to take your security to the next level:

1. Set up a P.O. box or a mailbox at a commercial mail receiving agency (CMRA), like Mail Boxes Etc. or The UPS Store, for your personal and business mail.
2. Transfer your home, investments, and other necessary assets to a trust or privacy LLC, as I discussed above.
3. Establish an alternate name or alias and, when possible, use it for entering into contracts for things like mobile phones and utilities. Be careful not to violate any laws. Remember, privacy, not fraud, is your goal.
4. Never give out your SSN, address, or personal data to *anyone* except a government agency that absolutely *must* have it.

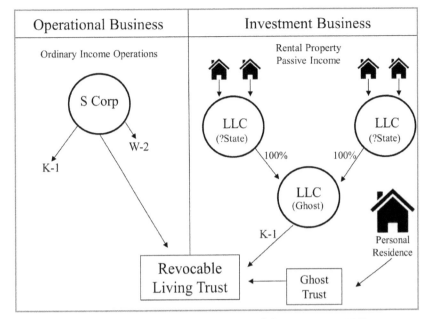

Figure 18.1 – **Secrecy and the Privacy/Ghost Trust or LLC**

Figure 18.1 shows how you may set up a privacy LLC to serve in your asset protection and business structure.

Level Three Security: Ghost Address and Cash Only

Certainly this level takes a tremendous amount of work and attention to detail. If you are living at this level of security, your habits and daily procedures will be significantly impacted. In fact, it may even require you to move from your current home to "reset" a lot of your personal information that is in the public eye. However, you may need to go to this level if you have a stalker, criminal, or general threat to your safety or financial security. The following are basic guidelines for Level Three:

1. Obtain a ghost address. This is similar to a P.O. box or CMRA, but is actually a physical street address you can give to others as necessary. This is also different from a Ghost Trust or LLC (Those are structures with your name nowhere to be found). This is an address that you can use locally for deliveries or when a street or physical address is needed.

2. Move, purchase a home for cash or rent with an alias, and use your ghost address for any utilities or paperwork.
3. Pay for everything with cash.
4. Set up email under an alias.
5. In general, use your alias more aggressively—but always legally—to maintain personal privacy.
6. Follow specific rules when traveling. There are numerous privacy blogs where you can learn tips for what information to share when booking travel. For example, in the film *Jack Reacher*, the protagonist travels via bus when he needs to lie low.
7. Have *no* information about yourself or your work habits in public view. Close your Facebook account—sorry.

Going Offshore

Most experts agree that a foreign asset protection trust and offshore bank account can provide significant secrecy benefits. However, the cost and time necessary to do it right need to be carefully considered. It truly is a legitimate structure and procedure, but it's something that usually only the very wealthy use.

The asset protection benefits of going offshore can also pose an extremely formidable barrier against fraudulent lawsuits, judgment creditors, and so on. Some individuals in high-risk occupations who may need to leave town in the middle of the night find comfort in having an account and credit card offshore that can be accessed quickly and secretly.

One cautionary note: Even if you take assets offshore, I never advocate hiding assets or income from the IRS. Ultimately, all your income-producing activities need to be on your tax return. Don't mess around with the IRS. It's not worth it.

Game Plan Takeaway and Action Items

Certainly, improved personal security and secrecy need to be more of a priority. Don't take identity theft lightly. In fact, the very week

I was editing this book, I had a close family member call me because someone had opened a credit card in her name. The threat is real. I myself have started to more diligently implement Level One and some Level Two security measures.

- Review Level One security measures and determine your initial steps for improving your privacy.
- Sign up for privacy blogs and newsletters to stay aware of trends and issues on privacy and identity protection.
- Begin monitoring your credit with a reporting agency (see Chapter 7 as well).
- Consider Level Two security measures if you have significant assets, a visible lifestyle, or a high-risk occupation.

19

PROTECTING YOUR HOME FROM A LAWSUIT

—— CASE STUDY ——

t was one of the most emotional legal meetings I have ever had with a client. Under the pressure of a major lawsuit, a husband and wife were desperate to find ways to protect their assets, principally their home.

They had lived there for more than 25 years, almost their entire marriage. They had raised their kids in the home and had hoped to retire there and have their grandchildren visit on a regular basis. Regrettably, the outlook was bleak, and their dreams probably weren't going to be realized.

Their story was all too familiar. They had signed a business contract with a distributor, their business had taken a turn for the worse, and the financing and debts had spiraled out of control. The distributor was taking the lead in the lawsuit.

My clients hadn't done any proactive planning to protect their home equity, and they would have to sell the home to pay off the debts. Even if they went into bankruptcy, which they wanted to avoid, the homestead exemption (which can protect a certain amount of the value of a home from creditors) in their state was meager.

The plan came down to selling the house for the greatest possible value and settling the debts at a discount. This is how people commonly lose their homes. It's sad when I see it up close, and I wish more people would take active steps to protect their home's value. This couple had serious regrets and wanted to warn others not to fall into the same predicament. Listen to their plea.

We typically don't hear news stories about creditors throwing debtors out of their homes and onto the street. It's much less dramatic and more discreet than that.

Usually what occurs is that collection threats start to pile up on the kitchen table, lawsuits get filed, and when the homeowners realize what the future holds, they sell the house for the highest possible price before the bankruptcy court or creditors can sell it for a lower value, thus somewhat minimizing the damage. Hence the lack of public drama when someone loses their home to litigation. In this chapter, we'll go over some plays that can help you protect your home.

Common Roadblocks to Protecting Home Equity

For most of us, our home is one of our most valuable assets. It truly is our castle. But it can also be one of our most vulnerable assets. Although you need to protect it at all costs—and I'll present some options and strategies for doing so below—I want to address several dilemmas that create significant hurdles to salvaging the complete value of a home:

- *Sale of Home Tax Exemption vs. Asset Protection.* As we covered in Chapter 16, recall there are IRS rules regarding the home sale tax exclusion, which allows you to not pay taxes on $250,000 in profit if you're single or $500,000 in profit for couples if you've lived in the home for two of the past five years. Many people will place their personal residence into an LLC, thinking they have automatically created better asset protection. In reality, the asset protection is questionable at best. To put your home in an LLC is contrary to the purposes of an LLC. If the LLC isn't used for business or investment purposes, but for personal use, the LLC won't provide much protection at all for a personal residence. If you try to morph your home into an investment and pay rent to yourself or some crazy scheme, then you may shoot yourself in the foot for utilizing the sale of home exemption I mentioned above.

- *The Moving Target of Equity.* The second dilemma is that your property is hopefully continually increasing in value. The equity in someone's home is oftentimes one of their most valuable assets, and hopefully in the long run consistently increasing. Regrettably, you are therefore forced to protect a level of equity that is constantly changing. So it is important to realize that any plan to protect your home requires you to frequently and regularly update your protection strategy.

- *To Pay Off or Not to Pay Off.* Most of us have been taught that it is a wise long-term policy to pay down our mortgage until our home is completely paid off. This inevitably will increase the equity in our home until it is just one big asset as a target. Many view paying off their home as the pinnacle of their life's work. Regrettably, a creditor or plaintiff will view this as the "golden egg" in a lawsuit. Please be open to protecting your equity in creative ways. I'm not saying it's bad to pay off your mortgage and own your home free and clear. However, it is naive to pay off your home without realizing you are also seriously exposing yourself to a loss in the event of a lawsuit.

Knowing these three major issues about the precarious position of retaining a home's value is a key to being able to keep the value of your home in check, even if things go south for your business.

Six Ways to Protect Your Home in a Lawsuit

There are six major ways to protect your home in a potential lawsuit that we should cover; they will vary based on what state you live in, your marital status, and the amount of equity involved.

There are more than six ways to defend your home, but some can be quite expensive and aggressive and aren't usually used by mainstream lawyers and planners. However, the list below comprises what I believe to be the most common, effective, and legally accepted methods to protect your home.

With all these strategies, I can't emphasize enough that it's critical you implement them or at least consider their effectiveness in your situation *before* a cause of action arises. Please note that I didn't say "lawsuit," but "cause of action." For example, you can't start trying to protect your home the day after a car accident, even though the lawsuit over the accident may occur years later.

Asset protection for your home needs to start *now*, when there is a clear blue sky, not when the storm clouds come.

1. Maximize the Homestead Exemption

This is a statutory exemption available in most states that protects a certain amount of the value of a person's home from a creditor or bankruptcy. Essentially, if a creditor comes after you in a lawsuit and forces the sale of your home, they only get what's left after selling fees, the mortgage balance, and your homestead exemption amount.

In states like Florida and Texas, citizens enjoy an unlimited homestead exemption, and it's very difficult for creditors to ever get a debtor's home. O.J. Simpson exploited this law by buying an expensive home in Florida to avoid the civil judgment against him in the deaths of Nicole Brown Simpson and Ronald Goldman, and since then,

Florida has modified the law to prevent new residents from pulling the same trick. However, it can still be a powerful tool for citizens in several states if properly implemented.

Forty-eight states have a "Homestead Exemption" to one degree or another, and the amount and rules on how to qualify for and satisfy the requirements of the exemption vary. For example, 21 states require that a homeowner file the appropriate paperwork to qualify for the exemption. See Appendix A for a table of homestead exemption rules by state.

So if homeowners want to take advantage of this exemption, it is essential that they have a general understanding of their state's law and consult with their asset-protection professional.

2. Protect the Home with Tenancy by the Entirety

If your state allows it, you can title your personal residence as "tenancy by the entirety," which offers unique protection: If one spouse is sued, the property cannot be attached or bifurcated by the lawsuit. Essentially, tenancy by the entirety holds that if a husband gets into a terrible lawsuit, it's not fair that the wife loses the house when the lawsuit had nothing to do with her (or vice versa). There are 25 states that have this law on the books, including Hawaii (as if you needed another reason to move to the Aloha State). See Appendix B for a list of states with tenancy by the entirety laws.

3. Implement an Equity Stripping Plan

Equity stripping is the strategy of placing a lien on your home with a mortgage and removing the equity by replacing it with a loan. This makes your home much less attractive to a potential creditor who wants to take it to satisfy a judgment.

The trick is in the implementation of the loan. Ideally, a traditional home equity line of credit (HELOC) or even a first mortgage lien, wherein you use the loan proceeds to invest and create additional wealth, can be a perfect fit. It's legitimate, and it's difficult for a creditor to challenge in court and step in front of a valid lienholder on the title to your primary residence.

Some homeowners implement a "smoke and mirrors" strategy by creating a shell company and placing a lien on their home with the shell company. This essentially clouds the title and gives the public (i.e., anyone doing a title or asset search) the impression that the lien on your home is maxed out and there isn't any equity to be had in a lawsuit. This strategy can be successful in dissuading a lawsuit, but in a court battle, a judge or plaintiff's attorney would slice right through the structure once they discovered the lien wasn't tied to an actual loan with a third party. While this strategy may not hold up in court, there is no tax ramification and nothing illegal about having a lien on your own home. It is simply a way to put the public face you desire on the amount of potential equity in your home.

4. *Create a Domestic Asset Protection Trust (DAPT)*

A DAPT is a self-settled trust created and protected under certain state statutes that offers another method of protecting assets. As a nation, we are becoming more and more comfortable with this type of trust. More than 17 states have these laws on the books, and each year, another state adopts some version of DAPT law. In Chapter 21, I explain the DAPT more thoroughly. For now, it is important to note that the DAPT is excellent for protecting a personal residence, cabin, beach house, or farm that you plan on keeping for life (or

---

CRITICAL ALERT!
THE IRREVOCABLE TRUST

The irrevocable trust is a close second to the Nevada entity for the most classically oversold structure offered at seminars around the country (see Chapter 3 wherein I discuss the Nevada scam). This is a type of trust typically based on common law or pieces and parts of state statutes referenced together to create what is sometimes called a "self-settled spendthrift trust." Yes, they sound complicated, and they are. They can also have a lot of tax ramifications that need to be carefully considered.

CRITICAL ALERT!, CONTINUED

However, do they provide asset protection? Yes, they certainly do when designed and implemented properly. The problem is that they can be expensive and, as I said, complicated for the average person to implement and maintain. But the promoters and scam artists at a seminar won't explain to you the gift tax, tax returns, and trust tax rates, and that the word "irrevocable" is quite literally that. While effective, these structures can be very dangerous and should only be considered after careful examination and when properly drafted with competent legal and tax counsel.

With that said, there are many variations of irrevocable trusts. The DAPT I previously mentioned and discuss more fully in Chapter 21 is a type of irrevocable trust, but the state legislatures that have adopted DAPT statutes have worked hard to make the DAPT laws clear and concise so that those implementing them know what they are getting into and understand the protection the DAPT offers.

Bottom line, an irrevocable trust that isn't tailored to a client's situation could cause more harm than good. And although these trusts are very effective, it is important to conduct a cost-benefit analysis before implementing such a plan. These are truly for the wealthy, not for new investors or business owners.

What about revocable trusts? While they have their uses, they do *not* provide asset protection.

When people think of a trust owning their home, they usually think of a revocable living trust (RLT), and frankly they should. The RLT, which I discuss in Chapter 24, is a fantastic trust structure for holding a personal residence for estate-planning purposes and avoiding probate, but it does not provide any asset protection whatsoever.

---

making very minor moves or changes, if necessary). In most states, the longer you keep the assets in a DAPT, the better protection the DAPT provides.

5. Put the Home Title in the Low-Risk Spouse's Name

In some situations, one spouse may have a "risk issue" with their lifestyle or business and removing their name from the title of the home could help protect it. The effectiveness of this strategy varies dramatically from state to state; it's critical to consult with an attorney who understands the law in your state or can at least research it to confirm your current standing. I also discuss the issues of asset protection in marriage and a potential divorce in more detail in Chapter 20. It's critical you consider these issues in marriage versus a third-party lawsuit and which is more important or riskier.

6. Purchase Umbrella Insurance

Umbrella insurance is just that—it's insurance that covers a variety of situations that could possibly create a claim. It can be very affordable, whether designed as a personal umbrella, a business umbrella, or both.

I'm a huge fan of ensuring my clients have proper insurance coverage. Any attorney or CPA who recommends you simply rely on legal structures and not buy insurance is taking a serious risk on your behalf.

Game Plan Takeaway and Action Items

In summary, it is clear that all of us need to take some active steps to better protect our equity in our home. However, it isn't clear which strategy is best for everyone. States have different laws, and of course, people have different situations. Consult with an attorney and proceed cautiously.

- Run the math and determine how much equity is exposed in your property.
- Know what the homestead exemption is in your state and if it's automatic or if you need to file a form to obtain protection.
- Learn if your state allows for tenancy by the entirety, and if so, make sure your title reflects it.

- If you still have exposed equity in your home, consider an equity stripping strategy or a DAPT.
- Finally, an umbrella insurance policy can be a good decision for anyone with a business, a home with equity, or other assets.

ASSET PROTECTION IN MARRIAGE AND DIVORCE

—— CASE STUDY ——

According to news reports, when actor Mel Gibson divorced from his wife of 31 years, the couple did not have a prenuptial agreement. Estimates of Gibson's wealth at the time were as high as $850 million, and it was widely speculated that his wife's property settlement was about $425 million, not to mention potentially half of any residual income from his films for the rest of his life.

I know we all love our significant others, but ask yourself if you would be willing to give them 50 percent of your current net worth, plus 50 percent of your future income.

By comparison, when Tiger Woods married his now ex-wife Elin Nordegren in 2004, it was widely believed that they signed a prenup. Upon their divorce nearly six years later, Woods was worth an estimated $600 million. However, in their case, most sources reported that Nordegren received around $100 million, or roughly one-sixth of Woods' net worth, rather than half. I can't say the prenup was the only or even the main reason for this difference, but anyone who followed the unveiling of Woods' infidelities in 2010 would likely agree that he got a good deal.

Most of us do not live in Mel Gibson's or Tiger Woods' world, but I think we would agree that the difference between one-half and one-sixth of our net worth is huge. The rules of law apply whether you are worth $600 million or $60,000.

Divorce can be the greatest threat to your assets if you are married, and most of us do get married. However, it's surprising how few people plan financially for what is probably the biggest decision of their lives. According to a 2010 *USA Today* article, less than 5 percent of all married people have a marital property agreement.

People who have been through nasty divorces—with each spouse trying to dig into the other's financial and personal affairs, hiring investigators to find any piece of dirt they can use for leverage in child custody, property division, alimony, etc.—have learned the consequences of failing to plan.

Moreover, many couples fail to realize that a marital property agreement can be a vital asset protection strategy that can protect *both* spouses from third-party creditors. Let's explore some ways that you can protect yourself and your assets in marriage . . . and divorce.

Who Owns What?

In general, property acquired by spouses during a marriage is the joint property of the spouses. This is called "community property"

GOOD TO KNOW:
MARITAL PROPERTY AGREEMENTS

Prenuptial and postnuptial agreements are both considered marital property agreements, and they need to include specific terms and be executed under certain conditions to be valid. Regrettably, a couple can't simply sit down by themselves and sign an agreement regarding the finances in their marriage. They must consult with separate attorneys.

---

in community property states and "marital property" in common law states. For this chapter, I'll use the term "marital property."

Any property that one spouse acquired (e.g., wages, real estate, securities, retirement savings, etc.) during the marriage is considered marital property unless it can be traced to separate property, which I explain below. Wages earned during marriage is one of the most common examples of marital property.

All other property is generally considered "separate property," including property obtained by inheritance and property obtained

---

GOOD TO KNOW:
COMMUNITY PROPERTY VS. COMMON LAW

Early in the history of our country, a few states adopted a legal principle called "community property." Essentially, in a community property state, if a property is acquired during marriage, it will be presumed community property unless an effort is made to designate it as sole and separate property. Thus, joint equal ownership is automatically presumed by law in the absence of specific evidence. In common law states, property isn't automatically presumed to be "community" or equally shared. Thus, property titled in the name of one spouse or acquired by just one spouse may be treated as separate property and must go through a separate analysis to determine whether it is marital property.

---

by a spouse prior to the marriage. Moreover, the income generated from the separate property remains separate as well. Therefore, if you inherit a rental property from your parents, then generally the rents from that unit would also be considered separate property. Of course, this general rule depends on whether the assets are commingled with marital property (see below).

The Risk of Commingling

Many people don't realize that although property may enter the marriage as separate property (e.g., a rental that one spouse owned prior to the marriage) or be acquired during the marriage (e.g., an inheritance), the character of some or all of the property can change during the marriage based on the spouses' conduct.

For example, if a wife owned a rental prior to the marriage but during the marriage used her weekly paycheck to remodel the rental, most states would deem all or a portion of the remodel is marital property because the wife used marital property (i.e., her paycheck) to pay for it. On the other hand, if the wife could prove that the remodel was paid for by rents received (which is separate property), then the remodel would remain the wife's separate property.

Many people do not take the time to account for their separate and marital assets and have no idea of the importance of, much less a plan for, maintaining separation between the two. Indeed, the easiest and most common mistake spouses make during the marriage is commingling their separate and marital property. In the example above regarding the remodel, if the wife deposited her rent checks into the same bank account in which she deposited her wages, she would be commingling her separate property (rent checks) with her marital property (wages). If she then used a check from this account to fund the remodel, it would be impossible for her to prove that the money came from her rent checks as opposed to her wages, and therefore the remodel most likely would be considered a marital asset.

Moreover, if the husband's creditors wanted to go after the wife's bank account, it would be very difficult for her to demonstrate that the account is her separate property if she had been depositing her wages in that account for years. From an asset protection standpoint, it is very important to keep separate accounts for marital assets and separate assets.

Rules in a Community Property State

In community property states, the method of holding title does not determine whether the property will be considered marital or separate. For example, many people in community property states assume that if they title property acquired during marriage in their name as their "sole and separate property," that makes it separate property. Not necessarily. You need additional clear, written evidence of this intent.

Thus, in a community property state, if a property was acquired during marriage, it will be presumed community property. The issue for the court during a divorce would be whether the spouse claiming a separate property interest can prove that he or she met the written requirements to convert the community property into separate property (this is called a *transmutation*). States have specific rules governing transmutations. You should always check with your attorney to determine the proper requirements for a transmutation and consult your CPA on possible tax consequences.

There are nine community property states—Arizona, California, Idaho, Louisiana, Nevada, New Mexico, Texas, Washington, and Wisconsin—and it's important to understand how these unique rules can affect your assets. While not a community property state, Alaska does allow couples to opt into a community property arrangement; property is separate unless both parties agree to make it community property through a community property agreement or a community property trust.

Division of Property in Common Law States

In common law states, property titled in the name of one spouse is treated as the separate property of that spouse. Therefore, asset protection against creditors usually entails titling the asset in the name

CHAPTER 20 • Asset Protection in Marriage and Divorce

of the spouse with the lowest risk. However, in a divorce, the property will still be distributed depending on whether it is considered marital property or separate property, using the general characterization rules I've already discussed.

In these states, the court generally divides marital property equally unless somehow that would be inequitable. However, courts generally have wide latitude to determine what is equitable in any given situation and may take factors like age, health, future income, and amount of assets into account. Some courts also allow marital misconduct (infidelity, domestic abuse, etc.) to be relevant considerations.

This is what is scary about divorce courts. What a judge may deem equitable can be very different from what you think is equitable, and who holds the title has less of an impact than you'd expect in determining how property is divided in a divorce. This is why you need to take it upon yourself to make these decisions using a marital property agreement before you ever stand in front of a divorce court judge.

Creating a Valid Marital Agreement

Therefore, to protect your assets, marital agreements, whether prenuptial or postnuptial, are extremely important and must comply with technical rules. If the rules aren't followed for preparing and entering into the agreement, they will do little to protect the parties and their assets from each other in a divorce.

Rules can vary from state to state, and it's important to make sure you have an attorney prepare or at least review your marital agreement. Some (but not all) of the rules that states require for a valid marital property agreement are:

1. Each party must have a separate attorney to advise them on their rights and obligations in the marital agreement.
2. Each spouse must provide full disclosure of their assets and liabilities so that each spouse can be fully informed prior to entering into the agreement.

3. The parties should always be given adequate time and opportunity to consider the terms of the agreement. Any argument that the negotiating process was unfair may be grounds for invalidating the agreement. For example, many courts will not enforce premarital agreements entered into at the eleventh hour before the marriage.

Marital Agreements and Asset Protection

The marital agreement is actually quite critical when employing the asset protection strategy of placing assets in the lower-risk spouse's name. In Chapter 19, I discuss this strategy in more detail. Of course, such a strategy needs to be carefully considered and weighed against the hopefully unlikely possibility of a future divorce. But as you are already discussing this dire outcome when drafting a marital agreement, it's important to also consider the asset protection strategies that may be involved.

Estate Planning and Marital Planning

As I discuss in Chapter 26, the primary benefit of setting up a revocable living trust (RLT) before or during marriage is for estate planning and to make sure the proper beneficiaries of each spouse receive the correct assets in the proper manner. With an RLT, the creators or grantors of the trust remain the trustees and have the right to change the trust while they are alive.

Many married couples will implement a joint RLT. This can fly in the face of any prenuptial or postnuptial planning. It is essential that any sort of marital agreement be coordinated with RLTs to confirm and memorialize each spouse's separate and/or marital property. Often, if there is a marital agreement being prepared or in place, I recommend the couple use separate RLTs to further show the separation of assets for marital and asset planning protection.

Still, planning for divorce and estate planning are very different, so it's important to have a comprehensive discussion with an attorney (or two attorneys, in the case of marital agreements) when making these plans.

Using Irrevocable Trusts to Avoid Marital Planning

Some individuals never want to have the prenup conversation and search for options to protect their assets from divorce while avoiding ruining a relationship or causing an awkward situation. This is where an irrevocable trust could play a role for someone contemplating getting married in the near future.

Generally, trusts can be revocable, whereby the person creating the trust reserves the right to revoke the trust. But an irrevocable trust is one where the person creating the trust has no power to revoke it. As such, an irrevocable trust can be an effective tool that removes assets from your estate, making them unreachable by creditors or a divorcing spouse.

If you transfer assets to an irrevocable trust before a future marriage, the assets are no longer your property but are property of the trust. However, a significant drawback is that you may forfeit a great deal of control and beneficial enjoyment of the property. There could also be gift tax consequences. Therefore, you should discuss the pros and cons of using an irrevocable trust for future marital planning with *both* your attorney and your CPA.

Game Plan Takeaway and Action Items

Whether you are a celebrity like Mel Gibson, married to an athlete as was Elin Nordegren, or simply a regular American with assets in a marriage, you have to consider divorce as a potential threat to your wealth. Divorce is certainly one of the most emotionally and financially draining experiences a person can go through.

It's easy to live in denial regarding the potential for divorce, but we should be realistic. Experts agree that the divorce rate in the U.S. is difficult to determine accurately, but we do know it's too high— and devastating when it does occur. Don't ignore the possibility of divorce when doing proper marital, estate, and asset protection planning.

- If you are getting married soon, consider a prenuptial agreement.
- If you are already married, consider a postnuptial agreement.

- Make sure you are keeping property separate and not commingling assets or funds if it has already been identified as such.
- Consider your estate planning goals at the same time you are implementing any marital agreement.
- If still single, you may want to set up an irrevocable trust to sidestep the prenup discussion.

CUTTING-EDGE ASSET PROTECTION STRATEGIES

―――― CASE STUDY ――――

When O. J. Simpson played for the Buffalo Bills, he received an interesting benefit in his compensation plan: a defined benefit retirement plan, which is similar to a 401(k) or IRA. For Simpson, the plan meant that upon retirement from the NFL, he would be paid approximately $25,000 a month for the rest of his life as a pension.

Fifteen years later, on June 17, 1994, he was charged with committing a double murder. Although he was found criminally innocent of the crime in 1995, he later lost a civil judgment brought by the murder victims' families. The jury in that case found that Simpson committed both "homicides willfully and wrongfully." The families obtained a combined judgment against him in the amount of $33.5 million.

At the date of the final civil judgment on appeal, Simpson's retirement plan was reported by the court to be valued at $4.1 million and untouchable by the plaintiffs under federal law.

Moreover, Simpson moved to Florida in 1999 and purchased a multimillion-dollar home to avail himself of Florida's unlimited homestead exemption, wherein creditors cannot touch an individual's home or its equity. Although this was somewhat limited by the 2005 Bankruptcy Code Amendments, Florida still has one of the broadest homestead provisions in the U.S.

In 2006, Simpson began to pursue the publication of a book, *If I Did It*, and hoped to keep the profits from its sale. However, in July 2007, a federal bankruptcy judge awarded the rights to the book to the Goldman family. Although the family would ultimately receive 90 percent of the profits to help satisfy the civil suit judgment against Simpson, they were still prevented from going after his retirement plan.

Then, in October 2008, Simpson was found guilty of entering a room in the Palace Station Hotel & Casino in Las Vegas along with a group of men and committing multiple felonies, including criminal conspiracy, kidnapping, assault, robbery, and use of a deadly weapon. Simpson received the harshest punishment and was sentenced to 33 years in prison with the possibility of parole after about nine years.

The amazing fact: Throughout this entire saga, by relying on various federal and state exemptions, Simpson was able to protect his assets. This case is an extreme one, and I'd never suggest emulating a criminal like Simpson. However, it does provide an excellent example of how powerful retirement plans and the homestead exemption are as asset protection tools.

As with the O. J. Simpson case, we often see asset protection strategies getting tested in court and gaining traction with different state legislatures throughout the country. Even though these more advanced tactics can sometimes be complex and expensive to set up and maintain, they can offer a huge payoff by insulating a family's assets from creditors. Once you've implemented the basic strategies, some of which I explained in Chapter 17, it may be time for you to investigate more advanced tactics.

Review Your Assets and Potential Risks

First, it's important to review your personal net worth and the growth of your assets on a regular basis. At the same time, you should assess the risks in your life and where a potential lawsuit and cause of action could arise. By going through this process, you can determine what level of protection you need.

Next, focus on your most valuable assets, and develop asset protection structures and strategies that can be applied to specific assets and risks. At this level of planning, it's important not to take a scattershot approach but rather target your methods after cost-benefit analyses and second opinions from qualified professionals.

When I'm working with clients, once we have some ideas as to which plans to implement, I encourage them not to overdo it by trying to accomplish too much at once. It can sometimes be overwhelming to implement new entities, trusts, structures, and procedures for asset protection. If you're ready to pull your hair out due to the time involved and the administrative headaches required for your plan, it's clearly not worth it. Make sure you go into any advanced asset protection procedure with your eyes wide open about the costs and how your professional advisor expects you to maintain the plan.

That said, if you have valuable assets that need to be protected and potential risks that could threaten them, it's important to take your asset protection beyond the basics.

Here are some advanced and cutting-edge strategies that might benefit you, depending on your situation.

Charging Order Protection Entities

In a nutshell, a Charging Order Protection Entity (COPE) protects your assets from personal liabilities that arise outside your LLC or whatever entity is holding the asset. Some of you may be thinking, "That's what I thought my LLC was doing already! I was protecting my rental property by putting it in an LLC." However, that may not be the case in every state. What you were doing was protecting yourself or your other assets from liabilities that could potentially arise from your rental, not the other way around. LLCs were developed with the primary purpose of protecting *you* from the *rental*, not protecting the *rental* from *yourself*.

This is a legal principle, developed in courts and even codified under some state laws, that allows you, the owner of an asset, to protect its equity inside an entity such as an LLC or limited partnership (LP). Thus, by putting an asset like a real estate property or an investment account in the right type of COPE, you have protected the asset.

The effect of this law is that a judge will give an order charging a debtor to pay creditors from the revenue of an entity but not allow the creditor to foreclose on or dissolve the entity to get at the asset. However, this protection isn't provided in every state. In 2019, there are now 20 states that provide COPE protection for LLCs, while 29 provide the same protection through an LP (Louisiana is the only state without LP or COPE protection for assets). See Appendix C for a table of states that currently provide this type of protection.

Because of the limited access to COPEs in a variety of states, some people are tempted to set up entities in states like Delaware, Nevada, or Wyoming. This can be effective if completed properly, but it can also add setup and maintenance costs because you will also have to register your entity in the state where you are doing business. There is also the argument that once you register an entity as a "foreign" entity in the state where the asset is actually held, you subject yourself to the law of the state, which can undermine the COPE.

Now, it's understandable that a structure such as this might appear sexy and exciting to implement. However, because of its cost and complexity, I don't recommend this for the brand-new investor but

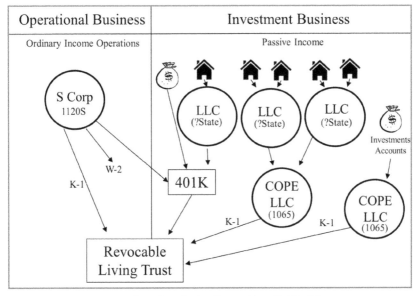

Figure 21.1 – **Charging Order Protection Entity Diagram**

rather the investor with significant assets to protect. Nonetheless, I often see nonlawyer, self-professed gurus selling structures such as this for thousands of dollars and making outrageous promises of protection and ease of maintenance. Be sure to get price quotes and opinions from various bona fide law firms before implementing a COPE. With all these considerations in mind, Figure 21.1 shows how a COPE should be structured to provide maximum protection.

Foreign Charging Order Protection Entities

Using a foreign COPE is an important extra step when clients have significant assets. In fact, some of you may remember the disclaimers from 2012 presidential candidate Mitt Romney regarding his foreign assets in entities and trusts and the ensuing discussion.

As Romney clearly explained in his public statements, foreign COPEs aren't used to avoid taxes but for additional privacy and asset protection. U.S. citizens are required to report their worldwide income on their tax returns, whether or not their assets are held within a COPE. As such, the IRS has been very aggressive in recent years in going after Americans trying to shelter income in foreign tax havens. However, after complying with tax reporting procedures, a foreign entity such as a COPE *can* dissuade a creditor from pursuing a lawsuit when they see the legal costs necessary to track down assets abroad.

Domestic Asset Protection Trusts

This is one of the hottest structures in asset protection today. I discuss domestic asset protection trusts (DAPT) briefly in Chapter 19 in regard to protecting your primary residence and consider this to be the best use for a DAPT.

Essentially, a DAPT is an irrevocable self-settled trust created and protected under state statute. Once you place your assets in the trust, after a certain amount of time (which will vary by state), the assets are protected indefinitely from future creditors. What makes DAPTs so popular is that they don't require you to file a separate tax return, nor do they have gift tax consequences. They are relatively affordable and easy to set up and maintain. A DAPT can hold your personal residence, stock brokerage accounts, or LLCs that own your rentals. Moreover, it is ultimately coordinated with your revocable living trust and enhances your estate plan (but doesn't replace it).

One of the unique and critical requirements that makes the DAPT effective is that the donor must appoint a third-party trustee to approve distributions. This requirement is what protects you from your creditors because, in effect, the trustee won't distribute assets if you're under threat of a judgment from a creditor.

While a DAPT can own rental property LLCs, I typically have concerns when they are used for this structure because of the third-party trustee requirement and steps that need to be taken for distributions. For example, if you want money or assets out of the DAPT, you need to request the distribution from your trustee. This will typically be a friendly trustee who looks out for potential creditors against you before making a distribution, but it's an extra step that can be cumbersome.

Rather, I recommend a DAPT for assets that you will have for a very long time or make few changes to—such as a personal residence, farm,

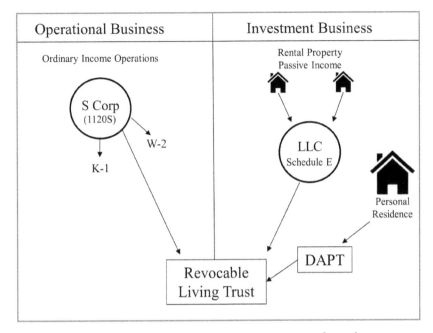

Figure 21.2 – **Domestic Asset Protection Trust (DAPT)**

cabin, etc. In those cases, managing a DAPT and its assets can be simple, affordable, and straightforward. Moreover, you can be designated as the investment trustee, allowing you to make decisions regarding the sale and acquisition of assets within the DAPT. You just can't be the distribution trustee. Figure 21.2 is a visual representation of what your personal asset protection structure may look like with a DAPT.

DAPT Locations

There are 17 states that currently have DAPT laws on their books: Alaska, Delaware, Hawaii, Michigan, Mississippi, Missouri, Nevada, New Hampshire, Ohio, Oklahoma, Rhode Island, South Dakota, Tennessee, Utah, Virginia, West Virginia, and Wyoming.

Clearly, if you live and own property in a state with a DAPT statute, you should be confident in the law you are relying on. The DAPT should do its job and protect your assets.

However, if you live in a state without a DAPT law but want to set up a DAPT in another state that allows it, there is still great debate as to the effectiveness of a DAPT set up in a state other than where you live and/or where the subject property is located. The reason why you may still wish to forge this path is that you will undoubtedly be creating another hoop for a creditor's attorney to jump through when coming after your assets. Essentially, non-DAPT states aren't declaring they *won't* recognize the DAPT, and under the "full faith and credit" clause of the U.S. Constitution, an asset owner can make an excellent argument in court to keep a creditor at bay.

Yes, in the end, the DAPT could ultimately fail when challenged in your home state by a creditor. At that point, it would be unlikely you could keep a creditor from reaching the assets held in your DAPT. But again, in some instances, the amount of time, money, and resources needed to reach the assets could potentially dissuade creditors from pursuing them.

So with all that said, you do not have to live in or have assets in a DAPT state to avail yourself of this strategy. In fact, Utah (where I have a home office) is a fantastic state in which to domicile the DAPT. Utah enacted a new and much more robust DAPT statute in 2013 that provides significant benefits compared to other states. When drafted carefully and executed correctly, the Utah DAPT provides the following benefits:

- *Assets placed in the trust are protected against future creditors imme-diately.* Nevada's statute, for example, doesn't begin protecting assets against future creditors until the assets have been in the trust for two years.
- *Assets placed in the trust are protected against existing creditors after two years.* This is similar to Nevada; however, that statute of limitations is reduced to 120 days if the settlor/grantor/donor of the DAPT sends out notices to all known creditors and publish-es notice of the DAPT for creditors the settlor isn't aware of.
- *A lawyer can serve as the trustee.* For an affordable, annual flat fee, you can avoid paying a trust company a percentage of the trust assets to serve as the trustee.
- *There are some exceptions for child support, alimony, federal and state taxes, or pre-existing torts.* There are limits to DAPTs, and one

can't expect to use them to get out of every possible debt. It is in our best interest as a society to limit their scope.

• *No tax issues when selling your personal residence.* Placing your personal residence in a DAPT does not hinder your use of the sale of home tax exemption to avoid paying taxes on any gain when you sell that residence, as long as the trust is drafted as a "grantor" trust.

Bottom line: Even in the courts of states that do not have a DAPT statute, a would-be litigant will still likely have to expend considerable resources to unwind and reverse the transfer of assets into a DAPT.

Retirement Plans

Retirement plans (IRAs, 401(k)s, etc.) have to be the most amazing and affordable methods of asset protection. You can build wealth at the same time you are protecting it from creditors.

In 1974, Congress passed the Employee Retirement Income Security Act (ERISA) to create minimum standards for pension plans and to protect the interests of employees in benefit plans offered by employers. One of the key features of this law is the anti-alienation provision that helps guarantee employees will actually receive the benefits promised by their employers by preventing creditors from collecting against the debtor's retirement plan. The Supreme Court has upheld this law.

The ERISA exemption is what O. J. Simpson relied on in making sure his multimillion-dollar retirement plan was not taken from him. The defined benefit retirement plan established by the NFL for its players is rarely going to be subject to the claims of a creditor. If you have a small business, you may choose to set up your own retirement plan or even a 401(k) and obtain the same asset protection Simpson had. I discuss the options and tax benefits of retirement plans in more depth in Chapter 24.

In this asset protection context, there are really two types of retirement plans: those that are covered by ERISA, such as a 401(k), and those that are not. Protection afforded to non-ERISA plans (such as IRAs, SIMPLEs, SEPs, and KEOGHs) varies from state to state. Thankfully, most states provide protection for these retirement accounts; in fact, payments from the retirement plans are protected as well as the cash value itself. However, there are a few states that don't provide any protection at all or set dollar limits on what is protected, and your IRA could be lost to an unforeseen liability or debt. Some states didn't want to provide unlimited protection for the entire amount within a retirement plan and have put limits or only protect a certain amount. Bottom line, if you are relying on your retirement plan as an asset protection vehicle, make sure you understand the rules in your state.

Figure 21.3 shows all the potential advanced asset protection strategies and where they may fit in your overall plan.

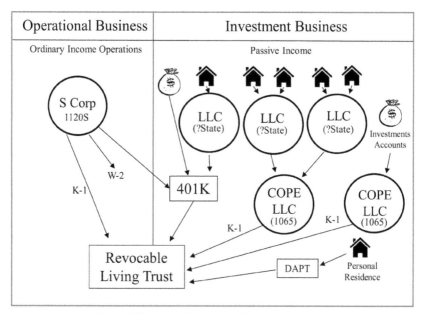

Figure 21.3 – **Master Diagram of Advanced Asset Protection Strategies**

Game Plan Takeaway and Action Items

It's imperative to tailor your asset protection plan to your specific needs and not overdo it. I committed this cardinal sin of asset protection when I was a brand-new lawyer by creating elaborate structures for clients when they didn't have the bookkeeping and maintenance temperament for such a structure. Yes, they asked me for the "top of the line" plan, but it was like giving the keys to a Ferrari to a teenager. They wanted it, but they quickly realized it was too much to handle.

However, if you start with the basics and add one structure at a time, in the long haul it will be much easier to manage. Rome wasn't built in a day, and you don't have to build your asset protection plan all at once either.

- Create a personal financial statement and list your assets at net equity value.
- Determine where your greatest risks and greatest assets reside.
- Focus on your most valuable assets and greatest risks first.
- Don't try to accomplish too much at first and take your time implementing a plan.
- Consider a COPE, DAPT, or retirement plan for advanced asset protection planning when the time is right.
- Beware of fraudulent transfers and maintain whatever plan you implement properly.

THE PROPER APPROACH TO PARTNERS AND INVESTORS

Athletes and teams commonly partner with other organizations, sponsors, and training systems to implement their game plan and take their team to the next level. In your business, partnering with the right individuals can be the difference between success and failure. The trick is bringing on the partners properly so your plan doesn't backfire.

22

DOCUMENTING A PARTNERSHIP

—— CASE STUDY ——

'll never forget this classic case: I had an appointment with a client who wanted to talk about their partner and the business problems they were having.

We met in the conference room, and my new client told an elaborate story of how she and her husband brought on a new partner in their business. Their plans with the new partner sounded great and would allow them to take the business to the next level.

She talked about how much money the partner would bring into the business, the new and improved duties of the client and her husband, and the duties of the new investor/partner. She explained the amazing potential of the business and how they would share the future profits.

Of course I was anxious to hear what was going wrong, and she stated simply that her new partner hadn't put in all the money he promised (but a good portion of it) and wasn't doing the duties he had agreed to do.

I asked for the partnership agreement. I can visualize what she handed me to this day: one sheet of paper with one paragraph at the top that said the partner would put in X dollars and do the following. It was four to six sentences long.

It could easily have been written on a napkin from Denny's. Needless to say, the battle began and was a story of "she said, he said." Nothing else was in writing but a few short emails. It was ugly.

The early stages of many partnerships are nearly identical to the one above. When I have an initial meeting with new partners, clients rarely ask, "How do I protect myself when going into business with someone?"—although that is what they should be asking. Instead they ask, "How do we split the profit from the revenue each month?" (Or the sale of the property or the sale of the business . . . you get the picture.)

For some reason, in all these partnership meetings, the skies are always blue, and there isn't a rain cloud in sight. They don't seem to realize that there *will* be problems down the road and times when they won't like what their partner is or isn't doing. We can be our own worst enemy when we don't take the time and effort to properly enter into a partnership. I see so many investors and small-business owners lose their businesses and sometimes everything, including their savings, to poor documentation and a partnership gone bad. Don't do that. Instead, use the plays in this chapter to protect yourself and your potential partner.

Pre-Partnership Vetting and Documentation

You would be astounded at the number of clients I meet with who literally know nothing about their partner's background, their approach to business, and their vision for the partnership. They rush into the relationship so quickly that they don't even gather this fundamental knowledge about their partner.

Here are some issues to consider before you ink the deal:

- Obviously, only go into business with those you trust. I always advise my clients to vet everyone in their business dealings, whether it be a contractor, a tenant, etc. This could mean conducting background checks and calling personal references. This is especially true with your business partner(s) and is by far the most important way to protect yourself when entering a partnership.
- Address potential issues before they become issues. Talk about worst-case scenarios. If your partner isn't willing to do so, for whatever reason, you have the wrong partner.
- Read and understand your partnership documents *before* you sign them. A good attorney can help you identify possible issues and present solutions, but ultimately you and your business partner(s) need to take ownership of the agreement and share a thorough understanding of how it will govern your business.
- Consider getting separate counsel if using the same attorney as your partner(s) is presenting concerns.
- If you live in a community property state, have every business partner's spouse sign the partnership/operating agreement and any amendments. The spouse presumably has an ownership interest in the business, and you want them to agree to the provisions of the partnership/operating agreement. This is especially important regarding the method of valuing the business when buying out a partner in the event of a divorce.

Setting Up the Partnership

Creating the partnership agreement and setting up the proper entity/ structure for the partnership are the two most important steps in the partnership process, perhaps even more important than analyzing the merits of the business itself. You could have the most successful moneymaking idea in the world, but if the foundation for the partnership is faulty, the business will ultimately fail.

Understanding the mechanics of how your business will be managed is the key to designing your partnership agreement and documenting the terms. While the list of items to consider in a solid partnership agreement is indefinable—every partnership is different—I've narrowed it down to my top ten:

1. *Partner roles in signing and authorizations.* Have a very clear understanding of what the managers or officers of the business are authorized to do on behalf of the company.
2. *Duties and responsibilities of each partner.* There should be a description of each partner's responsibilities and duties so each partner knows what to expect from the other. Furthermore, there should be predetermined consequences for partners not completing their duties.
3. *Contributions of capital.* What amount of time, money, and assets is each partner contributing to the partnership? This includes the initial contributions as well as additional contributions that may be necessary to continue operating the business in the future.
4. *Rights to distributions, profits, compensation, and losses.* Any right of the partners to receive discretionary or mandatory distributions, which includes a return of any or all of their contributions, needs to be clearly and specifically set forth in the partnership agreement.
5. *Unanimous vote requirements.* Which events or decisions will require a unanimous vote of the business partners? This question can be answered in many different ways, and there isn't a right or wrong answer. But it's crucial that you and your business partners decide the procedure together from the outset.
6. *Dissolution or exit strategy.* The partnership agreement should indicate the events upon which the partnership is to be dissolved and its affairs wound up. It's possible the business concept and model don't lend themselves to answering this question. But, for example, in a real estate deal, it's important

to have a timeline and possible triggering events that will lead to either selling the property or buying out one of the partners if they don't want to stick around for the long haul.

7. *A buy-sell provision or separate buy-sell agreement.* This is a type of agreement that addresses major changes in the partnership arrangement. For example, what if one of the partners voluntarily or involuntarily leaves the partnership? How is she bought out? What happens if you want to sell your ownership interest—should your business partner have a right to buy it before you sell it to a third party? What if your business partner dies? Or gets divorced? Or files for bankruptcy? Or just wants to retire? Again, there is no right answer to these questions. The point is that they get answered by you and your business partner(s) and are documented in the partnership agreement.

8. *Expulsion provision.* Carefully consider this provision, which is a double-edged sword. The benefit of such a provision is that you can put in writing when a partner can be forced out of the business. For example, you and your partners could agree that if one partner isn't pulling his weight, he can be forced out. But be certain that your well-deserved three-week vacation to Tahiti doesn't trigger the expulsion clause.

9. *Noncompete provision.* For example, you and your business partner(s) may agree that if one of the partners leaves the business, they cannot open a competing business or work for a competing business within a certain number of miles and for a certain period of time.

10. *Miscellaneous provisions.* Some examples include a provision for attorney's fees for the nonbreaching party if they win a lawsuit, a mediation or binding arbitration clause so you don't have to go to court if you don't want to, or a venue or choice of law provision on which state law would be applied in a contract dispute and where the dispute would be litigated.

The above is certainly not a complete list of all the issues you should consider when forming a partnership; however, it is a good start. Make sure you sit down with your partner(s) to discuss the best- *and* worst-case scenarios. Have a competent and honest attorney represent the company or have each partner hire an attorney to review the partnership documents and address the above issues, as well as the individual and specific needs of your and your partners' particular situation.

CRITICAL ALERT!
THE HANDSHAKE AGREEMENT

For some bizarre reason, many small-business owners think it is more expensive to hire a lawyer for one hour to review a contract than it is to risk a multi-thousand-dollar investment to an email chain or a handshake.

In the U.S., a contract can be created with a simple verbal understanding; not even a handshake is required. Emails are also now considered binding contracts in court and can drag you into unsuspecting relationships and claims.

You may say, "Well, if emails are considered binding, then great! Why do I need a contract? I have the emails that state our relationship and understanding. That's all I need." This statement could not be further from the truth.

As I just enumerated, there are many considerations that need to be addressed, documented, and clarified in a partnership agreement. In a handshake agreement or email chain, subsequent conversations and correspondence can modify or completely change the original terms. At the very least, get your agreement in writing and reviewed by an attorney.

The Best Entity for a Partnership

Another related question partners should ask their attorney is, "What documentation should we have to ensure the success of our partnership and protect one another from the business and the other's actions?"

In most cases, the best structure for a partnership is the LLC. I realize there are unique situations where a corporation or a limited partnership might make sense; however, those are the exception and not the rule. In fact, if you need to save taxes, it's typical to have each member's share of the LLC owned by an S corp. (See Chapter 4 for the benefits of an S corp.)

There are three significant reasons why the LLC is such a perfect entity for partnerships (something I discuss in more detail in Chapter 3). Here is a brief summary of these benefits:

1. Its limited liability protection shields you from the acts of your partner (and vice versa). Without it, you have unlimited vicarious liability.
2. The operating agreement and corresponding initial minutes and formation documents are fantastic documents to define all of the partnership terms.
3. The flexibility of the LLC is beneficial for allocating profits, losses, and capital as well as for allowing individual partners to do their own tax planning after they receive their allocated share of profit.

Possible Partnership Structures

There are a couple of ways you can structure a partnership: with a holding company or an operational partnership. The holding company is best for rentals, not operations. The self-employment tax can be disastrous in an operational partnership LLC and difficult to plan around. See Figure 22.1 on page 260 for a visual of how a holding company might be structured.

In an operational partnership, the LLC is still a great entity for the partnership, but having individual S corps for each participating partner can be hugely beneficial for individual tax planning and tax savings (see Figure 22.2 on page 260).

Partnership Management Tips

After all the documentation has been completed and you begin operating as a partnership, you should follow several procedures for a successful venture.

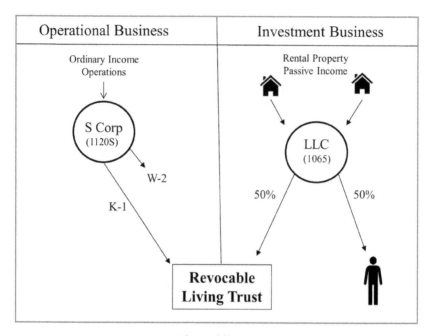

Figure 22.1 – **The Holding Company LLC**

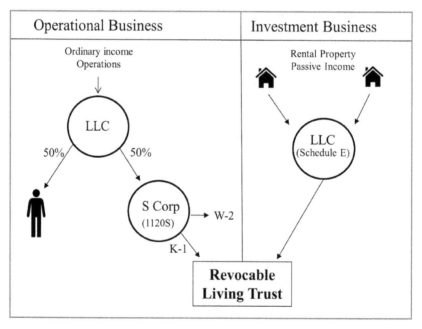

Figure 22.2 – **The Operational Company LLC**

Here are the top three habits that will help a partnership succeed:

1. *Communication and documentation.* As the business partnership evolves, record and document anything that is contrary to your initial partnership/operating agreement. A good partnership/operating agreement will allow for revisions due to changing circumstances, but these should always be in writing and signed by each business partner.
2. *Be involved in your business.* Don't ever think a partnership is a turnkey operation. People who aren't in constant communication with their partners will soon find themselves on the outside and in a dispute. Clearly understand your duties and responsibilities and fulfill the expectations of your partners or readdress what those expectations should be.
3. *Bookkeeping and tax deposits.* Don't cut corners on bookkeeping and finances. This is the lifeblood of your business and will determine when and how your profits are distributed. Making sure your tax deposits are made on time and in the right amounts is also the backbone of good tax planning in your partnership. Beware of "phantom income," which is income from the partnership that exists on paper but has no corresponding distributions. This can wreak havoc on a partner's individual tax return without proper bookkeeping and planning.

Game Plan Takeaway and Action Items

In the case study above, the relationship fell apart, and it took a lot of time, money, and heartache to unwind the partnership. And it wasn't just the legal fees that hit them hard—it was the wasted opportunity cost and the progress the business could have made during that same period of time.

Partnering is great. Partnering can make you more effective, influential, and successful and make you more money—but only if it's done right. Be cautious and careful.

- Do a background check on potential partners and speak to their references.

- Discuss the good and bad scenarios to understand everyone's positions.
- Document the partnership and get it reviewed by an attorney.
- Consider an LLC for asset protection from your partner's actions, and use the operating agreement as the foundation for the partnership.
- Stay involved in your partnership and communicate regularly, taking notes on changes in your duties or financial agreements.
- Operate like best friends and follow through with your commitments.

23

BRINGING ON INVESTORS

─── CASE STUDY ───

My client was grateful to not end up in jail.

The situation started out innocently and seemingly benign. He wanted to raise money to expand his real estate business. This was back in 2005 and 2006 and he was "killing it."

He was honest and hard-working. He found some friends and associates who were busy with their day jobs and wanted to invest money with him to cash in on some of his success. I'm not sure if my client thought of them as partners, lenders, or investors. Frankly, I don't think he knew the difference. I just know he promised a rate of return, a share of the bottom line, and in his mind, expected them to just sit back and watch. He probably would have defined them as "silent investors."

Well, we all know what happened in 2007 and 2008. Real estate prices plummeted, deals essentially came to a standstill, and my client was left trying to explain the situation to his investors.

They had invested in a "security," as defined by the Securities and Exchange Commission (SEC). They had relied on my client's promises and lost their money. For all intents and purposes, my client was just as guilty as Bernie Madoff and could have shared a jail cell with him.

Nonetheless, my client begged for mercy and patience. He promised to work hard and rebound with real estate deals in the future. He was lucky to receive their mercy because they could have easily brought in local and federal prosecutors. Many investors did just that, and many people like my client went to jail.

Ultimately, my client survived financially and stayed out of criminal court, but it certainly cost him years of his life in stress, worry, and an ulcer trying to find solutions and work through the process.

Hindsight is 20/20. What would he have done differently if he knew the market was going to crash? Better yet, what could he have done differently with his legal documentation that would have sidestepped any issues? With what he knows now, a little legal planning would have resolved the issues quickly and efficiently with no personal exposure. You can learn those same rules.

There comes a time in the lifespan of just about every business when the potential for substantial growth comes to fruition and additional capital is necessary to make that growth happen. It's at these moments that you'll probably start looking for people to invest in your business.

When raising capital, the options boil down to three types: investors, lenders, and partners. For example, some potential investors will want to become partners in the venture and have some control or voting rights in making decisions. They may also want to take greater risks in hopes of a greater reward. Other partners may want a fixed rate of return on their investment and less risk. This would be considered an "investor" where they don't have any real vote or control over the investment. Others may want less risk, or even some sort of security for their investment and thus act as a "lender" who takes a lien against property or stock in the company.

A party to your business will rarely fit into more than one of these categories. This is a critical point. Only with careful planning could a party be *both* a partner and a lender, or an investor and a lender. Each title comes with a different set of documents, benefits, duties, and responsibilities. In this chapter, I'll walk you through some best practices for taking on investors.

Investors vs. Silent Partners

This important issue for categorizing investors all comes down to expectations, and your expectations are just as important as theirs.

GOOD TO KNOW:
THE PARTICIPATING NOTE

If a party lends you money for a project wherein they receive a fixed rate of return (for example, an interest rate or points) but then also receive a share of the profit when the property or business sells, then they are a partner and not a lender. This agreement is documented in a participating loan note, showing that the lender is expecting to share in profits over and above a fair interest rate. I can't emphasize this enough: If you have this type of note and the money your lender is receiving looks like it's because she is a partner, then at the end of the day, she is now firmly in the partnership category for tax and personal liability exposure. You can't call her a partner when it's convenient and a lender when it's not.

Silent partners generally want to "set it and forget it" when it comes to their investments. They want to invest money in an enterprise, not worry about or spend time and effort helping the business make decisions, and still see a significant return on their investment. The scary part here is the term *significant return*. These investors are looking for greater returns than they could garner from publicly traded stocks, bonds, and mutual funds, all of which are generally safer investments. Silent partners are taking a risk investing with you, so they usually want a bigger bang for their buck.

You may simply want someone who gives you money, sits back, doesn't get involved, and waits for your success or failure. They don't have a say in what you do or how you do it.

Based on the two perspectives above, the person I just described is actually an investor. *Silent partners are investors.*

The SEC sometimes agrees. The SEC calls a money partner an investor if they are investing in what the SEC terms a *security*. To meet those requirements, the investor has to have:

1. Been given a promise or an expectation for a return
2. Invested money
3. Rely wholly on someone else's efforts in the business

They don't have a say in the business, and so while you might call them a silent partner, they qualify as an investor to the SEC. This distinction is extremely important, and misunderstanding it could land you in jail if you lose their money.

Avoiding the SEC Investor Classification

While bringing an investor into your business can be a great way to raise needed capital, it also takes careful planning. Doing it in the wrong way can be considered the issuance of a security under federal law, which will place you under the jurisdiction of the SEC.

The SEC was created by the federal government in response to the stock market crash of 1929, which sparked the Great Depression. The SEC's job is to "require that investors receive financial and other significant information concerning securities being offered for public sale" and "prohibit deceit, misrepresentations, and other fraud in the sale of securities." You do not want to get involved with the enforcement arm of the SEC. It's akin to being pursued by the IRS— certainly not anyone's idea of a good time.

There are three primary ways to bring an investor into your business without incurring the wrath of the SEC:

1. Bring them on as a partner
2. Treat the silent partner as a lender
3. Register your company with the SEC under "Regulation D offerings" to offer a security to your investor

Bringing On a Money Partner as a True Business Partner

Bringing on a money partner as a business partner has several pros and cons. First, you can avoid the SEC registration issue, and your partner can now share in the profits. It saves you extra legal work, and you may even get the help and advice of an excellent partner.

However, by bringing them on as a partner, you must involve them in voting and decision-making. The words *silent partner* should never escape your lips, and they should never be treated in that manner. The reasoning is this: By not treating them as a silent partner, they can't complain later that they didn't know what was going on or didn't have any say in the operations if the business fails.

Of course, the potential drawback in this situation is that you legitimately have to address their concerns on a regular basis. In fact, the documentation from the beginning of the relationship needs to reflect that they are a business partner. There isn't a loan or interest rate, and they have actual ownership in the underlying entity. In Chapter 22, I discuss how to document a partnership and the various issues to consider when doing so.

Treating Your Money Partner as a Lender

A lender relationship could be a great fit for you and your money partner. The positives include a fixed rate of return for your lender, which leaves them with much less risk in the venture. Moreover, if they are considered a lender, you don't have to listen to their complaints on how you run the business or follow through with their recommendations or advice. If you are looking for a silent partner and don't want to deal with the SEC, the lender classification may be the perfect fit. But, of course, they must be willing to live with a fixed rate of return.

As lenders, they cannot share in the profits of the business through some sort of percentage of ownership or back-door payment. This will drag you back into a potential SEC claim from them if you lose their money. They could also be unwittingly transformed into a partner (see "The Participating Note" sidebar on page 265), and now they are personally and vicariously liable for the operations of the business. They could even be targeted by your creditors if a creditor gets wind of your relationship.

Having a solid promissory note is great start. However, it really is just a start. A promissory note could still be considered a security under federal law. Nevertheless, the landmark 1990 U.S. Supreme Court case *Reves v. Ernst & Young* helped clarify the distinction between when a note is a security and when it is not. In that decision, the Court listed several categories of transactions that do not implicate federal securities laws. Among these categories are promissory notes "secured by a lien on a small business or some of its assets."

I often work with real estate investors who are looking to raise money to purchase, rehab, and flip residential real estate. When this kind of "fix & flip" business takes a loan from a silent partner, evidenced by a solid promissory note and secured with a first position deed of trust on the property being flipped, the note does not qualify as a security because it is "secured by a lien on a small business or some of its assets." This approach works best when the small business actually has some assets, such as real estate. Don't expect to avoid SEC scrutiny if you give a lender no more security on a loan than a lien on the assets of a business that, in reality, has few or no assets.

So follow this plan when documenting the lender's relationship: Use a promissory note and secure that note with a first position deed of trust on the real estate that is the subject of the deal, equipment in the business, the stock of the business, or a personal guarantee at the least. (A personal guarantee can set you up for personal liability issues, but it's typical in this situation and better than making the investor a partner.) Moreover, do not give the lender a piece of the profits or you risk creating a participating note, as discussed previously.

At a bare minimum, the promissory note and terms should include the following information:

1. The party making the loan and the party responsible to pay it back
2. The amount loaned and interest rate
3. How and when payments are to be made
4. Whether there is a penalty for repaying the loan early
5. The consequences of a default in the repayment of the loan

Documenting an Investor Deal with the SEC

While bringing on a lender can be a great option, some silent partners want more than just an interest rate return on their money. They want to share in the profits of the business without worrying about how to run the business; in other words, they want an equity position in the enterprise. This is our investor classification and needs to be documented as such.

A full-blown SEC-registered offering can cost hundreds of thousands, if not millions, of dollars in legal, accounting, and regulatory fees. However, there are several exemptions to the requirement to register a securities offering with the SEC. These exemptions are intended, as the SEC states, to "foster capital formation by lowering the cost of offering securities to the public."

The space in which small-business owners generally operate is called "Regulation D offerings." The good news is that the federal government passed, and the SEC implemented the "Jumpstart Our Business Startups" (JOBS) Act in 2012 and 2013, respectively. One key element of the JOBS Act was the elimination of the blanket prohibition on the general solicitation of Rule 506 under Regulation D offerings. Essentially, this change simplified the rules for raising capital to some degree and opened up more options for contacting potential investors.

These rules allow business owners to raise an unlimited amount of capital for their business and provide for public solicitation—so you can talk about the money you want to raise for your business anywhere you want, including online, and not just through personal networking and word-of-mouth. However, you need to meet the conditions that 1) all purchasers in the offering are accredited investors, and 2) the issuer takes reasonable steps to verify their accredited investor status.

Here is a short checklist for bringing on a silent partner as an investor:

- Consult with an experienced securities attorney to make sure a Regulation D offering makes sense and to choose the specific option that is best for you.
- Make sure your attorney files Form D with the SEC within the allotted time frame.
- Don't forget to make the necessary filings in each state where you will offer securities for sale.

The path of any Regulation D offering, particularly a Rule 506(c) offering, must be followed carefully to make sure that all parts and subparts of the rules and regulations are being satisfied. This is a path that a small-business owner would be foolish to follow without the guidance of an experienced and knowledgeable securities attorney. For this reason, bringing on a silent partner as an investor isn't cheap; expect to spend at least $15,000 in fees if you wish to raise capital in this manner.

The Crowdfunding Option

Crowdfunding is the newest method of raising capital for small businesses and startups, and many predict it will eventually be the primary method. In essence, crowdfunding relaxes the current securities law restrictions, which in years past, made it nearly impossible for a small business or budding entrepreneur to raise significant amounts of capital from others.

In crowdfunding, business owners are allowed to raise money with advertising and from a broader type of investor; however, they are limited on "how much" they can take from any one investor. This reduces the risk that someone could be taken advantage of and lose their life savings, but on the flip side, it provides a lot of options and flexibility for the business owner to raise capital.

Generally, there are four types of crowdfunding in the marketplace today:

1. *Rewards-based funding.* A business owner can offer a reward, a partial product, a service, or something typically related to the underlying business model as a benefit to the donor. With this strategy, the donor receives something but not ownership in the company. They are typically excited to be involved because of the product or the entrepreneur's story (something I'll discuss more below).

2. *Donation-based funding.* This type of crowdfunding offers the donor nothing in return except the satisfaction of helping the entrepreneur launch their business. Typically it is a little hard to persuade someone to just give you money out of the kindness of their heart, so your story should be truly compelling. Moreover, there is no deduction for the gift by the donor but no taxable income for the entrepreneur receiving the funds.

3. *Debt-based funding.* With this strategy, the donor is actually a lender and expects to be paid back. True, the terms are often generous, giving the entrepreneur ample time to launch their business and typically under much more favorable terms than a bank would offer. It seems to be easier to attract a "crowd" when they have an expectation of being paid back. Many experts have speculated that this could be one of the strongest crowdfunding models in years to come.

4. *Equity-based funding.* Finally, there is the option for a crowdfunding donor to receive actual equity and ownership in the company as an investor. This is where the SEC wants to define the rules to protect investors from scams and probably the most logical and typical for an investor to want a "piece" of the company in exchange for their investment.

Many small-business owners hear about crowdfunding and say, "Sign me up!" However, not all types of businesses are a good fit for crowdfunding. A service business is going to have a challenge, as is a business with a smaller vision or lack of scalability.

Moreover, experts emphasize that a successful crowdfunding project needs to have a great "story." Why are you doing this? What are you passionate about? How much do you need? What are your plans? Your story needs to be realistic, yet exciting and visionary. Most important, remember you are selling yourself almost more than your product or service. Meet with a crowdfunding consultant, and align yourself with the crowdfunding portal that fits your business model best. The consultant will also help you craft your story and produce compelling marketing pieces, including video, for your campaign.

Bottom line, if you think you have an idea that could benefit from crowdfunding, research the developing laws and industry. The crowd may love your idea, and nothing attracts business and sales like a crowd.

Game Plan Takeaway and Action Items

As I shared in the case study above, it is very easy to raise money from investors in the wrong way, creating criminal liability if things go south. Even if you do everything legally, you could still have investors chasing you down for years demanding their money back if you don't handle your fundraising properly. I took a call with two real estate developers as I was writing this and discussed with them the very principles in this chapter. It's a common concern that many business owners will face someday.

However, don't be discouraged when learning the rules regarding raising capital. Believe it or not, they are structured to protect you— the one raising the money—as much as the people providing the funds. If you know the rules, you can raise money for your business with confidence and not have to constantly worry about a lawsuit or criminal indictment.

- Review your business model and determine if raising capital will be good for your business.
- Understand the differences between investors, partners, and lenders.
- Create a viable pitch based on the type of investment and amount of money you are seeking.
- Meet with a securities or business attorney to assess your risk.
- Meet with a crowdfunding consultant if you are interested in pitching to the crowd.

PLANNING FOR THE NEXT SEASON

Successful coaches are constantly recruiting and looking to next year's season and the future roster. You must also take the time to look up from the hard work of your business and think about building wealth and cash flow for the future so you can have the financial freedom you are working so hard for.

24

RETIREMENT PLAN OPTIONS

—— CASE STUDY ——

John was having incredible success with his online marketing business. I knew he had been ignoring his tax and legal planning, and I was excited to meet and share some ideas.

After focusing on the basics of his business and tax situation—his S corp, payroll level, maximizing deductions, health care, and real estate ambitions—we were ready for the retirement plan deduction. As I suspected, he thought an IRA was his only option.

When I told him we could sock away close to $50,000 in a 401(k) and even consider a pension for putting away another six figures, he almost fell off his chair.

I further explained that he could self-direct his new 401(k), form an LLC or corporation, and shift future opportunities to or purchase unique investments in the new entity owned by his retirement plan. We talked about the tax savings and bringing a Roth into the mix, and we calculated future growth in the plan and long-term potential tax savings.

The energy and positive vibes in the room were palpable. Yes, he was still going to pay some taxes on his other income, but the opportunity to build tax-deferred wealth that was completely asset-protected absolutely blew him away.

Who says tax planning isn't exciting?

In the above case study, my client was ready to make significant contributions but didn't know how to proceed.

Regrettably, I meet with a lot of folks who have visions of grandeur and are excited to start a retirement plan, but don't have the discretionary income to do it. It sounds great, and they know they should start saving, but they need to get their house in order first.

Too many people get excited about what they *could* do with their retirement plan rather than get excited about what they *must* do to fund it. **Note: I discuss some of these habits in Chapter 1, and if you thought you were too smart for the first chapter and skipped ahead to these meatier chapters at the end, please go back and give it a read.**

With that said, once you are ready, there are four primary considerations in determining which retirement plan is best for any individual or family. They are:

1. How much can you deposit each month, quarter, or year?
2. What would be the tax impact of your decision—need a deduction now or not?
3. Do you want to "self-direct" your retirement plan? (See Chapter 25.)
4. Might you need to access the money before age 59½ for some reason?

Let's unpack some of these concepts a bit so you can create a section of your playbook that's all about saving for retirement.

Contribution Options

The first question I ask a client when meeting on this topic is how much they can and want to put away into a retirement plan. The issues of tax impact, self-directing, and withdrawal strategies are all secondary to this first important question.

An IRA could be a great fit for clients just starting out with retirement investing. However, for my clients whose businesses are doing well and can save more, there are other exciting options. To help illustrate your choices, I created a Tower (shown in Figure 24.1) to demonstrate how you can climb to greater heights of saving and building as your income grows, your ability to save increases, and your knowledge with investing blossoms.

At the bottom of the tower, I recommend most everyone start with at least a traditional IRA, even if you only save a few hundred dollars each month. The allowable yearly contribution to an IRA in 2019 is $6,000 ($7,000 if age 50 or over). As you have the ability to save more, you will graduate to a Roth IRA, and then if you need a deduction of

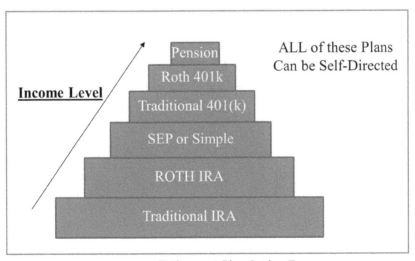

Figure 24.1 – **Retirement Plan Option Tower**

around $10,000, a SEP (for a limited time in your situation) may be a good fit based on your income and what you are trying to accomplish.

When you are willing and able to put away $15,000 or more, and possibly married, the power of the 401(k) is unsurpassed! In fact, the advent in recent years of the Solo 401(k) for the small-business owner is absolutely amazing. (I'll discuss this later in the chapter.)

For those who experience incredible financial success in their business and want to put away serious dollars, I'd first advise significant matching with a 401(k), adjusting salary levels, implementing profit sharing, possibly starting a pension plan, and exploring even more exotic and unique plans. I have had clients save $200,000 to $400,000 in deferred compensation plans annually. Many small-business owners are shocked at these numbers, thinking they can only save $6,000 to $10,000 at most in an IRA and perhaps $40,000 or more in a 401(k) each year. But the adage is true: The more money you make, the more you can save.

But remember, there is balance! I am not suggesting in any way, shape, or form that retirement plan funding, especially at significant levels, is more important than investing in real estate, building your business, or holding precious metals, just to name a few. Meet regularly with tax, legal, and financial professionals to create a well-balanced approach to the correct retirement plan, the funding amounts and investment strategy *within* the plan itself.

The Power of the Roth IRA and Roth 401(k)

Many individuals aim for the holy grail of retirement plans—the Roth structure, and they may be correct in that assumption. For those new to retirement planning, Roth accounts are initially funded with after-tax funds, meaning you pay tax on the money before it's deposited in the account. *Then* the funds grow tax-free and come out tax-free! Yes, there are sometimes contribution limits based on your situation, and you can only withdraw profit from the plan after five years or age 59^1/$_2$, whichever is longer. However, almost every financial model in existence shows that with the time value of money, the Roth will outperform the traditional IRA or 401(k) every time.

While a Roth IRA or Roth 401(k) costs more money to use initially because you must pay taxes on the contribution going in, rather than getting a tax deduction, it pays off significantly over time. If you can afford the initial cost of paying the taxes, I strongly encourage you to consider a Roth structure. (For those in higher income tax brackets facing contribution limits, I discuss a creative contribution strategy below.)

CONSIDERING TAX IMPLICATIONS

This is actually the easiest part of choosing the proper retirement plan. It's completely objective. Run the numbers! Do you get a tax deduction with the plan (e.g., a traditional plan), or do you pay tax first (e.g., a Roth)? How much is the deduction or the tax? Compare your options and recognize that these decisions may change from year to year as your income varies. The beauty of the new Solo 401(k) platform is that you can have both traditional and Roth accounts within the same plan and make contributions to both or either account from one year to the next depending on your taxable income and situation.

IRA vs. 401(k)

One question you might ask yourself is, "Will I need to access my retirement funds before age 59½ for some reason?" This is where things get very interesting, and we start to see the stark differences between an IRA and a 401(k). In Figure 24.2 on page 282, I highlight these differences. (This does not include the Roth plan; it operates under a slightly different set of rules.)

60-Day Rollover

This provision is unique to IRAs. It allows you to withdraw money for 60 days, use it for any purpose you like, keep and pay taxes on the profit (if you make money with the withdrawal), return the original withdrawal amount before the 60 days is up, and avoid any penalty or tax for the withdrawal.

IRA	401(k)
60-day roll over and use of cash	No 60-day rollover
72t distributions before 59 ½	No 72t Distribution
Borrowing not allowed	Can borrow up to 50k or 50% of the value
Both UDFI & UBTI apply	No UDFI when investing
Smaller contributions	Much larger contributions

Figure 24.2 – **IRA vs. 401(k)**

Strategy: Some investors will move some money out of a 401(k) to an IRA and use the 60-day rollover provision to access cash quickly for an investment or other project. This method is not allowed under a 401(k).

72t Distributions

Once your money has been rolled from a 401(k) to an IRA, or if the money originated in the IRA, you can make a special election/calculation based on your age and the value of the account to take regular distributions before you are 59½. The distributions need to continue at least five years or until you are 59½, whichever is longer.

Strategy: As you earn money in your 401(k), roll certain amounts to an IRA and make 72t distributions to avoid penalties while accessing your retirement funds well before retirement age.

401(k) Loans

First, this strategy isn't just for those with an employer who offers a 401(k). Many people don't realize how affordable and easy it is to set up their own 401(k) in their business. This is sometimes referred to as a Solo 401(k), and I discuss it more below. It comes in handy with this strategy: You can borrow up to 50 percent of your 401(k) or $50,000, whichever is less, and then use the funds for business or personal use with no strings attached. You cannot do this with an IRA. The loan term is typically more than five years; if you can't pay back the loan in that time, it is deemed an early distribution from the 401(k) that may be subject to penalties and/or taxes.

Strategy: Form a 401(k) in your small business, roll your IRA funds into the 401(k), lend them back to your business or to another entity for a business venture, and pay the tax-deductible interest back to your 401(k), which will receive this interest tax-free!

Contribution Levels

Consider the varying levels of company contributions that can be made with a 401(k) vs. an IRA. The "matching," as it is sometimes called, will be based on your payroll level, but it can significantly increase the amount you contribute.

Strategy: Consider a profit-sharing plan with your 401(k) to store away even more. If you have other employees, consider safe-harbor and "cliff" provisions, which allow you to increase contributions to your own account over time without having to put away as much for your employees.

Non-Recourse Loans

As I discuss in detail in Chapter 25, a retirement plan can borrow on its own to invest. This isn't a situation where you are borrowing from your IRA or 401(k); rather, your retirement plan actually applies for its own loan (called a non-recourse loan) to buy bigger and better assets, like cash-flow-producing real estate. This is great because many retirement plan owners feel limited on what they can creatively purchase because they don't have enough funds in their plan. Be aware that there is an unrelated debt-financed income (UDFI) tax on IRAs but not on 401(k)s.

Strategy: If you are going to leverage your IRA for a real estate deal, think twice and roll the money into a 401(k) first. Then borrow away and avoid any UDFI tax. Both types of retirement accounts can use non-recourse loans, but a 401(k) doesn't pay UDFI tax.

Small-Business Solo 401(k) Plan

A properly structured S corp is used best when business owners also build and contribute to a 401(k) plan. Years ago, the cost of setting up and maintaining a 401(k) was prohibitive for a single business owner. But in recent years, the benefits and flexibility of the Solo 401(k) have become astounding. A business owner can not only employ themselves and contribute to a 401(k), but they can also include their spouse or other family members in the plan.

As usual, there are a few rules to be aware of, but it is quite straightforward and easy to understand. Here are a few provisions related to the Solo 401(k) you should keep in mind as you interview professionals to help you implement your own plan.

- *Only W-2 salary income can be contributed to a 401(k).* You cannot make 401(k) contributions from your rental income, invest-ments, dividends, or net profit income that comes from your K-1. Thus, your salary level in your S corp is absolutely critical in this analysis. While many S corp owners seek to minimize their W-2 salary for self-employment tax purposes, you must also carefully consider your annual planned 401(k) contribu-tions. In other words, if you cut your salary too low, you won't be able to contribute the maximum amount to your 401(k). On the other hand, in order to make a large contribution to the 401(k), you may need to take an unnecessarily high W-2 salary from the S corp, This may not make sense for SE tax planning. There is a sweet spot and balance to this planning! Nevertheless, you'll still be able to make *excellent* annual contri-butions compared to that of an IRA.
- *Elective salary deferral limit.* In 2019, the deferral limit is $19,000 or 100 percent of your W-2, whichever is less. Thus, if you have at least $21,000 (approximately) of payroll income from the S corp, after FICA withholdings, you can contribute $19,000 to

your 401(k) account. If you are 50 or older, you can make an additional $6,000 annual contribution if you increase your payroll.

- *Putting your spouse on payroll.* As I mentioned earlier, many small-business owners can essentially double their contributions to the 401(k) by putting their spouse on the payroll as an employee, board member, or co-owner, knowing all of the money is staying in the family, so to speak. In 2019, a spouse's salary could be adjusted to put away a $19,000 ($25,000 if age 50 or over) elective deferral, and then an additional company match would be 25 percent of the salary. This could add up to a total contribution of approximately $30,000 with only a payroll of approximately $21,000)—something unheard of in an IRA!
- *The "match."* As mentioned above, another benefit of the 401(k) is the nonelective deferral of 25 percent of the payroll, otherwise referred to as the company match. Combined with the payroll deferral, in the example above, the total contribution in 2019 on approximately $21,000 of payroll would be $24,000 ($19,000 + $5000 and add another $6,000 if age 50 or over). In fact, depending on the payroll level, the total contribution with matching can now be as high as $56,000. Remember, if you make Roth contributions, you don't get a tax deduction because you pay the tax on the deferral amount as it's contributed. However, the company match will be deductible.

Now, here is the rub. Don't get fixated on contributing the maximum amount of $56,000. Based on the contribution equations, in order to contribute the maximum of $56,000, you need a W-2 salary from the S corp of $148,000. Also, keep in mind that if you have employees other than yourself or your spouse, you are required to implement an approved "matching" program of some sort.

Bottom line, maximizing the 401(k) is often difficult or impractical to accomplish with additional employees. Consequently, the 25-percent match deferral is best used in owner-only 401(k) plans unless you use safe-harbor plans or cliff provisions to minimize how much you may be required to contribute on behalf of your employees. Whenever you have multiple employees, it's critical to get opinions from several experts on multi-employer plans to build the best plan for your business.

The "Back Door" Roth IRA

There are two strategies that have arisen in recent years due to the income limitations on making contributions to Roth IRAs. It's no secret that the power of a Roth IRA cannot be matched over time, and even high-income earners want to take advantage of this option. Thus, I often advise clients on creative ways to use a Roth IRA.

The first is to use a Roth 401(k). As I mentioned above, you may want to contribute to a Roth IRA and are willing to pay the tax, but your income level won't allow you to make a contribution. However, if you have a business, you can avoid these income limitations by creating a Roth 401(k), which is typically part of every 401(k) established today. This will allow you to use the Roth strategy because you own a business—even though you have a higher personal income level.

The second strategy involves making nondeductible contributions to a traditional IRA and then converting those funds to a Roth IRA. In the end, you don't get a tax deduction on the amounts contributed, but the funds are held in a Roth IRA and are released tax-free upon retirement just like a typical Roth IRA.

If you can't start a Roth 401(k), here's how the "back door" Roth IRA works:

1. *Fund a new nondeductible traditional IRA.* This IRA is nondeductible because high-income earners who participate in a company retirement plan (or have a spouse who does) can't also make deductible contributions to an IRA. The account can, however, be funded by nondeductible amounts up to the IRA annual contribution amounts of $6,000 ($7,000 if age 50 or older). You will not get a tax deduction on the amounts contributed to the traditional IRA.

2. *Roll over funds from an old 401(k) from a previous job to an IRA.* A faster way to expedite this process is to transfer monies from a

401(k) instead and then ramp up the IRA value through a roll-over.

3. *Convert the nondeductible, traditional IRA to a Roth IRA.* In 2010, the limitations on Roth IRA conversions, which previously restricted Roth IRA conversions for high-income earners, were removed. As a result, all taxpayers can now convert traditional IRA funds to Roth IRAs.

This back door Roth IRA contribution strategy was first used in 2010, as it relied on the then-newfound ability to convert funds from traditional to Roth. It has been used by thousands of Americans ever since and is still alive and well today.

While I have presented the steps in a simple manner above, there are a number of issues to address before and when undertaking this strategy. But now you have an extra tool in your toolbox that you should at least consider using. The bottom line is that Roth IRAs can be established and funded by high-income earners. Don't find yourself left out of one of the greatest tax strategies offered to Americans.

How Do I Set Up a Roth IRA for My Kids?

Many don't realize how simple and easy it can be to establish Roth IRAs for their children. Some use them to coinvest those funds with their own Roth IRAs into real estate deals or startup companies. Some open brokerage accounts and teach their kids how to buy and sell stocks. Whatever your investment strategy, don't leave your kids out. Consider a Roth IRA a valuable tool for teaching your kids or grandkids how to invest and save for their college educations.

The only requirement for establishing a Roth IRA is that the account owner is at least 18 years old and has earned income. You may open a Roth IRA for your child under 18 as a custodial IRA. When the child reaches 18, he or she will take over as the responsible party for the account. If your child works in your business, on your rental properties or real estate investments, or even if they have a part-time or summer job, pay them some income so they can establish a Roth

IRA. Their earned income can then be contributed to the annual Roth IRA in 2019 at the current limit of $6,000 ($7,000 if 50 or older). (See Chapter 12 for a thorough discussion on the strategy of hiring family members.)

In all instances, the amounts contributed to a Roth IRA can be withdrawn penalty-free and tax-free. Earnings may be distributed penalty-free for the qualified higher education expenses of the child, though the earnings withdrawn can be subject to tax.

Can I Self-Direct my Retirement Plan?

Yes! You can self-direct any type of tax-deferred vehicle such as a 401(k), IRA, Roth IRA or 401(k), SEP, SIMPLE, Coverdell IRA (college IRA), or even an HSA (health savings account). This shocks the vast majority of my new clients. See Chapter 25 for some general options and strategies when it comes to self-directing.

The beauty of self-directing is that you can choose what you put into your retirement plan. Remember, a retirement plan is simply a vehicle—what you put in the car with you on your journey to retirement bliss is up to you! Invest in what you know best, not what your financial advisor knows best. They are the navigator, not the driver of the vehicle. Listen to their advice carefully, and then make the best decision without their outside pressure or undue influence.

Figure 24.3 on page 289 highlights this concept of putting what *you* want in your vehicle.

Game Plan Takeaway and Action Items

As I mentioned from the outset of this book, one of the key characteristics of my financially independent and wealthy clients is that they maintain a tax-deferred or tax-free retirement account. They all understand the importance of being well-diversified, and they find a balance between real estate and marketable securities based on their knowledge, life experiences, and risk tolerance. Many self-direct their retirement accounts. And they all contribute to their retirement accounts annually and have cultivated a lifetime habit of saving.

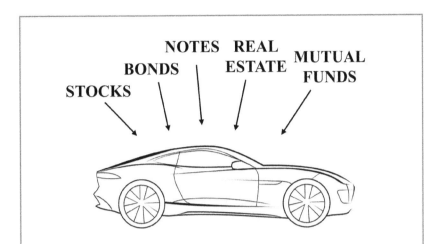

Figure 24.3 – **Retirement Vehicle**

- Determine how much you can save on a monthly, quarterly, or annual basis.
- Decide if you need a tax write-off or can afford to pay the taxes and use a Roth IRA or 401(k).
- Consider self-directing and make sure your plan offers such an option.
- If you can and want to contribute more than $10,000 a year, run the numbers on other types of plans rather than a basic IRA.

SELF-DIRECTING YOUR RETIREMENT FUNDS

— CASE STUDY —

During the 2012 presidential campaign, *The Wall Street Journal* reported that former Massachusetts governor and presidential candidate Mitt Romney had an IRA valued between $20 million and $100 million.

The article speculated about how those earnings were made and eventually concluded that, because there is no way he could have such significant returns in mutual funds or typical stock or bonds, he must have invested in companies he was consulting and working with while running his private equity firm, Bain Capital.

In other words, he "self-directed" his retirement account into investments with small companies that he knew.

Wall Street investment firms like Merrill Lynch must have cringed to have this become a point of public discussion. Never would a financial planner suggest self-directing or having their clients put their investment funds in a place where the planner wouldn't receive a commission on the investment. A Romney campaign aide who was questioned about Romney's investments and tax treatment said that ". . . it's the same for Governor Romney as it is for every citizen of the U.S."

This is true. Don't feel trapped into investing your IRA or other retirement plan into one of the menu options you get from your account custodian. There are other choices.

There are two important lessons to learn from Mitt Romney's $20 million IRA. First, you don't have to settle for a select group of mutual funds when investing your retirement plan. You can self-direct your IRA into all kinds of legal investments, including small companies such as Romney did. Other popular self-directed options are real estate, loans, or precious metals. You should seek to place your retirement account with a self-directed retirement plan custodian that will allow you to invest in any option allowed by law.

The second lesson to learn is that Romney found success with his IRA account by investing in what he knew best. Many of our clients express frustration about their retirement plans because the funds are invested in unfamiliar mutual funds, bonds, or stocks. They have no idea how the investments will turn out, and they don't have the skill or insight that would give them an advantage in their investments. However, many who self-direct their retirement plans have found success in investing in the options they understand, from real estate or a small startup company to building a unique and diverse investment portfolio.

Self-Directed IRA Basics

A self-directed IRA is an IRA (Roth, Traditional, SEP, Inherited IRA, SIMPLE) where the custodian of the account allows the IRA to invest into any investment allowed by law. These investments typically include real estate, promissory notes, precious metals, and private company stock. The usual reaction I hear from investors is, "Why haven't I ever heard of self-directed IRAs before, and why can I only invest my current retirement plan into mutual funds or stocks?" The reason is that the large financial institutions that manage most U.S. retirement accounts don't find it administratively feasible to hold real estate or publicly traded assets in retirement plans.

When instructing clients about self-directing, I always suggest they use the concept of "opportunity shifting." That is, avoid doing every deal in your own name, and every once in a while, shift an opportunity to your retirement account. Let your IRA, for example,

---

GOOD TO KNOW:
SELF-DIRECTING A 401(k)

You can also self-direct a 401(k). In Chapter 24, I discuss the considerations and options for choosing the best retirement plan based on your situation. Whichever tax-deferred vehicle you use, they can all be self-directed.

With a 401(k), you typically adopt a plan document under the umbrella of an entity, such as an S corp, and serve as the trustee of the plan. The plan has its own bank account and is allowed to invest in all the same types of investments as a self-directed IRA and under the same prohibited transaction rules.

The beauty of the 401(k) is that you can make larger contributions than you can to an IRA, borrow from the plan within limits, and use leverage within the 401(k) for projects while avoiding the dreaded unrelated debt-financed income (UDFI) tax that applies to IRAs.

---

do the deal and potentially defer the taxes or avoid them altogether if you have a Roth IRA or 401(k).

Self-Directed IRA Investment Choices

The most popular self-directed retirement account investments include rental real estate, secured real estate loans to others, small-business stock or LLC interest, and precious metals such as gold or silver. These investments are all allowed by law and can be great choices for investors with experience in these areas.

Under current law, a retirement account is only restricted from investing in the following:

- Collectibles such as art, stamps, coins, alcoholic beverages, or antiques
- Life insurance
- S corp stock
- Any investment that constitutes a prohibited transaction (discussed below)
- Any investment not allowed under federal law (e.g., a marijuana dispensary)

Avoiding Prohibited Transactions

When self-directing your retirement account, you must be aware of the prohibited transaction rules found in Internal Revenue Code 4975 and the Employee Retirement Income Security Act. These rules don't restrict what your account can invest in but rather whom your IRA may transact with. In short, the prohibited transaction rules restrict your retirement account from engaging in a transaction with a disqualified person.

The rationale behind the prohibited transaction rules is that the federal government doesn't want tax-advantaged accounts conducting transactions with parties who are close enough to the account owner that they could be designed to avoid or unfairly minimize tax by altering the true fair market value or price of the investment.

Disqualified persons include the account owner, his or her spouse, children, parents, and certain business partners. So, for example, your retirement account could not buy a rental property that is owned by your father.

The IRA must hold the property strictly for investment. The property may be leased to your cousin, friend, sister, or a random unrelated third party, but it cannot be leased or used by the IRA owner or the aforementioned prohibited family members or business partners. Only after the property has been distributed from the retirement account to the IRA owner may the owner or family members reside at or benefit from the property.

The IRA/LLC Structure

In a typical self-directed IRA investment, your IRA custodian holds your investment in their company name for your IRA's benefit (e.g., property is owned as ABC Trust Company FBO John Smith IRA), receives the income, and pays the expenses for the investment at the account owner's direction and instruction.

Many self-directed retirement account owners, particularly those buying real estate, use an IRA/limited liability company (LLC) as the vehicle to hold their retirement account assets. An IRA/LLC is a special type of LLC, which consists of an IRA (or other retirement account) investing its cash into a newly created LLC. The IRA/LLC can be managed by the IRA owner, who then directs the LLC; the LLC takes title to the assets, pays the expenses to the investment, and receives the income from the investment.

There are several restrictions to the IRA owner also being the manager, such as not receiving compensation or personal benefit from the IRA/LLC. However, the ability to control the LLC and its investments, the ability to make decisions, and the money saved by not needing a custodian may outweigh the restrictions of being your IRA's manager. There are many laws, as well as pros and cons, to consider, so please be sure to consult an attorney before establishing an IRA/LLC. Figure 25.1 on page 296 shows what an IRA/LLC structure may look like.

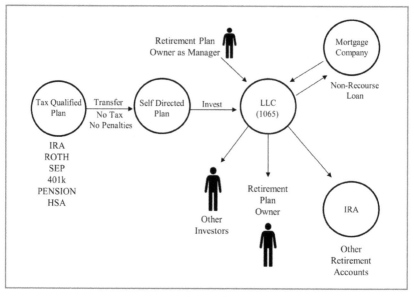

Figure 25.1 – **The IRA/LLC Structure**

Buying a Future Retirement Home with Your IRA

You can actually buy a future retirement home with your IRA, but you need to understand the rules and drawbacks before doing so. The strategy essentially works in two phases. First, the IRA purchases the property and owns it as an investment until the IRA owner decides to retire. Second, upon retirement of the IRA owner after age 59½, the owner distributes the property from the IRA to himself. Then he takes ownership of the property and may now use it and benefit from it personally.

Before proceeding down this path, you should consider a few key issues:

1. The property must be distributed from the IRA to the IRA owner before the owner or his family may use the property personally.
2. Distribution of the property from the IRA to the owner is called an in-kind distribution and results in taxes due for traditional IRAs.
3. For traditional IRAs, the custodian of the IRA will require a professional appraisal of the property before allowing it to be

distributed to the owner. The fair-market value of the property is then used to set the value of the distribution.

Because the tax burden upon distribution can be significant, this strategy is not without its drawbacks. Some owners will instead take partial distributions of the property over time, holding a portion of the property personally and a portion still in the IRA to spread out the tax consequences. However, if you can pull this off in a Roth IRA, you can distribute the retirement home to yourself tax-free when you are 59½ or have had the Roth for five years, whichever is longer.

UDFI and UBIT Taxes

There are two types of taxes that can blindside a self-directed IRA investor. It's important that an IRA investor enter their investment projects with their eyes wide open and evaluate if these taxes might impact them.

The first is called unrelated business income tax (UBIT). This tax doesn't apply to IRAs with passive investments like rental real estate or capital gains or on dividend profits from a C corp (i.e., what you get from publicly traded stock owned by your IRA), as those types of income are specifically exempt from UBIT tax. However, anything that creates ordinary income will trigger the tax—and it's serious. The UBIT tax rate could be as high as 37 percent. Not an insurmountable issue or deal breaker, but certainly needs to be calculated and considered.

A few examples of businesses that create UBIT are ones selling goods or services or a real estate project doing a development or rehabbing more than three properties a year. Being subject to UBIT tax isn't the end of the world, and there are some structuring options to minimize the tax, such as a C corp "blocker company," which can cut the tax rate in half in many instances. The new tax rate for corporations is 21 percent and would be the maximum tax rate your retirement plan would pay in this type of structure.

The second tax is the unrelated debt-financed income (UDFI) tax. This tax only applies if there is acquisition debt on the sale of the asset held by the IRA. It's the same rate as UBIT, but it only applies on the debt ratio of the asset. For example, if you sell a property worth $100,000 and the debt remaining on the property is $70,000, then the debt-to-equity ratio is 70 percent. Next, calculate the amount of profit on the property. Assume you purchased the property for $60,000 and the adjusted basis is $50,000. Your profit would be $50,000, and 70 percent of that profit would be subject to UDFI. That's $35,000 taxed under the UBIT tax table and paid on a Form 990-T.

The primary strategy to avoid UDFI is to move your assets from a self-directed IRA to a self-directed 401(k). UDFI does not apply to a 401(k).

Bottom line, if you are wanting to "do business" in your IRA or 401(k) (think service business, product sales, or manufacturing or development), you need to consider UBIT tax. It's ok to do this type of business in an IRA or 401(k), but it takes additional planning and strategy.

My partner at KKOS Lawyers, Mat Sorensen, has written *The Self-Directed IRA Handbook (now in its second edition, released in 2018)*, the most comprehensive and easy-to-understand book on the complex topic of UBIT as well as all the basics. Please refer to it for more information and education on self-directed IRAs. You can also visit his content packed website at www.sdirahandbook.com.

Asset Protection for Self-Directed IRAs

When analyzing asset protection for self-directed IRAs, we must consider two types of potential threats: first, a creditor from outside the IRA (like a creditor coming after you personally and wanting to collect against your IRA), and second, claims inside your IRA that could arise due to the operations of the business or the assets held by the IRA (like a tenant suing the IRA that owns the rental property).

- *Outside Liability.* Most IRA owners know that their IRA is generally protected from their personal creditors. Various federal and state laws provide protection that prohibits a creditor from collecting or seizing the assets of an IRA or other retirement plan. For example, if an individual personally defaults on a loan in their name and then gets a judgment against them, the creditor may collect against the individual's personal bank accounts and wages, but not their IRA. Even in the case of bankruptcy, a retirement plan is considered exempt from creditors. Because of these asset protection benefits, retirement plans are excellent places to hold assets.

- *Inside Liability.* This is the situation that shocks most IRA owners and is particularly important to self-directed IRA accounts because many hold businesses or assets that can create liability. Protections preventing a creditor of the IRA owner from seizing IRA assets *will not* apply if the liability arose *inside* the IRA. It's not your liability; it's the IRA's liability. Moreover, there have been many cases where creditors came after IRA owners as the directors of the IRA, which means you may have personal liability by directing the investment. For example, if a self-directed IRA owns a rental property and the tenant in that property slips and falls, the tenant can sue the self-directed IRA and the IRA owner who owned and leased the property to the tenant. Since the IRA is a revocable trust, each investment is in fact controlled by the IRA owner, as he could terminate the IRA at any time and take ownership in his personal name. You can read more about inside liability in Chapter 8.

The best solution to avoid personal liability when self-directing your IRA is to use an IRA/LLC, as I discussed previously, where you are the manager of the LLC and thus protected under its corporate veil.

Game Plan Takeaway and Action Items

Now, is self-directing for everyone? Absolutely not. If you listen to Jim Cramer on *Mad Money*, he will tell everyone that they are crazy to self-direct. However, this is the typical Wall Street approach to this topic: "Let *us* invest your money. We know best—not you!"

If you believe your financial advisor is more knowledgeable than you and/or you don't have the time to get more engaged in your retirement plan investments, then certainly stay away from self-directing. However, if you want more freedom and feel you have some great ideas on how your IRA could be making more money, then look into self-directing.

Bottom line: You have to be more engaged in your retirement planning. You know this. You probably feel guilty about it, and it's time you do something about it. Study more and get engaged, and whether you decide to self-direct or stay with your financial advisor, you will be informed—and pleasantly surprised by your many options and the potential you have to succeed in this area.

- Review the financial returns of your retirement account.
- Change the investments in your retirement account to what you know best.
- Consider an IRA/LLC structure for asset protection and management ease.
- Determine if your investments would be subject to UDFI/UBIT taxes and plan accordingly.
- There are many laws to consider when self-directing, so please be sure to consult an attorney before establishing an IRA/LLC.
- Consider rolling over old IRA or 401(k) money or opening a new account for your IRA, HSA, or Coverdell IRA at www.directedira.com.

FAMILY TRUSTS AND ESTATE PLANNING

---- CASE STUDY ----

I received the following email from one of my clients, and I share it here with their permission:

"My grandfather was very concerned about any of his wealth being lost to taxes and his kids having to deal with the probate process, so he planned ahead and consulted with an attorney to create a trust to pass his assets down to his children.

"Unfortunately, he waited until much later in life to establish the trust and did not fund the trust when he established it. He thought there would be plenty of time to do that 'later,' and didn't share some of the important details with the family.

"Shortly after it was established, he became very ill and entered the hospital. By the time he got out, he was not very coherent and had completely forgotten to put any assets into the trust. It wasn't until after he passed away that his attorney and our family discovered what had happened.

"He had a trust, but it was completely empty! This ended up causing some conflicts within the family concerning the inheritance of the business, which was settled by everyone's 'best guess' as to what he would have wanted.

"He was able to transfer some of his wealth down the generations via other means, such as buying fully funded whole-life insurance policies for all his grandchildren, but the whole purpose of creating the trust did not work out in the end."

Estate planning doesn't have to end this way. This is a classic story of having the best of intentions, yet leaving a mess to the family, which can end in fights, lawsuits, and probate court.

Millions of Americans die each year without any type of estate plan in place, and this forces their families into the court system, where they experience the high cost and time delay characteristic of probate proceedings. In fact, more than 50 percent of Americans don't even have a will or any type of estate plan. With that said, does everybody need to be scared into a revocable living trust (RLT)? Certainly not!

Here is the truth: Not everybody needs an RLT. A simple will may be all some of us need to plan for our estate upon our demise.

There are three main reasons to implement an RLT:

1. You have provisions you may want to implement for minor children or children that act like minors and have special needs for managing their finances.

2. You wish for your family to avoid probate because you own a personal residence, business, or rental properties.

3. You wish to minimize estate tax with a marital bypass trust.

A quality estate plan typically includes an RLT as well as a number of ancillary documents such as a will, powers of attorney for finances and health care, an advance medical directive or living will, burial instructions, a directive for organ donation, final instructions, etc. In this chapter, we'll cover the basic plays you need to know to plan your estate.

Avoiding Probate with a Revocable Living Trust

One of the key reasons for using an RLT is to avoid probate, which means avoiding attorneys, judges, courts, and the state sticking their noses into family affairs. Probate is essentially the court's process of determining if the will is valid and then executing its provisions. If there isn't a will, then the court distributes the assets according to state law.

In addition to helping your family avoid probate, the RLT becomes the instruction manual for how the estate is to be distributed among the beneficiaries. The process is administered by the trustee you appoint and avoids a tremendous amount of wasted time and money spent going through court.

In order to make sure the trust does its job, it needs to be funded by holding title to four main assets:

1. Real estate (typically your personal residence)
2. Entities (such as corporations and LLCs for rentals)
3. Investment accounts (including retirement accounts with see-through provisions)
4. Life insurance (so that minor children receive it constructively)

Figure 26.1 on page 304 shows an example of a typical family trust structure.

Estate Tax and the A-B Trust Strategy

In the late hours of December 31, 2012, lawmakers in Washington, DC passed the American Taxpayer Relief Act of 2012. Under the

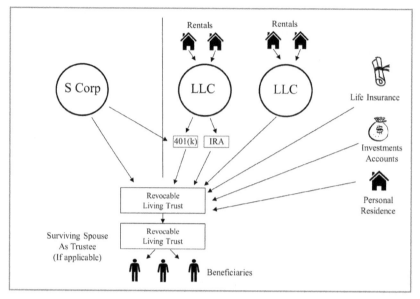

Figure 26.1 – **Estate Planning Diagram**

"fiscal cliff legislation," as it came to be known, the estate and gift tax exemption was set at $5 million. This means that the first $5 million of an individual's estate may be inherited (at death) or gifted (during life) before any estate or gift tax is due. This exemption amount is adjusted each year for inflation. Now in 2019, the estate and gift tax exemption is $11.4 million per individual. This means that an individual can leave $11.4 million to their beneficiaries and pay no federal estate or gift tax, while a married couple under an A-B (bypass) trust structure will be able to shield $22.8 million.

As mentioned above, with a marital bypass trust, often referred to as an A-B Trust, a married couple can take advantage of both personal exemptions and thus double how much they can leave to their family without estate tax. This is a special trust that creates two subsequent trusts upon the death of the first spouse, and thereby doubles the estate tax exemption. Obviously this is a very complex aspect of estate planning and is typically only undertaken when a family's net worth is more than $11 to $12 million in 2019.

Don't Gift Property with a Low Tax Basis

When you gift property during your lifetime, the tax basis in the asset transfers to the person who receives the gift. In other words, if you have a property you bought for $100,000 that is now worth $300,000, the person receiving the gift would get your $100,000 tax basis so that when they sell the property, they pay capital gains taxes on anything above $100,000. When someone inherits property upon death, however, they receive tax basis in the property at the fair market value at the date of death. So if the basis to the owner was $100,000, but the fair market value was $300,000 at their death, the heir would get the property at a $300,000 tax basis. When they later sell the property, they will only pay taxes on any gain above $300,000—as opposed to $100,000 if the gift had been made during the lifetime of the donor. Make sure these types of properties are transferred to the trust and inherited by the family, not gifted to them during life.

CRITICAL ALERT!
TOP THREE MISTAKES IN DIY ESTATE PLANS

Families can easily and affordably prepare basic estate planning documents online these days. However, this increase in affordability and convenience found on the web has created a false sense of security and inadequate planning that has caused disasters for many families. Many do-it-yourself estate plans fail to provide the benefits and protections that are included in a well-drafted and carefully planned estate.

Below are the top three mistakes I've seen made by individuals who have completed their estate plan on their own. Two of the mistakes listed below are based on actual clients who hired our firm to represent them in a lawsuit with other heirs in probate court due to the fact that their parents made the drastic error of completing their estate plan on their own.

CRITICAL ALERT!, CONTINUED

1. *Improper signatures and witnesses for wills.* Most states require the signature of the person creating the will as well as two witnesses to the will. The only exception to the two-witness requirement in most states is a holographic will, which is a handwritten will with the signature of the person creating the will. No matter how good it looks or how many terms are included, failure to adhere to the signature and witness requirements invalidates the entire will.

2. *Failure to fund the trust.* Most individuals who create an RLT on their own fail to actually fund it with the assets from their trust. Funding a trust means that you put the assets you want to be controlled by the trust in the name of the trust. For example, if you want your home to be subject to the terms in your trust, then you need to deed the home out of your personal name and into the name of the trust. If the property is not deeded into the trust, it falls outside the trust terms, and your heirs will need to go to probate court to get a judge to approve any transfers of title following your death.

3. *General do-it-yourself forms may not address your unique situation.* Most families have at least one situation unique to their estate that is typically not covered by standardized documents found on the web. For example, you might have a child who is financially irresponsible, but the rest of your children are not. Do you know how to use prepackaged forms to create an adequate plan that considers the financially troubled child while not adversely affecting the inheritance of your other children? Or maybe you have an estate that has more debt than assets. Do you know how to plan the estate to leave the most to your family and the least to your creditors? The list could go on and on. My point is that the unique situations that arise are rarely handled properly when you're doing your estate plan on your own.

Creative Provisions for Children

Many parents and even grandparents don't realize how creative they can be in distributing their assets upon their passing. I realize that some folks believe it's immoral to control their children or family with money after their passing, but others feel they have a duty to leave their hard-earned assets in a constructive manner for their descendants' posterity. Whatever your position may be on the degree of control you want to exercise from the grave, here are a few options to consider:

- Require your trustee to hold children's inheritance in trust until they reach the age of 25, 30, or 35. Give it to them in stages, e.g., a third at age 25, a third at age 30, and the final third at age 35.
- Use a joint trust for minor children until the oldest reaches age 18. Then split up the trust into individual trusts for each child. This makes it easier for the trustee to manage the trust while the children are minors. Then when different children pursue business, education, marriage, or even world travel, their trust is accounted for separately from the others.
- Consider having the trustee give the guardian of your children a specific amount each month to take care of the living costs of your minor children (room, board, clothing, school supplies, etc.). It could be something like $1,000 a month, adjusted for inflation as of the date of your trust.
- Place restrictions on inheritance if there is drug or alcohol abuse. An attorney can insert a provision that prevents a distribution to any child with an abuse problem and allow for the trustee to hold their funds in the trust until they have their life under control.
- Give the inheritance in matching funds, distributing $1 for every $1 the child earns.
- Give them a bonus for graduating from certain levels of college or do not allow full distribution until they obtain a certain level of higher education. However, still distribute funds for school or any secondary education program, skills training course, etc.

- Distribute funds for education. Or use their GPA as a "carrot." In other words, distribute funds only if children maintain a minimum GPA that you set. You could also tie funds for tuition or books to GPA to help keep the children focused on finishing school, rather than becoming career students.
- Distribute a certain amount of funds for a wedding.
- Distribute funds for church service, volunteering for the Peace Corps, or joining the military for a certain number of years.
- Distribute funds to start a business upon the presentation of an acceptable business plan to the trustee. Name a board of advisors to approve any small business or investments by the children.

Disinheriting a Child

Perhaps you have a child whom you'd like to disinherit from your estate. If so, don't just leave their name out of the will and think this will accomplish your goals as the laws in most states will presume you intended to have them inherit unless you specifically state otherwise. Following your spouse, your children are the presumed heirs to your estate by law in the absence of an estate plan. As a result, it is important to include a complete list of your children in the estate plan and to specifically mention any child who will not be an heir by stating something like, "It is the intention of the settlor [you] to disinherit the following child from the estate." It's that simple: just clearly indicate in writing that you specifically intend them not to inherit your estate, and they're out.

Don't Forget Fido: Pets in Your Estate Plan

It's absolutely crucial to consider your loved ones in your estate planning, and that loved one can extend to your pets as well. What will happen to your "best friend" if you pass away? Someone has to care for them, and that's why remembering them in your Will or Trust is vital. In fact, the Revocable Living Trust is a perfect place to have a plan for your pet: the one that loves you unconditionally and doesn't ask for money.

Believe it or not, every year thousands of pets are euthanized when the pet owner dies and no one wants to be the guardian of the pet. The reality is, however, if someone was designated in advance *and* given a financial incentive to take care of the pet, this disaster could be avoided.

We ask every client during the estate plan drafting process if they own a pet and have a section to deal with such matters. There are some important questions you need to have answers for when you are ready to sit down with your legal team and draft a provision for your pet. You will need to identify:

- Who will be the guardian of the pet?
- Will they receive any compensation for performing this service?
- Who will be the "back up" in case the primary caregiver isn't able to continue?
- Where do you want your animal buried?
- Have you set aside funds for someone to care for your pet and, ultimately, to pay for costs associated with their death?

These are all important and sensitive topics for a loving pet or animal owner and should address these issues in their revocable living trust.

The Living Will/Health-Care Directive

A living will is a legal document that can be used to make decisions as to whether you want to be on life-sustaining support or whether you want to pull the plug if you are brain dead or in a persistent vegetative state.

Dealing with the death of a spouse or other close family member is one of the most difficult situations a person will face. However, that experience is made even more difficult when family members must make life-ending decisions for their loved ones. A well-drafted estate plan includes a living will, aka a health-care directive, whereby a person makes a legal decision for themselves about whether they want to be placed on life-sustaining support or whether they want to be removed from the support if they are brain dead or in a persistent vegetative state.

CRITICAL ALERT!
WHY EVERYONE NEEDS A LIVING WILL

The recent case of Marlise Munoz reminds us all of one important decision we should not leave to others: whether we want to remain on life support or not.

Marlise Munoz suffered a pulmonary embolism and was taken to a hospital in her city of Fort Worth. She was pronounced brain dead two days later. Marlise was 14 weeks pregnant and, under Texas law, her body was required to be left on life support even though it was unknown whether the fetus would be able to survive.

Erick Munoz, Marlise's husband, attempted to have her life support and ventilation removed after being told she was brain dead and seeing his wife in the hospital. He stated she had previously expressed to him that she would not want to be kept on life support if she was in a vegetative state and had completed a valid advance directive to that effect as well. This would have typically been the end of the story, and the machines would have been removed so Marlise could pass according to her wishes. However, there was a twist.

Officials at the hospital wouldn't carry out the wishes of Marlise and her advance directive because she was pregnant and claimed the advance directive was irrelevant. They pointed out that advance directives, like Marlise's, contain the line: "I understand that under Texas law this directive has no effect if I have been diagnosed as pregnant." And they claimed that the legislature had shown a clear interest in the protection of the unborn. This is also true in 11 other states.

Despite Mr. Munoz's requests to the hospital that his wife be removed from life-sustaining support, the hospital refused, and Mr. Munoz was forced to file a legal action to have the ventilation and feeding tube removed. Mr. Munoz stated to the court that it was difficult to "endure the pain of

CRITICAL ALERT!, CONTINUED

watching my wife's dead body be treated as if she were still alive. . . . One of the most painful parts of watching my wife's deceased body lie trapped in a hospital bed each day is the soulless look in her eyes. Her eyes, once full of the life, are now empty and dead."

Almost two months later, a Texas court finally approved the removal of life support, and Mr. Munoz was finally able to lay his wife's body to rest.

Although there was a unique aspect to the Munoz case, it again was a great reminder for all of us of the need to carefully consider these issues in advance and implement a living will or advance directive for our loved ones.

The living will can be relied on by family members. It also allows a person to declare if they wish to be an organ donor and/or want their body to be used for medical research. Hospitals are authorized and protected by law when they rely on a living will, and it makes family decisions at a hospital so much easier.

Using an Estate Closer

An estate closer is someone who helps the trustee, executor, or beneficiaries with the closing of an estate. A good estate closer is with the trustee and executor from the beginning of the estate and offers a support throughout the entire process, helping with court forms, accounting, and tax returns. Essentially, the estate closer helps the trustee or executor with every aspect of the estate all the way to the end.

An estate closer will direct the following procedures if and when necessary:

1. Direct the probate proceedings with an attorney for any necessary assets
2. Prepare the fiduciary return for a trust if applicable

3. Prepare an estate tax return if estate tax is owed

4. Prepare the final personal 1040 tax return of the deceased

5. Prepare any and all gift tax returns if necessary

6. Complete a detailed accounting of all the assets

7. Track any income while the estate is being settled

8. Coordinate the transfer of the assets to the beneficiaries

9. Provide emotional support and guidance to the family from start to finish

As you can imagine, all these complex tasks can be a significant burden to a family when they have never had to deal with such a situation. Not only are they trying to grieve and comfort other family members, but they can also be saddled with duties they aren't equipped to handle.

The estate closer can help the family through these financial tasks as well as many of the emotional issues of dividing up money and personal property. There are a lot of strategies to splitting up assets fairly. Some property should be sold immediately, while other assets may need to be held by the estate until the time is right to liquidate and distribute the assets to the beneficiaries.

The estate closer can also help identify fraud. Regrettably, fraud can be a common problem in an estate wherein one family member in control takes advantage of the others. Sadly, many families don't prosecute the guilty parties because they don't want to tear the family even further apart. The fact that no one is held accountable for these terrible acts of fraud makes it an even greater travesty.

As tempting as it might be to save a few dollars by not employing a competent estate closer, it is never a good idea for the trustee to shortcut the process just to try to save a few weeks or months of administration. Handling the trustee's responsibilities properly at all stages is always the best course of action and could prevent major fraud against the estate.

Game Plan Takeaway and Action Items

The real benefit of a revocable living trust is that the structure allows a grantor or grantors to control, affect, and influence future generations. Think of your own family. How many of us can say we know the detailed life history of a grandparent or great-grandparent? I suspect very few. However, if that same relative had created a trust for our education and tried to positively influence our lives through an inheritance, I would argue that many of us would be very interested in the life history, personality, and character of such a grandparent.

Leaving your family with an organized estate plan for your affairs is something they will truly appreciate. After your passing, that plan will allow them to focus on mourning and emotional wellness rather than financial or court issues.

If you've already completed your estate plan on your own, consider having a lawyer review your documents and goals to ensure you have the right plan for your family. Or, if you know you're in need of a new plan, you can revoke the old do-it-yourself plan and replace it with one that has been carefully considered by an attorney experienced in estate planning.

- At the very least, complete a handwritten will.
- Create a binder and organize a list of your financial affairs for your family.
- Consider a comprehensive estate plan to organize your affairs.
- If you have an estate plan, make sure it's been reviewed in the past five years.
- Make sure your trust is funded.

POST-GAME WRAP-UP

I n 2014, NFL quarterback Peyton Manning broke the career touchdown record. Over the years, sports analysts have consistently praised Manning for his ability to walk up to the line in a no-huddle offense and call out a successful play based on what he sees on the defensive side of the ball.

As an armchair spectator, you may think this is a relatively simple exercise for someone with Manning's experience. However, don't let his amazing athletic talent trick you into thinking he and his teammates don't have complicated and well-thought-out game plans for each football game. In fact, it's not uncommon for an NFL offensive coordinator to have multiple game plans to account for the different circumstances that can occur during a game and to even plan from quarter to quarter as the scrimmage evolves.

Entrepreneurs are unique individuals, but they can't expect to walk into complex business situations and make last-minute calls like Peyton Manning. Successful business owners plan ahead. They strategize, visualize, consult with professionals and partners, and plan in advance for the challenges they may face in their business. They make game plans.

For example, if you don't make important tax-planning decisions during the year or even near year-end, you can't expect that a last-minute April 14th decision will bail you out—essentially trying to call a "Hail Mary" play to throw a touchdown with your tax return. You will inevitably pay more in taxes because of your lack of foresight and planning.

Win or lose, there are always takeaways after a game. It's important to review both the good and the bad of what just happened. The same goes for business and financial affairs: You need to constantly review and update your game plans to ensure success and avoid repeating mistakes.

Build a team of professionals in the different technical disciplines supporting your business: accounting, taxes, banking, insurance, financial planning, litigation, business planning, and estate planning. Have regular meetings with these licensed and bona fide professionals. Be careful of "coaches" who give advice in areas in which they aren't licensed.

Develop regular game plans for the day, week, and month with manageable tasks you can complete. Prioritize, starting with the most important and impactful strategies that will improve your business or personal financial life, and don't let the busy work distract you from your goals.

Review your game plans after each season of your business, or after each project. Consider what you could have done better, what you may have done wrong, and what worked that is worth repeating.

A game plan needs to be updated and improved upon as you develop as a business owner and your business matures. A plan that worked for you two years ago may not be what you need for your business to succeed this year.

At the very least, you should implement a monthly game plan. This could be to make overall progress in your business or be a combination of smaller game plans that address the variety of issues I set forth in this book.

Here are some steps to consider when implementing a regular game plan.

Step 1: Create Your Game Plan Structure

Create the necessary sections for your game plan that address what is most critical in your business for both the particular time period you are focusing on and future success.

Below I have listed some questions, issues, and topics you may consider when building and maintaining a game plan. Of course these are just a starting point as you review and update your game plan on a regular basis.

- *Organizational or management issues.* Are there any legal or tax planning items that need to be dealt with? Are there facility issues to address? Are there any employees that need to be moved, trained, promoted, or terminated? What structural issues need to be planned for over the next three, six, or 12 months?
- *Product development.* How is your product or service mix doing? Do you need to change prices, add another product or service to your lineup, or start developing a new offering you want to roll out in the future? Could your customer service be improved upon? What needs to be modified or completely changed due to the current market and economy?
- *Systemization.* How do you deliver your products or services? Are they being delivered in the most efficient and effective manner possible? How can you improve to save time and money? Every employee and member of your organization needs to understand the system that produces your product or service and the role they play in that system.
- *Hatting.* Does everyone in your organization understand what "hat" they are wearing and the tasks they need to complete each

day? What are their responsibilities, and are they being held accountable to accomplish them?

- *Personal training and education.* Do you currently have all the necessary business and trade skills specific to your product mix to provide a valuable final product or service? What are the next books you plan on reading? What training and management videos are you watching? What is your plan for continuing your education as a business owner?

- *Employees and vendors.* If you have employees, do you have a quality set of policies and procedures and an employee handbook? Do all your employees understand their duties and responsibilities? What are your future plans for training, team-building, and social events? Are all of your vendors performing up to your expectations and guidelines? Do you need to send out any of your required services for bids to see if you can save money or get better service with new vendors?

- *Retirement and estate planning.* Are you setting aside some money each month for savings? Do you have a tax-deferred structure or plan in place? Are you living below your means, and have you considered where you could save money? Are you considering buying rental property? Is your estate plan completed and up to date?

- *Managing by statistics.* Do you have a system to report sales, costs, production, budget-to-actual figures, etc.? Do you have numbers for everything, and do you track them and manage by them? Do you set goals that can be tracked by objective criteria? Do you review these numbers every time you open your game plan? Do you hold yourself accountable if you're not reaching your goals?

- *Marketing tasks.* What are the items in your marketing plan you need to implement now or put into your game plan for the future to make sure you follow through on them?

Step 2: Create a Timeline for Your Action Items

Don't stress about this process. All your objectives and tasks from the different sections above should be commingled in an overall timeline.

You should certainly create checklists for each of your game plans and strategies that are critical to your success. I suggest you put them all into one master timeline that should be broken into three-month, six-month, and 12-month periods. Hold yourself accountable to these timelines and checklists. They will help keep you on track!

Step 3: Revisit Your Game Plan Regularly

As I stated above, I suggest you update your plan monthly and at the very least redraft it every three months. And you should be carrying it with you everywhere you go. Review it constantly and stay disciplined! Make notes on your plan whenever you have a brilliant idea. Don't say to yourself, "I need to do that next quarter when I review my plan." Write it down now!

Step 4: Manage by Statistics

Your numbers and reports, even if you are only keeping track and reporting to yourself, will consistently tell you if you are headed in the right direction. Don't get discouraged if the numbers aren't what you hoped for. Make changes as needed—being a business owner means change. Don't be afraid of it. Embrace it and become accustomed to it.

My sincere hope is that several of the case studies and topics I covered in this book apply to issues you are currently facing in the operations and growth of your business. Don't give up, and keep playing the game. With smart planning and hard work, you can develop winning game plans over and over again and ultimately reach your American Dream.

APPENDICES

A team needs the details, stats, and data to make good decisions. Here are some useful resources in the appendices to help you in your game-winning strategies.

HOMESTEAD EXEMPTION BY STATE

The homestead exemption, which is available in most states, protects some of the value of a person's home from a creditor or bankruptcy. If you are forced to sell your home due to a lawsuit, the creditor only gets what's left over after selling fees, the mortgage balance, and your homestead exemption amount. This amount varies by state, which is explained in the table below. There is more detail on the homestead exemption in Chapter 19.

The information provided in this table is general and is intended only to serve as initial guidance in your research. It is absolutely critical that you review the specific and current laws of your state and determine which state exemptions you may qualify for and the amounts for that exemption.

Column 1 is the dollar amount that is exempt for those who are single.

Column 2 is the dollar amount that is exempt for those who are married.

Column 3 indicates property interests that qualify for the homestead exemption, other than a typical residence.

Column 4 indicates whether the exemption is automatic. If not, you will need to research the proper procedure to file for the exemption in your jurisdiction.

Column 5 indicates whether a spouse can claim the exemption even if their name is not on the property title.

States	Column 1 Single Exemption Amount	Column 2 Married Exemption Amount	Column 3 Other Interests Protected Including a Typical Home	Column 4 Automatic Exemption	Column 5 Title Affects the Claim
Alabama	$15,000	$30,000	Mobile Home	No	No
Alaska	$72,900	$72,900		Yes	No
Arizona	$150,000	$150,000	Condominium, Cooperative, Mobile Home	Yes	No
Arkansas	$2,500	$2,500		Yes	No
California[1]	$75,000	$100,000	Mobile Home, Boat, Stock Cooperative, Planned Development, Condominium Apartment	Both	No
Colorado[2]	$75,000	$150,000	Mobile Home, House trailer Farms	Yes	No
Connecticut[3]	$75,000	$150,000	Mobile Home, Cooperative	Yes	No
Delaware	$125,000	$125,000	Manufactured Home	Yes	No
District of Columbia	Unlimited	Unlimited	Cooperative	Yes	No
Florida	Unlimited	Unlimited	Mobile Home, Leaseholds	No	No
Georgia	$21,500	$43,000	Cooperative	No	No
Hawaii	$20,000	$30,000	Any Rights to Immediate Possession	Yes	No
Idaho	$100,000	$100,000	Mobile Home	Yes	No

States	Column 1 Single Exemption Amount	Column 2 Married Exemption Amount	Column 3 Other Interests Protected Including a Typical Home	Column 4 Automatic Exemption	Column 5 Title Affects the Claim
Illinois	$15,000	$30,000	Farm, Cooperative, Condominium, or Lease for Residence	Yes	No
Indiana	$19,300	$38,600		No	No
Iowa	Unlimited	Unlimited		No	No
Kansas	Unlimited	Unlimited	Mobile Home, Farm	No	No
Kentucky	$5,000	$10,000		No	No
Louisiana	$35,000	$35,000		Yes	No
Maine[4]	$47,500	$95,000	Cooperative	Yes	No
Maryland	$22,975	$22,975	Permanent Manufactured Home	No	No
Massachusetts	$500,000	$500,000	Mobile Home, Condominium, Cooperative	Yes	No
Michigan	$30,000	$30,000		Yes	No
Minnesota[5]	$390,000	$390,000	"Dwelling Place"	Yes	No
Mississippi[6]	$75,000	$75,000		No	No
Missouri	$15,000	$15,000		Yes	No
Montana	$250,000	$250,000	Mobile Home	Yes	Yes
Nebraska	$60,000	$60,000		Yes	Yes
Nevada	$550,000	$550,000	Cooperative, Condominium, Mobile Home	No	No
New Hampshire	$100,000	$200,000	Mobile Home	No	Yes

States	Column 1 Single Exemption Amount	Column 2 Married Exemption Amount	Column 3 Other Interests Protected Including a Typical Home	Column 4 Automatic Exemption	Column 5 Title Affects the Claim
New Jersey	None	None		N/A	N/A
New Mexico	$60,000	$120,000		No	No
New York[7]	$82,775 to $165,550	$165,550 to $331,000	Cooperative, Condominium, Mobile Home	Yes	No
North Carolina	$35,000	$70,000	Cooperative	No	No
North Dakota	$100,000	$100,000		No	Yes
Ohio	$136,925			Yes	No
Oklahoma	Unlimited	Unlimited	Mobile Home	Yes	No
Oregon	$40,000	$50,000	Mobile Home, Floating Home	No	Yes
Pennsylvania	None	None		N/A	N/A
Rhode Island	$500,000	$500,000		No	No
South Carolina	$58,255	$116,510	Cooperative	Yes	No
South Dakota	Unlimited	Unlimited	Mobile Home	No	Yes
Tennessee[8]	$5,000	$7,500		No	No
Texas	Unlimited	Unlimited		Yes	No
Utah[9]	$20,000	$40,000	Mobile Home	No	Yes
Vermont	$125,000	$250,000		No	No
Virginia[10]	$5,000	$10,000		No	No
Washington	$125,000	$125,000	Mobile Home	Yes	Yes
West Virginia	$25,000	$50,000	Any Property Interest Used as Residence	Yes	No
Wisconsin	$75,000	$150,000		No	Yes
Wyoming	$20,000	$40,000		Yes	Yes

[1] Exemption is $175,000 if the debtor or debtor's spouse is over 65 years old, has a physical or mental disability that makes them unable to work, or is 55 with a gross income of less than $25,000 if single or $35,000 if married.

APPENDIX A ◦ Homestead Exemption by State

[2] Exemption is $105,000 if the debtor or debtor's spouse or dependent is 60 years old or older, or has a physical or mental disability that makes them unable to work. Sale proceeds exempt two years.

[3] Exemption is $125,000 if the money judgment arises out of services provided at a hospital.

[4] Exemption is $95,000 if the debtor or debtor's spouse is 60 years old or older, or has a physical or mental disability that makes them unable to work. Joint exemption is $190,000.

[5] If the property is used primarily for agriculture, the exemption amount is $975,000.

[6] Exemption is $30,000 if the property is a mobile home or trailer.

[7] Depends on the county where the debtor resides: not to exceed $165,550 for the counties of Kings, Queens, New York, Bronx, Richmond, Nassau, Suffolk, Rockland, Westchester, and Putnam; $131,325 for the counties of Dutchess, Albany, Columbia, Orange, Saratoga, and Ulster; and $82,775 for all remaining counties.

[8] Exemption for an unmarried individual who is 62 years old is $12,500. If the debtors are a married couple and one spouse is over 62 and the other is younger, the exemption is $20,000. For a married couple, both over 62, the exemption is $25,000.

[9] Exemption is $5,000/$10,000 if the property is not the primary residence.

[10] Exemption is $10,000 if the debtor is 65 years or older.

B

TENANTS BY THE ENTIRETY BY STATE

If your state allows it, you can title your personal residence as "tenancy by the entirety," which offers the following protection: If one spouse is sued, your home cannot be attached or bifurcated by the lawsuit. I cover this concept in more depth in Chapter 19.

The information provided in this table is general and is intended only to serve as initial guidance in your research. It is absolutely critical that you review the specific and current laws of your state to determine what the laws specifically provide for tenants by the entirety.

Column 1 indicates the states without tenancy by the entirety laws.

Column 2 indicates the states that are considered Modified Bar Jurisdictions. These are states in which a creditor can obtain rights to the debtor's portion of the personal residence if married, but only after the debtor's part is no longer absolute, such as in cases of divorce or death.

Column 3 indicates the states that are considered Full Bar Jurisdictions. These are the best states under this type of asset protection, and are states in which a creditor has no rights against the personal residence of a married couple, so long as only one of the spouses is liable for the debt to the creditor. If both spouses are liable for the debt, then tenancy by the entirety provides no protection for the personal residence.

States	Column 1 Not Available	Column 2 Modified Bar Jurisdiction	Column 3 Full Bar Jurisdiction
Alabama	X		
Alaska		X	
Arizona	X		
Arkansas		X	
California	X		
Colorado	X		
Connecticut	X		
Delaware			X
District of Columbia			X
Florida			X
Georgia	X		
Hawaii			X
Idaho	X		
Illinois		X	
Indiana			X
Iowa	X		
Kansas	X		
Kentucky		X	
Louisiana	X		
Maine	X		
Maryland			X
Massachusetts		X	
Michigan			X
Minnesota	X		
Mississippi			X
Missouri			X
Montana	X		
Nebraska	X		
Nevada	X		
New Hampshire	X		
New Jersey		X	

APPENDIX B ◦ Tenants by the Entirety by State

States	Column 1 Not Available	Column 2 Modified Bar Jurisdiction	Column 3 Full Bar Jurisdiction
New Mexico	X		
New York		X	
North Carolina			X
North Dakota	X		
Ohio	X		
Oklahoma		X	
Oregon		X	
Pennsylvania			X
Rhode Island			X
South Carolina	X		
South Dakota	X		
Tennessee			X
Texas	X		
Utah	X		
Vermont			X
Virginia			X
Washington	X		
West Virginia	X		
Wisconsin	X		
Wyoming			X

C

CHARGING ORDER PROTECTION ENTITIES (COPE) AND SERIES LLC BY STATE

This table covers two asset protection strategies. First, the Charging Order Protection Entity (COPE) protects your assets from personal liabilities that arise outside your LLC, or whatever entity is holding the asset. An LLC protects your personal assets from the liabilities of your business; a COPE protects your business from your personal liabilities. You can read more about COPEs in Chapter 21.

Series LLCs allow you to have mini-LLCs under a parent LLC, giving you limited personal liability from claims arising from multiple rental properties or operations without the extra costs or headaches of maintaining multiple LLCs for your different properties or business ventures. The debts, obligations, and liabilities of each mini-series are only enforceable against the assets of that series, not against the assets of the parent LLC or any other series. You can find more information on this concept in Chapter 3.

The information provided in this table is general and is intended only to serve as initial guidance in your research. It is absolutely critical that you review the specific and current laws of your state and determine which type of entity best fits your situation and asset protection plan.

Column 1 indicates the states that are considered **Type 1 LPs: Foreclosure States**. These are the states providing moderate protection from outside creditors. These laws provide that a creditor may foreclose upon a limited partner's interest in the limited partnership (LP), thus divesting the partner of her ownership and stepping into her shoes as a limited partner in the LP. However, the creditor cannot force the dissolution of the LP and will have to comply with the voting rights it is given in the LP as a substitute or replacement limited partner. These laws are based on the relatively new Uniform Limited Partnership Act of 2001, which specifically classifies a charging order as a lien that can be foreclosed upon.

Column 2 indicates the states that are considered **Type 2 LPs: Charging Order States**. These are the states providing the best asset protection from outside creditors. These laws provide that the exclusive remedy for creditors seeking to satisfy a debt with an LP interest is to obtain a charging order for future distributions from the LP to the limited partner. The creditor cannot force foreclosure of the interest or dissolution of the partnership. It is important to note that state case law is going to be extremely determinative as to the effectiveness of the charging order protection.

Column 3 indicates the states that are considered **Type 1 LLCs: Dissolution States**. These are the states with the worst LLC statutes for protection from outside creditors. These laws are based on Section 503 of the Uniform LLC Act of 1996 and allow creditors to force the dissolution of the LLC and receive a pro rata share of the LLC's assets upon dissolution.

Column 4 indicates the states that are considered **Type 2 LLCs: Foreclosure States**. These are the states providing moderate LLC protection from outside creditors. These laws provide that a creditor may foreclose upon a member/debtor's interest and actually take away their interest in the LLC, thus stepping into their shoes. However, the creditor cannot force the dissolution of the LLC and will have to comply with the voting rights it is given in the LLC as a substitute or replacement member. These laws are based on Section 504 of the Uniform LLC Act of 1996, or Section 703 of the Revised Uniform Limited Partnership Act of 1976, which does not specifically bar creditors from seeking foreclosure. Specific case law for these states and how a creditor's claim may be treated will be the determining factor.

Column 5 indicates the states that are considered **Type 3 LLCs: Charging Order States**. These are the states that provide the best asset protection from outside creditors. These laws provide that the exclusive remedy for creditors seeking to satisfy a debt with an LLC interest is to obtain a charging order for future distributions from the LLC to the member/debtor. The creditor cannot force foreclosure of the interest or dissolution of the company.

Column 6 indicates states that have **Series LLC** statutes/laws and thus provide for the Series LLC.

States	Column 1 Type 1- LP Foreclosure States	Column 2 Type 2- LP Charging Order States	Column 3 Type 1- LLC Dissolution States	Column 4 Type 2- LLC Foreclosure States	Column 5 Type 3- LLC Charging Order States	Column 6 Series LLC States
Alabama[1]		X			X	X
Alaska		X		X		
Arizona		X			X	
Arkansas		X	X			
California		X		X		
Colorado		X		X		
Connecticut		X	X			
Delaware		X			X	X
District of Columbia		X		X		X
Florida		X		X		
Georgia		X		X		
Hawaii		X		X		
Idaho		X		X		
Illinois		X		X		X
Indiana		X			X	
Iowa		X		X		X
Kansas		X		X		X
Kentucky		X		X		
Louisiana	X		X			
Maine		X			X	
Maryland		X		X		
Massachusetts		X		X		
Michigan		X			X	
Minnesota[2]		X		X		X2
Mississippi		X			X	
Missouri		X		X		X
Montana		X		X		X
Nebraska		X		X		
Nevada		X			X	X
New Hampshire		X	X			

States	Column 1	Column 2	Column 3	Column 4	Column 5	Column 6
	Type 1- LP Foreclosure States	Type 2- LP Charging Order States	Type 1- LLC Dissolution States	Type 2- LLC Foreclosure States	Type 3- LLC Charging Order States	Series LLC States
New Jersey		X			X	
New Mexico		X		X		
New York		X	X			
North Carolina		X			X	
North Dakota[3]		X			X	X
Ohio		X			X	
Oklahoma		X			X	X
Oregon		X		X		
Pennsylvania		X		X		
Rhode Island		X			X	
South Carolina		X		X		
South Dakota		X			X	
Tennessee		X			X	X
Texas		X			X	X
Utah		X		X		X
Vermont		X		X		
Virginia		X			X	
Washington		X		X		
West Virginia		X			X	
Wisconsin		X		X		X
Wyoming		X			X	

[1] Effective 1/1/2017, the LLC Act will expressly prohibit foreclosure.

[2] Minnesota does not permit forming Series LLC's but does recognize Series LLCs formed out of State.

[1] North Dakota allows Series LLCs, but does not specifically provide for a liability shield between the different series.

INDEX

home equity, 219–227

homestead exemption, 200, 220, 222–223, 240, 323–328

from inside and outside liability, 89–90

life insurance, 201–202

LLCs and, 29

in marriage and divorce. *See* marriage, asset protection in

myths, 196–197

planning your strategies, 241

privacy planning, 207–216

for rental property investments, 97–100

retirement plans, 239–240, 247–248

S corps and, 36, 37, 45

for self-directed IRAs, 298–299

tenancy by the entirety, 200–201

umbrella insurance, 100–101, 199, 226

audit protection, 15, 96, 112, 165, 167, 170, 178, 180

B

bankruptcy, 205–206

board of advisors, xix, 95–97, 110, 147, 308

bookkeeping, 163–171

about, 163–164, 170–171

accounting systems, 165–169

audit protection and, 15, 96, 112, 165, 167, 170, 178, 180

decision making and, 165

receipts, 110–111, 112, 167, 170, 178, 180

separate accounting for each business, 164–165

smartphones for, 169–170

tax savings and, 165

business credit. *See* corporate credit

business entities. *See also* asset protection; C corporations; limited liability companies; partnerships; S corporations; sole proprietorships

business goals and, 19

cancellation of, 97

corporate credit and, 19–20

costs and requirements, 20

determining which is right for your business, 14–21

do-it-yourself entity formation, 18

filing taxes as proper entity, 175–176

investors and, 17

location and, 19

marketing and, 19

partners and, 17

business insurance, 199

buy-sell agreements, 257

C

C corporations (C corps), 48–56

finding trustworthy advisors, 55

purpose, 48–49, 56

S corps and, 38

small-business owners and, 49–55

taxes and, 49–54

capital, raising, 263–273

about, 272–273

CPSIA information can be obtained
at www.ICGtesting.com
Printed in the USA
JSHW020154211221
21411JS00008B/21